# SPELLING THE EASY WAY

**JOSEPH MERSAND**

Formerly Associate Professor of Education
York College of the City University of New York

**FRANCIS GRIFFITH**

Emeritus Professor of Education
Hofstra University, Hempstead, New York

**BARRON'S EDUCATIONAL SERIES, INC.**

Woodbury, New York/London/Toronto

*All inquiries should be addressed to:*
Barron's Educational Series, Inc.
113 Crossways Park Drive
Woodbury, New York 11797

*Library of Congress Catalog Card No. 82-4042*

Paper Edition
International Standard Book No. 0-8120-2502-4

**Library of Congress Cataloging in Publication Data**
Mersand, Joseph E., 1907–
   Spelling the easy way.

   (The Easy Way)
   Rev. ed. of: Spelling your way to success. 1974.
   Summary: Discusses the importance of good spelling,
explains the general rules of English spelling, and
examines some troublesome spelling problems.
   1. English language—Orthography and spelling.
[1. English language—Spelling]  I. Griffith, Francis J.
II. Title.  III. Series.
PE1145.2.M39  1982      428.1      82-4042
ISBN 0-8120-2502-4 (pbk.)         AACR2

PRINTED IN THE UNITED STATES OF AMERICA
2 3 4 5   049   9 8 7 6 5 4 3 2

# Contents

Troublesome Words

Measuring Your Progress

# A Word about This Series

Barron's has developed the "Easy Way" series to help you master the subjects you want to learn—or *need* to learn for school and jobs. Each book is clearly organized and filled with practical, straightforward information to promote rapid learning. The authors are respected educators with years of teaching experience in their fields.

If you're a student, these are the books you'll want to turn to for a valuable overview of coursework or for help in navigating the rough spots you encounter. Most of them contain numerous examples and exercises to give you that extra margin of skill and confidence that pays off in better grades.

If you're already out of school, you'll find that these books are an ideal source of self-improvement. Use them to brush up on the basics of English and math. Build your vocabulary. Or teach yourself new skills like typing and foreign languages.

Whatever your goals, you can count on this series to help you learn the "Easy Way"—not with gimmicks and magic shortcuts (for there are no shortcuts to real learning), but through clear, expert instruction that you can follow at your own pace. We're sure you'll want to return to this series again and again to meet your learning needs.

# Introduction

Interest in spelling correctly is probably as old as writing. More than 2,000 years ago, The Greek philosopher Aristotle said:

"It is possible to spell a word correctly by chance, or because someone prompts you, but you are a scholar only if you spell it correctly *because you know how*."

Apparently the Greek schoolboy and adult had difficulties with spelling much the same way as so many of us today.

That spelling is troublesome and difficult to many people is obvious from the many complaints that have been made about the poor spelling practices of employees in business as well as students in high school and college. In a recent survey, one hundred presidents of the largest business concerns in the United States were asked their opinions about the competence in English of high school and college graduates of the last five to ten years. Over twenty of these executives indicated that spelling needed great improvement. Here are some typical comments:

"Inability to spell simple words used in business communications, such as *receive, recommend, all right*."

"They cannot spell common every day words."

"Spelling is a lost art that should be revived."

"Their spelling has been atrocious."

"High school graduates exhibit a noticeable deficiency in ability to spell."

These are the opinions held not only by many business executives but by many college teachers and college presidents as well. Parents who compare their own achievements as students with those of their children today are also among the severe critics of today's spellers.

The recent emphasis upon the basics in education implies emphasis on correct spelling. Although all sorts of machines can perform acts more speedily than the human mind, no machine can express a person's thoughts. And if that person is a poor speller, the machine, no matter how costly and intricate, will make the same spelling mistakes.

Of the production of spelling books, there seems to be no end. From the famous blue-backed speller of Noah Webster in 1783 to the ever-increasing number in our own times, books on spelling have been numerous. A new book in this field can be justified if it endeavors to combine the knowledge of the experts in the field of spelling with more effective presentation and better methods for mastering this important subject. If the author by his manner of presenting the important subject of spelling, through clearly stated rules, copious exercises, and numerous examples will make you interested in improving your spelling, then you will be well along the way to becoming a better speller. Like so many other aspects of learning, we learn best what we are interested in and what we really want to learn.

Most chapters in the book have one or more exercises designed to fix in your memory and to make habitual the principles of correct spelling. It is imperative that you do these exercises carefully. Note the errors that you have made and review until you spell these troublesome words effortlessly. A few minutes a day over a period of time should suffice to achieve your objectives. The exercises are of various types, in accordance with the best methods of teaching.

Above all, you must try to use as many of the words you have been studying as soon as and as often as possible. Memorizing the rules will not be of much help unless you apply them.

Lord Chesterfield, who said so many wise things to his son in his famous letters, also considered the subject of spelling.

"Orthography is so absolutely necessary for a man of letters, or a gentleman, that one false spelling may fix ridicule upon him for the rest of his life, and I know a man of quality who never recovered the ridicule of having spelled *wholesome* without the *w*."[1]

His remark about orthography (or correct spelling) which applied to the aristocratic gentleman of his day is now pertinent to everyone who wishes to be considered an educated man.

Even one of our founding fathers, Thomas Jefferson, expressed himself on this subject to his daughter, in whose education he was so interested:

"Take care that you never spell a word wrong. Always before you write a word, consider how it is spelled, and if you do not remember, turn to a dictionary. It produces great praise to a lady to spell well."

Whether from the viewpoint of good social etiquette, success in school and college work or promotion in your chosen profession, you cannot afford to remain a poor speller. This book will help you to become a good one.

The authors wish to express their thanks to Estelle J. Mersand and Kathryn O'D. Griffith; and to David Sharp, Mrs. Margaret C. Chandler, Miss Bidabee Gloster and Miss Gladys D. Roche for their assistance in preparing and editing the manuscript.

Joseph Mersand
Francis Griffith

[1] Lord Chesterfield, *Letters to His Son*, 1750.

# 10,000 Word Ready Reference Spelling List

# 10,000 Word Ready Reference Spelling List

## How to Use This List

*Spelling*. The words in this reference list are spelled according to American usage.

When two spellings are valid, both are listed:

dem·a·gogue, dem·a·gog

*Dividing words at the end of a line*. Centered dots indicate division points at which a hyphen may be put at the end of a line of typing or writing. For example, *baccalaureate* (*bac·ca·lau·re·ate*) may be ended on one line with

bac-
bacca-
baccalau-
baccalaure-

and continued on the next line, respectively, with

-calaureate
-laureate
-reate
-ate

2

Note, however, that a single initial letter or a single terminal letter is not cut off. The following words, for example, are not hyphenated:

|          |        |
|----------|--------|
| abound   | icy    |
| o'clock  | seamy  |

*Plurals*. Most English nouns form their plural by adding *s*. These regular plurals are not shown in the reference list. Irregular plurals are shown:

> la·bo·ra·to·ry (–ries)
> knife (knives)
> lar·ynx (la·ryn·ges *or* lar·ynx·es)
> las·so (las·sos *or* las·soes)
> la·tex (la·ti·ces *or* la·tex·es)
> oc·to·pus (–pus·es *or* –pi)

*Definitions*. Brief definitions of confusing pairs of words are given:

> arc (something arched or curved; see *ark*)
> ark (a boat; a repository for Torah scrolls; see *arc*)
> af·fect (to influence; see *effect*)
> ef·fect (to accomplish; see *affect*)

Brief definitions of foreign words and phrases are also given:

> ad va·lo·rem (Latin: according to value)
> a pri·o·ri (Latin: reasoning from self-evident proposition)

# 10,000
# Words

A

aback
aba·cus (–cus·es)
aban·don
aban·don·ment
abase
abase·ment
abash
abate·ment
ab·bey
ab·bot
ab·bre·vi·ate
ab·bre·vi·a·tion
ab·di·cate
ab·di·ca·tion
ab·do·men
ab·dom·i·nal
ab·duct
ab·duc·tion
ab·er·ra·tion
abet
abet·ted
ab·hor
ab·hor·rence
abide
abil·i·ty (–ties)
ab·ject
ab·jur·ing
able-bod·ied
ab·lu·tion
ably
ab·ne·ga·tion
ab·nor·mal·i·ty (–ties)
ab·nor·mal·ly
aboard
abol·ish
ab·o·li·tion
A-bomb
abom·i·na·ble
abort
abor·tion
abound
about-face
above·board
above men·tioned
abra·sive
abreast
abridge
abridg·ment, abridge·ment
abroad
ab·ro·gate

abrupt
ab·scess
ab·scond
ab·sence
ab·so·lute
ab·solve
ab·sorb
ab·stain
ab·strac·tion
abun·dant
abut·ment
abys·mal
abyss
ac·cede
ac·cel·er·ate
ac·cent
ac·cept (to receive; see
    except)
ac·ces·so·ry, ac·ces·sa·ry
    (–ries)
ac·ces·si·ble
ac·ci·dent
ac·claim
ac·cli·mate
ac·cli·ma·tize
ac·co·lade
ac·com·mo·date
ac·com·mo·da·tion
ac·com·pa·nist
ac·com·pa·ny
ac·com·plice
ac·com·plish
ac·cord
ac·cost
ac·count
ac·coun·tant
ac·cru·al
ac·cu·mu·late
ac·cu·ra·cy
ac·cuse
ac·e·tate
acet·y·lene
achieve
ac·knowl·edge
acous·tics
ac·quain·tance
ac·qui·esce
ac·quire
ac·qui·si·tion
ac·quit·tal

acre
acre·age
ac·ri·mo·ni·ous
across
ac·tiv·i·ty (–ties)
ac·tu·al
ac·tu·ar·i·al
ac·tu·ary
acu·punc·ture
ad·ap·ta·tion
ad·dict
ad·di·tion·al
ad·dress·ee
ad·duce
ad·e·noid
ad·e·quate
ad·here
ad·he·sive
ad hoc (Latin: pertaining to
    the case at hand)
ad ho·mi·nem (Latin:
    argument based on
    personality)
adieu (adieus or adieux)
    (French: farewell)
ad in·fi·ni·tum (Latin:
    without end)
ad·ja·cent
ad·jec·tive
ad·join·ing
ad·journ
ad·journ·ment
ad·ju·di·cate
ad·junct
ad·just·able
ad·ju·tant
ad-lib (Latin: without
    preparation)
ad·min·is·ter
ad·min·is·trate
ad·min·is·tra·tion
ad·min·is·tra·tor
ad·mi·ra·ble
ad·mis·si·ble
ad nau·se·am (Latin: to a
    sickening degree)
ad·o·les·cent
adopt
ad·re·nal
adroit

ad·u·la·tion
ad va·lo·rem (Latin:
  according to value)
ad·van·ta·geous
ad·ven·tur·ous
ad·ver·sary (–sar·ies)
ad·ver·si·ty (–ties)
ad·ver·tise·ment
ad·vice (recommendation;
  see *advise*)
ad·vis·able
ad·vise (to give advice; see
  *advice*)
ad·vis·er, ad·vi·sor
ad·vo·cate
aer·ate
ae·ri·al (relating to the air)
aer·i·al (antenna)
aero·dy·nam·ics
aero·nau·tics
aero·sol
aes·thet·ics
af·fa·ble
af·fect (to influence; see
  *effect*)
af·fec·tion·ate
af·fi·da·vit
af·fil·i·ate
af·fin·i·ty (–ties)
af·fir·ma·tive
af·flic·tion
af·flu·ent
af·ford
af·fray
af·front
af·ghan
afore·men·tioned
afraid
af·ter·ward, af·ter·wards
again
agen·cy (–cies)
agen·da
agent
ag·glom·er·ate
ag·gran·dize·ment
ag·gra·vate
ag·gres·sion
ag·gres·sive
ag·grieved
aghast
ag·ile

agil·i·ty (–ties)
ag·i·tate
ag·i·ta·tor
ag·nos·tic
ag·on·ize
agrar·i·an
agree·able
ag·ri·cul·ture
agron·o·my
aid (to give assistance, a
  subsidy; see *aide*)
aide (military assistant; see
  *aid*)
air-con·di·tion
air con·di·tion·er
air force
air·line
air·port
aisle
a la carte (French: each
  item is priced separately)
alac·ri·ty
al·ba·tross
al·bu·men
al·che·my
al·co·hol
al·ge·bra
al·ga (al·gae)
alias
al·i·bi
alien·ate
align·ment, aline·ment
al·i·men·ta·ry
al·i·mo·ny (–nies)
alive
al·ka·li (–lies *or* –lis)
al·lay (relieve; see *alley,
  ally*)
al·le·ga·tion
al·lege
al·le·giance
al·le·go·ry (–ries)
al·ler·gy (–gies)
al·le·vi·ate
al·ley (narrow passage; see
  *allay, ally*)
al·li·ance
al·li·ga·tor
al·lit·er·ate
al·lit·er·a·tion
al·lo·cate

al·lot
al·lot·ment
all·over (repeated design;
  see *all over*)
all over (everywhere; see
  *allover*)
al·low
al·low·able
al·low·ance
al·loy
all right
al·lude (to refer; see *elude*)
al·lure
al·lu·sion
al·ly (an associate; see
  *allay, alley*)
al·ma·nac
al·mond
al·most
alms
alo·ha
alone
aloud
al·pha·bet
al·pha·bet·ize
al·ready
al·tar (structure used in
  religious ceremonies; see
  *alter*)
al·ter (to change; see *altar*)
al·ter·ation
al·ter·ca·tion
al·ter·nate
al·ter·na·tive
al·though
al·tim·e·ter
al·ti·tude
al·to·geth·er
al·tru·ism
al·um
alu·mi·num
alum·na (–nae)
alum·nus (–ni)
al·ways
amal·gam·ate
am·a·teur
am·a·to·ry
amaze
am·bas·sa·dor
am·bi·dex·trous
am·bi·ence, am·bi·ance

am·bi·gu·i·ty (–ties)
am·big·u·ous
am·bi·tious
am·biv·a·lence
am·bu·lance
am·bu·la·to·ry
ame·lio·rate
ame·na·ble
amend·ment
ame·ni·ty (–ties)
am·e·thyst
ami·a·ble
am·i·ca·ble
am·i·ty (–ties)
am·mo·nia
am·mu·ni·tion
am·ne·sia
am·nes·ty (–ties)
am·nio·cen·te·sis
amoe·ba (–bas or –bae)
amor·al
am·o·rous
amor·phous
am·or·ti·za·tion
amor·tize
amount
am·phet·amine
am·phib·i·an
am·phi·the·ater
am·pli·fy
am·pu·tate
amuse·ment
anach·ro·nism
an·al·ge·sic
anal·o·gous
anal·o·gy
anal·y·sis
an·a·lyst
an·a·lyze
an·ar·chy
anath·e·ma
anat·o·my
an·ces·tor
an·ces·try
anchor
an·cho·vy (–vies or –vy)
an·cient
an·cil·lary
an·ec·dote
an·es·the·sia
an·eu·rysm, an·eu·rism

an·gel (heavenly
   messenger; see angle)
an·gle (geometric figure;
   see angel)
an·guish
an·i·mate
an·i·mos·i·ty (–ties)
an·nals
an·neal
an·nex (noun), an·nex
   (verb)
an·ni·hi·late
an·ni·ver·sa·ry (–ries)
an·no·tate
an·nounce·ment
an·nounc·er
an·noy
an·nu·al
an·nu·ity (–ities)
an·nul
an·nun·ci·ate
anoint
anom·a·ly (–lies)
anon·y·mous
an·swer
ant (insect; see aunt)
an·tag·o·nize
an·te·ced·ent
an·te·date
an·te·lope
an·ten·na
an·te·ri·or
an·te·room
an·them
an·thol·o·gy (–gies)
an·thra·cite
an·thro·pol·o·gy
an·ti·bi·ot·ic
an·tic
an·tic·i·pate
an·ti·cli·max
an·ti·dote
an·ti·his·ta·mine
an·ti·pas·to
an·tip·a·thy (thies)
an·ti·pol·lu·tion
an·ti·quar·i·an
an·tique
an·tiq·ui·ty (–ties)
an·ti·sep·tic
an·ti·so·cial

an·tith·e·sis (–e·ses)
ant·onym
anx·i·ety (–eties)
anx·ious
aor·ta
apart·heid
apart·ment
ap·a·thy
aper·i·tif
ap·er·ture
apex
aph·o·rism
aph·ro·dis·i·ac
aplomb
apoc·a·lypse
apoc·ry·phal
apo·gee
apol·o·gize
apol·o·gy (–gies)
ap·o·plec·tic
ap·o·plexy
apos·tle
apos·tro·phe
apo·the·o·sis (–ses)
ap·pall, ap·pal
ap·pa·ra·tus (–tus·es or
   –tus)
ap·par·el
ap·par·ent
ap·pa·ri·tion
ap·peal
ap·pear·ance
ap·pease
ap·pel·lant
ap·pe·late
ap·pend·age
ap·pen·dec·to·my (–mies)
ap·pen·di·ci·tis
ap·pen·dix (–dix·es or
   –di·ces)
ap·per·tain
ap·pe·tite
ap·pe·tiz·er
ap·plaud
ap·plause
ap·pli·ance
ap·pli·ca·ble
ap·pli·ca·tion
ap·pli·ca·tor
ap·plied
ap·ply

ap·point·ment
ap·por·tion
ap·pose
ap·praise
ap·pre·ci·ate
ap·pre·hend
ap·pren·tice
ap·prise
ap·proach
ap·pro·ba·tion
ap·pro·pri·ate
ap·pro·pri·a·tion
ap·prov·al
ap·prox·i·mate
apri·cot
a pri·o·ri (Latin: reasoning
  from self-evident
  propositions)
ap·ro·pos
ap·ti·tude
apt·ly
aquar·i·um
aquat·ic
aq·ue·duct
ar·bi·ter
ar·bi·trary
ar·bi·trate
ar·bi·tra·tor
ar·bor
arc (curved line; see *ark*)
ar·cade
arch
ar·chae·ol·o·gy
ar·cha·ic
ar·chery
ar·che·type
ar·chi·pel·a·go (–goes)
ar·chi·tect
ar·chi·tec·tur·al
ar·chi·tec·ture
ar·chive
arc·tic
ar·dent
ar·dor
ar·du·ous
ar·ea
are·na
ar·gue
aria
ar·id

ar·is·toc·ra·cy (–cies)
aris·to·crat
arith·me·tic
ark (boat; see *arc*)
ar·ma·ment
ar·ma·ture
ar·mi·stice
ar·moire
ar·mor
ar·my (ar·mies)
aro·ma
arouse
ar·raign
ar·range
ar·ray
ar·rears
ar·rest
ar·riv·al
ar·rive
ar·ro·gance
ar·se·nic
ar·son
ar·te·ri·al
ar·te·rio·scle·ro·sis
ar·tery (–ter·ies)
ar·thri·tis
ar·ti·choke
ar·ti·cle
ar·tic·u·late
ar·ti·fact
ar·ti·fice
ar·ti·fi·cial
ar·ti·san
ar·tis·tic
as·bes·tos, as·bes·tus
as·cend
as·cen·sion
as·cent (climb; see *assent*)
as·cer·tain
as·cet·ic
as·cribe
asep·tic
askew
as·par·a·gus (–gus·es)
as·pect
as·per·i·ty (–ties)
as·per·sion
as·phalt
as·phyx·i·ate
as·pire

as·pi·rin
as·sail
as·sas·sin
as·sas·si·na·tion
as·sault
as·sem·ble
as·sem·bly (–blies)
as·sent (to agree; see
  *ascent*)
as·sert
as·sess·ment
as·set
as·sid·u·ous
as·sign·ment
as·sim·i·late
as·sis·tant
as·so·ci·a·tion
as·so·nance
as·sort·ment
as·suage
as·sump·tion
as·sur·ance
as·ter·isk
as·ter·oid
asth·ma
astig·ma·tism
as·trin·gent
as·trol·o·gy
as·tro·naut
as·tron·o·mer
as·tro·nom·i·cal,
  as·tro·nom·ic
as·tron·o·my (–mies)
as·tute
asun·der
asy·lum
asym·met·ric,
  asym·met·ri·cal
at·a·vism
athe·ist
ath·lete
ath·let·ic
at·mo·sphere
atom·ic
aton·al
atone·ment
atro·cious
at·ro·phy
at·tach
at·ta·ché

at·tack
at·tain
at·tempt
at·ten·dance
at·ten·tive
at·ten·u·ate
at·test
at·tic
at·tire
at·ti·tude
at·tor·ney
at·trac·tive
at·tri·bute
at·tri·tion
at·tune
atyp·i·cal
au·burn
auc·tion·eer
au·da·cious
au·dac·i·ty (–ties)
au·di·ble
au·di·ence
au·dio·vi·su·al
au·dit
au·di·tion
au·di·to·ri·um
au·ger
aug·ment
auld lang syne (Scottish:
   the good old times)
aunt (relative; see *ant*)
au·ral (relating to the ear;
   see *oral*)
au re·voir (French: good-
   bye)
au·ri·cle

aus·pic·es
aus·pi·cious
aus·tere
aus·ter·i·ty (–ties)
au·then·tic
au·then·ti·cate
au·then·tic·i·ty
au·thor
au·thor·i·ta·tive
au·thor·i·ty (–ties)
au·tho·ri·za·tion
au·tho·rize
au·to·bio·graph·i·cal,
   au·to·bio·graph·ic
au·to·bi·og·ra·phy (–phies)
au·toc·ra·cy (–cies)
au·to·crat
au·to·graph
au·to·mat·ed
au·to·mat·ic
au·to·mat·i·cal·ly
au·to·ma·tion
au·tom·a·ton
au·to·mo·bile
au·to·mo·tive
au·ton·o·mous
au·ton·o·my (–mies)
au·top·sy (–sies)
au·to·sug·ges·tion
au·tumn
aux·il·ia·ry (–ries)
avail·abil·i·ty (–ties)
avail·able
av·a·lanche
av·a·rice
av·a·ri·cious

avenge
av·e·nue
av·er·age
averse
aver·sion
avert
avi·ary (–ar·ies)
avi·a·tion
avi·a·tor
av·id
av·o·ca·do (–dos *or* –does)
av·o·ca·tion
avoid·able
avoid·ance
av·oir·du·pois (French:
   weight)
await
awake
awak·en·ing
award
aware
away
awe·some
aw·ful
awhile
awk·ward
aw·ning
awoke
ax·i·al
ax·i·om
ax·i·om·at·ic
ax·is (ax·es)
ax·le
aza·lea
az·i·muth
azure

**B**

bab·ble
ba·by (ba·bies)
ba·boon
bac·ca·lau·re·ate
bach·e·lor
ba·cil·lus (–li)
back·bone
back·fire
back·log
back·stop
back·ward
ba·con
bac·te·ri·al
bac·te·ri·ol·o·gy
bac·te·ri·um (–ria)
bad·ger
bad·i·nage
bad·min·ton
baf·fle
bag·gage
bail (security for due
    appearance; see *bale*)
bai·liff
bai·li·wick
bak·ery (–er·ies)
bak·ing
bal·ance
bal·co·ny (–nies)
bale (large bundle; see *bail*)
balk
bal·lad
bal·last
bal·le·ri·na
bal·let
bal·lis·tics
bal·loon
bal·lot
balm
ba·lo·ney, bo·lo·ney
bal·sa
bam·boo
ba·nal
ba·nana
ban·dage
ban·dan·na
ban·di·try
bane·ful
ban·ish
ban·is·ter
bank·rupt

bank·rupt·cy (–cies)
ban·ner
ban·quet
ban·ter
bap·tism
bap·tize
bar·be·cue
bare (exposed); see *bear,
    beer*)
ba·rom·e·ter
ba·ron (a lord of the realm;
    see *barren*)
bar·rack
bar·rel
bar·ren (not reproducing;
    see *baron*)
bar·rette (hair pin; see
    *beret*)
bar·ri·cade
bar·ri·er
bar·room
base (bottom; see *bass*)
bash·ful
ba·sic
ba·si·cal·ly
ba·sil·i·ca
ba·sis (ba·ses)
bas·ket·ry (–ries)
bass (a deep tone; see
    *base*)
bas·si·net
bas·soon
bas·tard
baste
bas·tion
bathe
bat·tal·ion
bat·tle
bau·ble
baux·ite
bay·o·net
bay·ou
ba·zaar (market; see
    *bizarre*)
beach (shore; see *beech*)
bea·con
beady
bear (an animal, to endure,
    to give birth; see *bare,
    beer*)

beard
beast
beau
beau·ti·ful
beau·ti·fy
beau·ty (–ties)
be·cause
bed·lam
bed·ou·in, bed·u·in
    (bed·ou·ins, bed·u·ins)
    *often in CAPS*
beech (tree; see *beach*)
beer (alcoholic beverage;
    see *bare, bear*)
be·fore
be·fud·dle
beg·gar
be·gin·ning
be·go·nia
be·grudge
be·guile
be·hav·ior
be·he·moth
be·hest
be·hold·en
be·hoove
beige
be·ing
be·la·bor
be·lat·ed
bel·fry (–fries)
be·lie
be·lief
be·lieve
bell (chime; see *belle*)
belle (beauty; see *bell*)
bel·lig·er·ent
bel·lows
be·neath
bene·dic·tion
bene·fac·tor
be·nef·i·cence
ben·e·fi·cial
ben·e·fi·cia·ry (–ries)
be·nev·o·lence
be·nign
ben·zene, ben·zine
be·queath
be·quest
be·reave

be·ret (woolen cap; see *barrette*)
ber·serk
berth (place; see *birth*)
be·siege
bes·tial
be·stow
be·tray
be·tween
be·twixt
bev·el
bev·er·age
bevy (bev·ies)
be·wail
bi·an·nu·al
bi·as (–es)
bi·ble
bib·li·cal
bib·li·og·ra·phy (–phies)
bib·lio·phile
bib·u·lous
bi·cam·er·al
bi·car·bon·ate
bi·cen·ten·ni·al
bi·ceps
bi·cy·cle
bi·en·ni·al
bier
bi·fo·cal
big·a·my
big·ot
big·ot·ry (–ries)
bi·ki·ni
bi·lat·er·al
bi·lin·ear
bi·lin·gual
bil·ious
bil·let
bil·let-doux (French: a love letter)
bil·liards
bil·lion
bi·na·ry
bin·au·ral
bind·ery (–er·ies)
bin·oc·u·lar
bio·chem·is·try
bio·de·grad·able
bio·graph·i·cal
bi·og·ra·phy (–phies)

bi·o·log·i·cal
bi·ol·o·gy
bi·op·sy
bi·par·ti·san
bi·ra·cial
birth (originate; see *berth*)
bis·cuit
bi·son
bisque
bit·ter
bi·tu·mi·nous
biv·ouac
bi·zarre (out of the ordinary; see *bazaar*)
black·mail
blar·ney
bla·sé
blas·phe·my (–mies)
bla·tant
bla·zon
blem·ish
blight
blind·ly
blithe
blitz·krieg (German: war conducted with great speed)
bliz·zard
bloc (group; see *block*)
block (hinder; see *bloc*)
block·ade
blos·som
blotch
blown
blud·geon
blue
blurb
boar (wild pig; see *bore*)
board (a piece of wood; see *bored*)
bod·ily
bo·gey
bog·gle
bo·lo·gna
bo·lo·ney, ba·lo·ney
bol·ster
bom·bard
bona fide (Latin: in good faith)
bo·nan·za

bond·age
bon·fire
bo·nus
bon voy·age (French: farewell)
book·keep·ing
boo·mer·ang
boon·dog·gle
boor·ish
bo·rax
bor·der
bore (to drill; past of *bear*; dull person; see *boar*)
bored (past of *bore*; see *board*)
born (from birth; see *borne*)
borne (past participle of *bear*; see *born*)
bor·ough (town; see *borrow*)
bor·row (to receive with intention of returning; see *borough*)
borscht (Russian: soup of beets and sour cream)
bo·som
bos·sy
bot·a·ny (–nies)
bot·tle
bot·tom
bou·doir (French: bedroom, private sitting room)
bough (tree limb; see *bow*)
bouil·la·baisse (French: fish stew)
bouil·lon
boul·der
bou·le·vard
bound·ary (–aries)
boun·te·ous
bou·quet
bour·bon
bour·geois (plural also bourgeois) (French: middle class)
bou·ton·niere (French: flower worn in buttonhole)
bo·vine

bow (to bend; see *bough*)
bow·el
boy·cott
brace·let
braid
braille
braise
brake (to stop; see *break*)
bram·ble
bras·siere
bra·va·do
brav·ery
bra·vo (bra·vos)
brawny
bra·zen
breach
breadth
break (to tear; see *brake*)
break·fast
breathe
breath·less
breech·es
breeze
breth·ren
bre·via·ry (–ries)
brev·i·ty
brib·ery
bric-a-brac
brid·al (relating to a bride;
    see *bridle*)
bridge
bri·dle (horse's headgear;
    see *bridal*)
brief
bri·gade
brig·a·dier
brig·and
bright
bril·liant
brine

bri·quette, bri·quet
bris·tle
brit·tle
broach (to open up a
    subject for discussion;
    see *brooch*)
broad·cast
bro·cade
bro·co·li, broc·o·li
bro·chure
brogue
bro·ker·age
bro·mide
bron·chi·al
brooch (ornament; see
    *broach*)
broth·er·ly
brow·beat
browse
bruise
brunet, brun·ette
brusque
bru·tal
bub·ble
buc·ca·neer
buck·et
bu·col·ic
bud·get
buf·fa·lo
buf·fet (verb: a blow with
    the hand)
buf·fet (noun: meal set out
    for self-service)
buf·foon
bug·a·boo
bu·gle
build
bul·le·tin
bul·lion
bul·wark

bump·kin
bump·tious
bun·ga·low
bun·gle
buoy·an·cy
bur·den
bu·reau
bu·reau·cra·cy (–cies)
bu·reau·crat
bur·geon
bur·glar
buri·al
bur·lesque
bur·ly
burnt
bur·ro (donkey; see
    *burrow*)
bur·row (a hole made in the
    ground by an animal; see
    *burro*)
bur·sar
bush·el
busi·ness
bus·tle
busy
butch·er
butte
but·tock
but·ton
but·tress
bux·om
buy (purchase; see *by*)
buzz
buz·zard
by (near; see *buy*)
by·pass
by-pro·duct
by·stand·er
by·way

**C**

ca·bal
ca·bana
cab·a·ret
cab·bage
cab·i·net
ca·ble
ca·boose
cache
ca·chet
ca·coph·o·ny (–nies)
cac·tus
ca·dav·er
ca·dence
caf·e·te·ria
caf·feine
ca·gey
cais·son
ca·jole
ca·lam·i·ty (–ties)
cal·ci·fy
cal·ci·um
cal·cu·late
cal·cu·la·tor
cal·cu·lus (–lus·es)
cal·en·dar (a system for
    fixing divisions of time in
    order; see *calender*)
cal·en·der (to press
    between rollers or plates)
cal·i·ber, cal·i·bre
cal·i·brate
cal·i·co
cal·is·then·ics
cal·lig·ra·pher
cal·lig·ra·phy
cal·lous (feeling no
    emotion; see *callus*)
cal·lus (hard, thickened
    area of skin; see *callous*)
cal·o·rie, cal·o·ry (–ries)
cal·um·ny (–nies)
ca·lyp·so
ca·ma·ra·de·rie
ca·mel·lia, ca·me·lia
cam·eo (cam·eos)
cam·i·sole
cam·ou·flage
cam·paign
cam·phor

ca·nal
can·a·pé (French: type of
    appetizer)
ca·nard
ca·nas·ta
can·cel
can·cel·la·tion,
    can·cel·ation
can·cer
can·des·cence
can·di·da·cy (–cies)
can·di·date
can·dle
can·dor
ca·nine
can·is·ter
can·ker
can·ni·bal
can·non (gun; see *canon*)
can·not
ca·noe
canon (dogma; see *cannon*)
can·o·py (–pies)
can·ta·loupe
can·tan·ker·ous
can·ta·ta
can·teen
can·ter (horse's gait; see
    *cantor*)
can·ti·cle
can·ti·le·ver
can·to
can·tor (synagogue official
    who sings liturgy; see
    *canter*)
can·vas (closely woven
    cloth; see *canvass*)
can·vass (examine votes;
    see *canvas*)
can·yon
ca·pa·bil·i·ty (–ties)
ca·pa·ble
ca·pa·cious
ca·pac·i·ty (–ties)
ca·per
cap·il·lary (–lar·ies)
cap·i·tal (seat of
    government; see *capitol*)
cap·i·tal·ism

cap·i·tol (building in which
    legislature meets; see
    *capital*)
ca·pit·u·late
ca·pon
ca·price
ca·pri·cious
cap·sule
cap·tain
cap·tion
cap·ti·vate
car·a·mel
car·at, kar·at (unit of
    weight; see *caret, carrot*)
car·a·van
car·bine
car·bo·hy·drate
car·bon
car·bun·cle
car·bu·re·tor
car·cass
car·cin·o·gen
car·di·ac
car·di·gan
car·di·nal
car·dio·gram
car·di·ol·o·gist
ca·reen
ca·reer
care·ful
ca·ress
car·et (printing symbol; see
    *carat, carrot*)
car·go
car·i·ca·ture
car·ies
car·il·lon
car·nage
car·nal
car·ni·val
car·niv·o·rous
car·ol
car·pen·ter
carp·ing
car·rel
car·riage
car·ri·er
car·ri·on

car·rot (vegetable; see
    *carat, caret*)
carte blanche (French: full
    discretionary power)
car·tog·ra·pher
car·ton
car·toon
car·tridge
cas·cade
case·work
cash·ier
cash·mere
ca·si·no
cas·ket
cas·se·role
cas·sette, ca·sette
cas·sock
cast (direct; see *caste*)
cas·ta·net
caste (class; see *cast*)
cas·ti·gate
cas·tle
cas·tor
ca·su·al·ty (–ties)
cat·a·clysm
cat·a·comb
cat·a·lep·sy (–sies)
cat·a·log, cat·a·logue
cat·a·lyst
cat·a·pult
cat·a·ract
ca·tarrh
ca·tas·tro·phe
cata·ton·ic
cat·e·chism
cat·e·go·rize
cat·e·go·ry (–ries)
ca·ter
cat·er·cor·ner, kit·ty-
    cor·ner
cat·er·pil·lar
ca·thar·sis
ca·the·dral
cath·e·ter
cath·o·lic (universal; see
    *Catholic*)
Cath·o·lic (member of a
    Catholic church; see
    *catholic*)
cat·sup, ketch·up

cau·cus
caught
caul·dron
cau·li·flow·er
caulk
caus·al
caus·tic
cau·tion
cau·tious
cav·al·cade
cav·a·lier
cav·al·ry (–ries)
cav·i·ar
cav·il
cav·i·ty (–tics)
ca·vort
cease
ce·dar
cede
ceil·ing
cel·e·brate
ce·leb·ri·ty (–ties)
ce·ler·i·ty
cel·ery (–er·ies)
ce·les·tial
cel·i·ba·cy
cell (microscopic mass; see
    *sell*)
cel·lar (basement; see
    *seller*)
cel·lo
cel·lo·phane
cel·lu·loid
ce·ment
cem·e·tery (–ter·ies)
cen·ser (incense burner;
    see *censor*)
cen·sor (supervisor of
    conduct and morals; see
    *censer*)
cen·sure
cen·sus
cent (monetary unit; see
    *sent*)
cen·te·na·ry (–ries)
cen·ten·ni·al
cen·ter·piece
cen·ti·grade
cen·ti·me·ter
cen·trif·u·gal

cen·trip·e·tal
cen·tu·ry (–ries)
ce·phal·ic
ce·ram·ic
ce·re·al (prepared grain;
    see *serial*)
cer·e·bel·lum
ce·re·bral
cer·e·mo·ny (–nies)
ce·rise
cer·tain
cer·tif·i·cate
cer·ti·fy
cer·ti·tude
ces·sa·tion
ces·sion
cess·pool
chafe
chaff
cha·grin
chair·man
cha·let
chal·ice
chalk
chal·lenge
chal·lis (chal·lises)
cham·ber·lain
cham·bray
cha·me·leon
cham·ois
cham·pagne
cham·pi·on
chan·cel·lor
chan·cery (–cer·ies)
chan·de·lier
change
chan·nel
chan·tey, chan·ty
    (chan·teys, chan·ties)
Cha·nu·kah, Ha·nuk·kah
cha·os
chap·ar·ral
cha·peau (French: hat)
cha·pel
chap·er·on, chap·er·one
chap·lain
chap·ter
char·ac·ter
cha·rade
char·coal

charge
char·gé d'af·faires (French:
   a diplomat who
   substitutes for an
   ambassador)
char·i·ot
cha·ris·ma
char·i·ty (–ties)
char·la·tan
char·treuse
chary
chasm
chas·sis
chaste
chas·tise
chas·ti·ty
châ·teau (French: mansion)
chat·tel
chat·ty
chauf·feur
chau·vin·ism
check
chee·tah
chef
chem·i·cal
che·mise
che·mo·ther·a·py
che·nille
cher·ish
cher·ub
chess
che·va·lier
chev·ron
chic
chi·ca·nery (–ner·ies)
chick·a·dee
chic·o·ry (–ries)
chief
chif·fon
child (chil·dren)
chime
chim·ney
chim·pan·zee
chin·chil·la
chintz
chi·ro·prac·tor
chis·el
chiv·al·ry (–ries)
chlo·rine
chlo·ro·form

chlo·ro·phyll
choc·o·late
choir (group of singers; see
   *quire*)
chol·era
cho·les·ter·ol
chord
cho·re·og·ra·phy (–phies)
chorus
chor·tle
chris·ten
chro·mat·ic
chrome
chro·mo·some
chron·ic
chron·i·cle
chro·no·log·i·cal
chro·nol·o·gy (–gies)
chrys·a·lis (chry·sal·i·des,
   chrys·a·lis·es)
chry·san·the·mum
church
chute
ci·gar
cig·a·rette, cig·a·ret
cin·der
cin·e·ma
cin·na·mon
ci·pher
cir·cle
cir·cuit
cir·cu·lar
cir·cu·la·tion
cir·cum·cise
cir·cum·fer·ence
cir·cum·lo·cu·tion
cir·cum·scribe
cir·cum·spect
cir·cum·stance
cir·cum·stan·tial
cir·cum·vent
cir·rho·sis
cis·tern
cit·a·del
ci·ta·tion
cite (to quote; see *site*)
cit·i·zen
city
civ·ic
ci·vil·i·ty (–ties)

civ·i·li·za·tion
claim·ant
clair·voy·ance
clam·my
clam·or
clan·des·tine
clan·gor
claque
clar·et
clar·i·fy
clar·i·net
clar·i·on
clar·i·ty
clas·sic
clas·si·cal
clas·si·cist
clas·si·fied
class·less
clause
claus·tro·pho·bia
clav·i·chord
clav·i·cle
cleanse
clear·ance
cleave
clef
clem·en·cy (–cies)
cler·i·cal
cli·ché (French: trite
   expression)
click (slight sharp noise;
   see *clique*)
cli·en·tele
cliff
cli·mate
climb (to go upward; see
   *clime*)
clime (climate; see *climb*)
clin·ic
clique (exclusive group; see
   *click*)
clob·ber
clois·ter
clos·et
cloth
clothe
cloud
clout
clus·ter
clutch

co·ag·u·late
co·alesce
co·ali·tion
coarse (rough; see *couse*)
coax
co·bra
co·caine
cock·le·shell
cock·ney
co·coa
co·coon
cod·dle
co·de·fen·dant
co·deine
cod·ger
cod·i·cil
cod·i·fy
co·ed·u·ca·tion
co·ef·fi·cient
co·erce
cof·fers
cof·fin
co·gent
cog·i·tate
co·gnac
cog·ni·tion
cog·ni·zant
co·here
co·he·sive·ness
coif·fure
co·in·cide
col·an·der
col·ic
col·i·se·um
col·lab·o·rate
col·lapse
col·late
col·lat·er·al
col·league
col·lec·tive
col·lege
col·lide
col·lie
col·li·sion
col·lo·qui·al
col·lo·quy (–quies)
col·lu·sion
co·logne
co·lon

col·o·nel (army officer; see
    *kernel*)
co·lo·nial
col·on·nade
col·o·ny (–nies)
co·lo·phon
col·or
co·los·sal
col·umn
co·ma
comb
com·bat n., com·bat vb.
com·bi·na·tion
com·e·dy (–dies)
com·et
come·up·pance
com·fort·able
com·ma
com·man·deer
com·mand·ment
com·man·do
com·mem·o·rate
com·mence
com·mend
com·men·da·tion
com·men·su·rate
com·men·tary (–tar·ies)
com·men·ta·tor
com·merce
com·mer·cial
com·min·gle
com·mis·er·ate
com·mis·sar
com·mis·sary (–sar·ies)
com·mis·sion
com·mit
com·mit·tee
com·mode
com·mo·di·ous
com·mod·i·ty (–ties)
com·mo·dore
com·mon
com·mo·tion
com·mu·nal
com·mune
com·mu·ni·ca·ble
com·mu·ni·cate
com·mu·nion
com·mu·ni·qué

com·mu·nism
com·mu·nist
com·mu·ni·ty (–ties)
com·mute
com·pa·ny (–nies)
com·pan·ion
com·par·a·tive
com·pas·sion·ate
com·pat·i·ble
com·pel
com·pen·sate
com·pete
com·pe·tence
com·pe·ti·tion
com·pet·i·tor
com·pi·la·tion
com·pla·cent (self-satisfied;
    see *complaisant*)
com·plain
com·plais·ant (obliging; see
    *complacent*)
com·ple·ment (something
    that completes; see
    *compliment*)
com·plete
com·plex·i·ty (–ties)
com·pli·ant
com·pli·cate
com·plic·i·ty (–ties)
com·pli·ment (expression of
    praise; see *complement*)
com·ply
com·po·nent
com·pos·ite
com·po·si·tion
com·pos·i·tor
com·pound
com·pre·hend
com·pre·hen·sive
com·press
com·prise
com·pro·mise
comp·trol·ler, con·trol·ler
com·pul·sion
com·punc·tion
com·put·er
com·rade
con·ceal
con·cede

con·ceit
con·ceive
con·cen·trate
con·cen·tric
con·cept
con·cern
con·cert (noun), con·cert
  (verb)
con·cer·to
con·ces·sion
con·cil·i·ate
con·cise
con·clude
con·coct
con·com·i·tant
con·cord
con·course
con·crete
con·cu·bine
con·cu·pis·cent
con·cur·rent
con·cus·sion
con·dem·na·tion
con·dense
con·de·scend
con·di·ment
con·di·tion·al
con·do·lence
con·do·min·i·um
con·done
con·du·cive
con·duct (noun), con·duct
  (verb)
con·duit
con·fer·ence
con·fes·sion
con·fet·ti
con·fi·dant (one to whom
  secrets are entrusted;
  see *confident*)
con·fi·dante (a female
  confidant)
con·fi·dence
con·fi·dent (assured; see
  *confidant*)
con·fig·u·ra·tion
con·fine
con·firm
con·fis·cate

con·fla·gra·tion
con·flict
con·form
con·frere
con·fron·ta·tion
con·fu·sion
con·geal
con·ge·nial
con·gest
con·glom·er·ate
con·grat·u·late
con·gre·gate
con·gres·sio·nal
con·gru·ent
con·ic
co·ni·fer
con·jec·ture
con·ju·gal
con·ju·gate
con·junc·tion
con·jure
con·nect
con·nive
con·nois·seur
con·no·ta·tion
con·nu·bi·al
con·quer
con·quis·ta·dor (Spanish:
  one that conquers)
con·san·guin·i·ty (–ties)
con·science
con·sci·en·tious
con·scious
con·script (noun),
  con·script (verb)
con·se·crate
con·sec·u·tive
con·sen·sus
con·sent
con·se·quence
con·ser·va·tion
con·ser·va·tive
con·ser·va·to·ry (–ries)
con·sid·er
con·sign
con·sis·tent
con·sole (noun), con·sole
  (verb)
con·sol·i·date

con·som·mé
con·so·nance
con·spic·u·ous
con·spir·a·cy (–cies)
con·spir·a·tor
con·spire
con·sta·ble
con·stab·u·lary
con·stant
con·stel·la·tion
con·ster·na·tion
con·sti·pa·tion
con·stit·u·ent
con·sti·tute
con·sti·tu·tion
con·sti·tu·tion·al·i·ty
con·strain
con·strict
con·struc·tive
con·strue
con·sul
con·sul·ta·tion
con·sume
con·sum·er
con·sum·mate
con·sump·tion
con·tact
con·ta·gious
con·tain·er
con·tam·i·na·tion
con·tem·plate
con·tem·po·ra·ne·ous
con·tem·po·rary
con·tempt·ible
con·temp·tu·ous
con·tend
con·tent (noun), con·tent
  (verb, adjective)
con·tes·tant
con·text
con·tig·u·ous
con·ti·nence
con·ti·nent
con·tin·gen·cy (–cies)
con·tin·u·al
con·tin·u·um
con·tort
con·tour
con·tra·band

con·tra·cep·tion
con·trac·tion
con·trac·tu·al
con·tra·dict
con·tral·to
con·trary (–trar·ies)
con·trast (noun), con·trast (verb)
con·tra·vene
con·trib·ute
con·trite
con·trive
con·trol·ler, comp·trol·ler
con·tro·ver·sy (–sies)
con·tro·vert
con·tu·ma·cious
con·tu·me·li·ous
con·tu·sion
co·nun·drum
con·va·lesce
con·vene
con·ven·tion
con·ve·nience
con·verge
con·ver·sa·tion
con·ver·sion
con·vert·er
con·vey
con·vic·tion
con·vince
con·viv·ial
con·vo·ca·tion
con·vo·lu·tion
con·vulse
coo·lie
co·op·er·ate
co·or·di·nate
co·pi·ous
cop·u·late
co·quette
cor·dial
cor·don
cor·do·van
cor·du·roy
cor·nea
cor·ner
cor·net
cor·nu·co·pia
cor·ol·lary (–lar·ies)
cor·o·nary

cor·o·na·tion
cor·o·ner
cor·po·ral
cor·po·rate
cor·po·ra·tion
cor·po·re·al
corps (group; see *corpse*)
corpse (dead body; see *corps*)
cor·pu·lent
cor·pus·cle
cor·pus de·lic·ti (New Latin: fact necessary to prove a crime)
cor·ral
cor·rect
cor·rec·tion
cor·re·late
cor·re·la·tion
cor·re·spon·dence
cor·ri·dor
cor·rob·o·rate
cor·rode
cor·ro·sion
cor·rupt
cor·sage
cor·set
cor·tege, cor·tège
cor·ti·sone
co·sign·er
cos·met·ic
cos·mo·pol·i·tan
cos·mos
cos·tume
cost·ly
co·te·rie
cot·tage
cou·gar
could
coun·cil (advisory group; see *counsel*)
coun·sel (advice; see *council*)
coun·sel·or, coun·sel·lor
coun·te·nance
coun·ter·feit
coun·try
coup
coupe
cou·ple

cou·pon
cou·ra·geous
cou·ri·er
course (direction, customary procedure; see *coarse*)
cour·te·ous
cous·in
cou·tu·ri·er
cov·e·nant
co·vert
coy·ote
crab·by
cra·dle
cra·ni·al
cra·vat
cray·on
crease
cre·ativ·i·ty
crea·ture
crèche
cre·dence
cre·den·tial
cred·i·ble
cred·it
cre·do
cre·du·li·ty
cre·du·lous
cre·mate
cre·ole
cre·o·sote
crepe, crêpe
cre·scen·do
cres·cent
cre·tin
cre·vasse
crev·ice
cri·er
crim·i·nal
crim·i·nol·o·gy
cringe
crin·kle
crip·ple
cri·sis (–ses)
cris·py
cri·te·ri·on (–ria *or* –rions)
crit·i·cal
crit·i·cism
cri·tique
cro·chet

crotch·ety
crock·ery
croc·o·dile
cro·cus
crois·sant
cro·ny (–nies)
cro·quet
cross·road
crouch
crou·ton
crowd
cru·cial
cru·ci·fix (–fix·es)
cru·el
cruise
cru·sade
crutch
crux
cry
cryp·tic
crys·tal
cu·bi·cal (shaped like a cube; see *cubicle*)
cu·bi·cle (sleeping compartment; see *cubical*)

cud·dle
cud·gel
cui·sine
cul-de·sac (culs-de-sac) (French: street closed at one end)
cu·li·nary
cul·mi·nate
cul·pa·ble
cul·ti·vate
cul·tur·al
cum·ber·some
cu·mu·la·tive
cun·ning
cup·board
cu·po·la
cu·rate
cu·ra·tor
cur·few
cu·ri·ous
cur·rant (berry; see *current*)
cur·ren·cy (–cies)
cur·rent (present; see *currant*)
cur·ric·u·lum

cur·so·ry
cur·tail·ment
cur·tain
cur·te·sy (–sies)
curt·sy, curt·sey (curt·sies *or* curt·seys)
cur·va·ture
curve
cush·ion
cus·tard
cus·to·di·an
cus·to·dy (–dies)
cus·tom
cus·tom·ary
cus·tom·er
cu·ti·cle
cut·lery
cy·cle
cy·clone
cyl·in·der
cym·bal
cyn·ic
cy·press
cyst
czar, tsar

# D

dab·ble
dad·dy (daddies)
daf·fo·dil
dag·ger
da·guerre·o·type (French:
    an early photograph
    produced in a special
    manner)
dahl·ia
dai·ly
dai·ry
dai·sy (daisies)
dam·age
dam·ask
dam·sel
dance
dan·de·li·on
dan·druff
dan·ger·ous
dan·gle
dash·board
da·ta
date
daugh·ter
daunt·less
daw·dle
daz·zle
dea·con
dear (expensive; expression
    of endearment; see *deer*)
de·ba·cle
de·base·ment
de·bat·able
de·bauch
de·ben·ture
de·bil·i·tate
deb·it
deb·o·nair
de·brief
de·bris (plural also debris)
debt
debt·or
de·but
de·cade
dec·a·dence
de·caf·fein·ate
de·cal
de·cap·i·tate
de·cath·lon
de·cay

de·ceased
de·cree
de·ceit
de·ceive
de·cent
de·cen·tral·iza·tion
de·cep·tion
deci·bel
de·cide
de·cid·u·ous
dec·i·mal
dec·i·mate
de·ci·pher
de·ci·sion
dec·la·ma·tion
dec·la·ra·tion
de·clas·si·fy
de·clen·sion
dec·li·na·tion
de·cliv·i·ty (–ties)
dé·col·le·tage (French: low
    neckline)
de·com·pose
de·con·tam·i·nate
de·cor, dé·cor (French:
    decoration)
dec·o·rate
dec·o·rous
de·co·rum
de·coy (noun), de·coy
    (verb)
de·crease
de·crep·it
de·cry
ded·i·cate
de·duc·tion
deer (an animal; see *dear*)
de fac·to (New Latin: in
    reality)
def·a·ma·tion
de·fault
de·fec·tive
de·fen·dant
de·fense, de·fence
def·er·ence
de·fi·ance
de·fi·cien·cy (–cies)
def·i·cit
de·fine
def·i·nite

def·i·ni·tion
de·fo·li·ant
de·for·mi·ty (–ties)
de·fraud
de·fray
deft
de·fy
de·gen·er·ate
de·gree
de·hy·drate
de·i·fy
deign
de·i·ty (–ties)
de·lay
de·lec·ta·ble
del·e·gate
de·lete
del·e·te·ri·ous
de·lib·er·ate
del·i·cate
de·li·cious
de·light
de·lin·eate
de·lin·quent
de·lir·i·ous
de·liv·ery (–er·ies)
de·lude
del·uge
de·lu·sion
de·luxe
dem·a·gogue, dem·a·gog
de·mand
de·mean·or
de·mil·i·ta·rize
de·mise
demi·tasse
de·moc·ra·cy (–cies)
de·mol·ish
dem·on·strate
de·mor·al·ize
de·mur
de·mure
de·ni·al
den·i·grate
den·im
de·nom·i·na·tion
de·nom·i·na·tor
de·noue·ment (French:
    outcome)
de·nounce

dense
den·tal
den·tist·ry
de·odor·ant
de·part·ment
de·par·ture
de·pen·dent
de·pict
de·pil·a·to·ry (–ries)
de·plete
de·plor·able
de·por·ta·tion
de·pos·it
de·pos·i·to·ry (–ries)
de·pot
dep·re·cate
de·pre·ciate
dep·re·da·tion
de·pres·sion
de·pri·va·tion
depth
dep·u·ty (–ties)
de·reg·u·la·tion
der·e·lict
der·i·va·tion
der·ma·tol·o·gy
de·rog·a·to·ry
der·rick
de·scend·ant, de·scend·ent
de·scen·sion
de·scent
de·scribe
de·scrip·tion
des·e·crate
de·seg·re·ga·tion
de·sert (arid barren tract;
  see *dessert*)
des·ic·cate
de·sid·er·a·tum (–ta)
de·sign
des·ig·nate
de·sir·able
de·sist
des·o·la·tion
des·per·ate
de·spi·ca·ble
de·spise
de·spite
de·spon·dent
des·pot

des·sert (course served at
  end of meal; see *desert*)
des·ti·ny (–nies)
des·ti·tute
de·stroy
de·struc·tion
de·sue·tude
des·ul·to·ry
de·tach
de·tail
de·tect
de·ter·gent
de·te·ri·o·rate
de·ter·mi·na·tion
de·ter·rent
det·o·na·tion
de·tour
de·tract
det·ri·ment
deuce
de·val·u·a·tion
dev·as·tate
de·vel·op
de·vi·ate
de·vice (mechanism; see
  *devise*)
de·vi·ous
de·vise (to invent; see
  *device*)
de·void
de·vour
de·vout
dew (moisture; see *due*)
dex·ter·i·ty (–ties)
di·a·be·tes
di·a·bol·ic
di·a·dem
di·ag·no·sis (–no·ses)
di·ag·o·nal
di·a·gram·ing,
  di·a·gram·ming
di·a·lect
di·a·logue
di·am·e·ter
di·a·mond
di·a·per
di·a·phragm
di·ar·rhea
di·a·ry (–ries)
di·a·ther·my

di·a·tribe
di·chot·o·my (–mies)
dic·tate
dic·ta·tion
dic·ta·tor
dic·tio·nary (–nar·ies)
dic·tum (dic·ta, dic·tums)
di·dac·tic
die (to expire; see *dye*)
die·sel
di·etary
dif·fer·ence
dif·fer·en·tial
dif·fi·cult
dif·fi·dence
dif·fuse
di·gest·ible
dig·it
dig·i·tal·is
dig·ni·fy
dig·ni·tary (–tar·ies)
di·gress
di·lap·i·dat·ed
di·late
dil·a·tory
di·lem·ma
dil·et·tante
dil·i·gence
dil·ly·dal·ly
di·lute
di·men·sion
di·min·ish
di·min·u·tive
din·er (restaurant; see
  *dinner*)
di·nette
din·ghy (dinghies)
din·ner (meal; see *diner*)
di·no·saur
di·o·cese
di·ora·ma
diph·the·ria
diph·thong
di·plo·ma
di·plo·ma·cy
di·rec·tion
di·rec·tor·ate
dirge
dis·abil·i·ty
dis·ad·van·tage

dis·agree
dis·al·low
dis·ap·pear
dis·ap·point
dis·ap·prove
dis·ar·ma·ment
dis·arm·ing
dis·ar·range
dis·ar·ray
dis·as·so·ci·ate
dis·as·ter
dis·as·trous
dis·avow
dis·burse
disc, disk
dis·cern
dis·cern·ible, dis·cern·able
dis·ci·ple
dis·ci·pline
dis·claim·er
dis·clo·sure
dis·com·fort
dis·con·cert·ing
dis·con·nect
dis·con·so·late
dis·con·tin·ue
dis·cor·dant
dis·count
dis·cour·age
dis·cour·te·ous
dis·cov·ery (−er·ies)
dis·creet (showing
    discernment in speech;
    see *discrete*)
dis·crep·an·cy (−cies)
dis·crete (individually
    distinct; see *discreet*)
dis·cre·tion
dis·crim·i·nate
dis·cur·sive
dis·cus (disk; see *discuss*)
dis·cuss (to talk about; see
    *discus*)
dis·cus·sion
dis·dain
dis·ease
dis·em·bark
dis·en·chant
dis·en·fran·chise
dis·en·gage

dis·en·tan·gle
dis·gorge
dis·grace
dis·guise
dis·gust·ing
dis·har·mo·ny
dis·heart·en
di·shev·el
dis·hon·es·ty
dis·il·lu·sion
dis·in·cline
dis·in·fec·tant
dis·in·her·it
dis·in·te·grate
dis·in·ter
disk, disc
dis·lodge
dis·mal
dis·miss
dis·obe·di·ent
dis·obey
dis·or·ga·nized
dis·par·age
dis·pa·rate
dis·pas·sion·ate
dis·patch
dis·pel
dis·pens·able
dis·pen·sa·ry (−ries)
dis·pen·sa·tion
dis·perse
dis·plea·sure
dis·pose
dis·pos·sess
dis·pute
dis·pro·por·tion
dis·re·gard
dis·re·pair
dis·re·pute
dis·rupt
dis·sat·is·fy
dis·sect
dis·sem·ble
dis·sem·i·nate
dis·sen·sion, dis·sen·tion
dis·sent
dis·ser·ta·tion
dis·ser·vice
dis·si·dent
dis·sim·i·lar

dis·sim·u·late
dis·si·pate
dis·so·ci·ate
dis·so·lute
dis·solve
dis·so·nance
dis·suade
dis·taff
dis·tain
dis·tance
dis·taste·ful
dis·tem·per
dis·tinct
dis·tin·guish
dis·tor·tion
dis·tract
dis·traught
dis·tress
dis·tri·bu·tion
dis·tur·bance
dis·uni·ty
di·verge
di·verse
di·ver·si·fy
div·i·dend
di·vine
di·vis·i·ble
di·vi·sion
di·vi·sive
di·vorce
div·ot
di·vulge
doc·ile
dock·et
doc·tor
doc·trine
doc·u·ment
dod·der·ing
dodge
doe (female deer; see
    *dough*)
dog·ger·el
dog·ma
doi·ly
dole·ful
dol·lar
do·lor·ous
dol·phin
do·main
do·mes·tic

do·mi·cile

dom·i·nance

dom·i·neer

do·min·ion

dom·i·no

do·nate

don·key

do·nor

doo·dle

dor·mant

dor·mi·to·ry (–ries)

dor·sal

dos·age

dos·sier

dou·ble

doubt

douche

dough (flour mixture; money; see *doe*)

dough·nut

dour

douse, dowse

dow·a·ger

down·ward

dow·ry (dowries)

dox·ol·o·gy (–gies)

doz·en

draft

drag·net

drag·on

drain

dra·ma

drap·ery (–er·ies)

drawl

drea·ry

dredge

driv·el

driz·zle

droll

drom·e·dary (–dar·ies)

drought, drouth

drowsy

drudge

drug·gist

drunk·ard

dry

du·al (two parts; see *duel*)

du·bi·ous

duc·tile

dud·geon

due (owing; see *dew*)

du·el (combat; see *dual*)

du·et

duf·fel, duf·fle

dul·cet

dul·ci·mer

dumb·bell

dumb·found, dum·found

dun·ga·ree

dun·geon

du·plex

du·pli·cate

du·plic·i·ty (–ties)

du·ra·ble

du·ra·tion

du·ress

du·ti·ful

dwarf

dwin·dle

dye (color; see *die*)

dy·nam·ic

dy·na·mite

dy·nas·ty (–ties)

dys·en·tery (–ter·ies)

dys·lex·ia

dys·pha·sia

dys·tro·phy (–phies)

**E**

ea·ger
ea·gle
ear·ache
early
ear·nest
earn·ings
ear·ring
earth
ea·sel
ease·ment
eas·i·ly
east·ern
easy
eau de co·logne (French: cologne)
eaves·drop
eb·o·ny (–nies)
ebul·lient
ec·cen·tric
ec·cle·si·as·tic
ech·e·lon
echo (ech·oes)
éclair
eclec·tic
eclipse
ecol·o·gy
eco·nom·ic
ec·sta·sy (–sies)
ec·stat·ic
ec·u·men·i·cal
ecu·me·nism
ec·ze·ma
edge
ed·i·ble
edict
ed·i·fi·ca·tion
ed·i·fice
edi·tion
ed·i·tor
ed·u·ca·tion
ee·rie, ee·ry
ef·face
ef·fect (to accomplish; see *affect*)
ef·fem·i·nate
ef·fer·ves·cence
ef·fi·ca·cious
ef·fi·ca·cy (–cies)
ef·fi·cien·cy (–cies)
ef·fi·gy (–gies)

ef·fort·less
ef·fron·tery
ef·fu·sion
egal·i·tar·i·an
ego·cen·tric
ego·tist
egre·gious
eighth
ei·ther
ejac·u·late
elab·o·rate
elapse
elas·tic
ela·tion
el·bow
el·der·ly
elec·tion
elec·tor·al
elec·tric
elec·tro·car·dio·gram
elec·tro·cute
elec·trode
elec·trol·y·sis
elec·tron
el·ee·mos·y·nary
el·e·gance
ele·gi·ac
el·e·gy (–gies)
el·e·men·ta·ry
el·e·phant
el·e·va·tion
elev·en
elic·it (draw out; see *illicit*)
el·i·gi·ble
elim·i·nate
eli·sion
elite
elix·ir
el·lipse
el·o·cu·tion
elon·gate
elope
el·o·quence
elu·ci·date
elude (avoid; see *allude*)
elu·sive
ema·ci·at·ed
em·a·nate
eman·ci·pate
emas·cu·late

em·bar·go
em·bar·ka·tion
em·bar·rass
em·bas·sy (–sies)
em·bel·lish
em·ber
em·bez·zle
em·bit·ter
em·bla·zon
em·blem
em·body
em·brace
em·broi·der
em·broi·dery (–der·ies)
em·broil
em·bryo
em·bry·ol·o·gy
em·bry·on·ic
em·cee (also M.C.)
emend
em·er·ald
emerge
emer·gen·cy (–cies)
emer·i·tus (–ti)
em·ery (–er·ies)
emet·ic
em·i·grate (to leave one's country; see *immigrate*)
émi·gré, emi·gré
em·i·nence
em·is·sary
emis·sion
emol·lient
emol·u·ment
emo·tion
em·pa·thy
em·per·or
em·pha·sis
em·pha·size
em·phat·ic
em·pire
em·pir·i·cal
em·place·ment
em·ploy·able
em·ploy·ee, em·ploye
em·ploy·ment
em·po·ri·um
emp·ty
em·py·re·an
em·u·late

emul·si·fy
en·able
en·act·ment
enam·el
en·camp·ment
en·ceph·a·li·tis
  (en·ceph·a·lit·i·des)
en·chant
en·cir·cle
en·close, in·close
en·clo·sure
en·code
en·co·mi·um
en·com·pass
en·core
en·coun·ter
en·cour·age
en·croach
en·cum·ber
en·cum·brance
en·cyc·li·cal
en·cy·clo·pe·dia
en·dan·ger
en·dear·ment
en·deav·or
en·dem·ic
en·dive
end·less
en·do·crine
en·do·cri·nol·o·gy
en·dorse
en·dow·ment
en·dur·ance
en·dure
en·e·ma
en·e·my (–mies)
en·er·get·ic
en·er·gize
en·er·gy
en·er·vate
en·fran·chise
en·gage
en·gage·ment
en·gen·der
en·gi·neer
en·grave
en·gross
en·gulf
en·hance
enig·ma

en·join
en·joy·ment
en·large·ment
en·light·en·ment
en·list
en·liv·en
en masse
en·mesh
en·mi·ty (–ties)
en·no·ble
en·nui (French: boredom)
enor·mous
enough
en·plane
en·rage
en·rap·ture
en·rich
en·roll·ment
en route
en·sem·ble
en·shrine
en·sign
en·slave
en·sue
en·tail
en·tan·gle
en·ter·prise
en·ter·tain
en·thrall
en·throne
en·thu·si·asm
en·tice
en·tire·ly
en·tire·ty (–ties)
en·ti·tle
en·ti·ty (–ties)
en·tomb
en·to·mol·o·gy
en·tou·rage
en·trails
en·trance
en·trant
en·treat
en·trée, en·tree
en·trench
en·tre·pre·neur
en·trust
en·try
en·twine
enu·mer·ate

enun·ci·ate
enun·ci·a·tion
en·vel·op (enclose
  completely; see
  *envelope*)
en·ve·lope (container for
  letter; see *envelop*)
en·vi·able
en·vi·ous
en·vi·ron·ment
en·vi·rons
en·vi·sion
envoi (final stanza of
  ballade; see *envoy*)
en·voy (government
  representative; see *envoi*)
en·vy
en·zyme
eon
ep·au·let, ep·au·lette
  (French: shoulder
  ornament)
ephem·er·al
ep·ic
ep·i·cure
ep·i·dem·ic
epi·der·mis
ep·i·gram
ep·i·gram·mat·ic
ep·i·lep·sy
ep·i·logue
ep·i·sode
epis·tle
ep·i·thet
epit·o·me
ep·och·al
equa·ble
equal
equal·ize
equa·nim·i·ty (–ties)
equate
equa·tion
equa·tor
eques·tri·an
equi·dis·tant
equi·lat·er·al
equi·lib·ri·um
equine
equi·noc·tial
equi·nox

equip
equip·ment
eq·ui·ta·ble
eq·ui·ty (–ties)
equiv·a·lent
equiv·o·cate
era
erad·i·cate
eras·er (a device to remove marks; see *erasure*)
era·sure (act of erasing; see *eraser*)
ere
erec·tion
er·go (Latin: therefore, hence)
er·mine
erode
erog·e·nous
ero·sion
erot·ic
err
er·rand
er·rant
er·rat·ic
er·ro·ne·ous
er·ror
er·satz
erst·while
er·u·dite
erup·tion
es·ca·late
es·ca·la·tor
es·ca·pade
es·cape
es·ca·role
es·chew
es·cort
es·crow
esoph·a·gus
es·o·ter·ic
es·pe·cial·ly
es·pi·o·nage
es·pla·nade
es·pouse
espres·so
es·prit de corps (French: a common enthusiasm for the group)
es·quire

es·say (noun), es·say (verb)
es·sence
es·sen·tial
es·tab·lish
es·tate
es·teem
es·thet·ic
es·ti·ma·ble
es·ti·mate
es·trange
es·tu·ary (–ar·ies)
et cet·era (Latin: and so forth)
etch·ing
eter·nal
eter·ni·ty (–ties)
ether
ethe·re·al
eth·i·cal
eth·ics
eth·nic
ethos
eth·yl
eti·ol·o·gy
et·i·quette
étude
et·y·mol·o·gy (–gies)
eu·ca·lyp·tus (–ti)
eu·chre
eu·gen·ic
eu·lo·gy (–gies)
eu·nuch
eu·phe·mism
eu·phon·ic
eu·pho·ria
eu·re·ka
eu·tha·na·sia
evac·u·ate
evade
eval·u·ate
ev·a·nes·cence
evan·ge·list
evap·o·rate
eva·sion
even·tu·al·i·ty (–ties)
ev·ery·where
evict
ev·i·dent
evil
evince

evis·cer·ate
evoc·a·tive
evoke
evo·lu·tion
evolve
ex·ac·er·bate
ex·act
ex·act·ly
ex·ag·ger·ate
ex·alt
ex·am·i·na·tion
ex·am·ple
ex·as·per·ate
ex·ca·va·tion
ex·ceed
ex·cel
ex·cel·lent
ex·cel·si·or
ex·cept (leave out; see *accept*)
ex·cep·tion·al
ex·cerpt
ex·cess
ex·change
ex·che·quer
ex·cise (noun), ex·cise (verb)
ex·cite·ment
ex·claim
ex·cla·ma·tion
ex·clude
ex·clu·sive
ex·com·mu·ni·cate
ex·co·ri·ate
ex·cre·ment
ex·cru·ci·at·ing
ex·cur·sion
ex·cus·ably
ex·e·cra·ble
ex·e·cute
ex·e·cut·able
ex·ec·u·tive
ex·ec·u·tor
ex·e·ge·sis
ex·em·pla·ry
ex·em·pli·fy
ex·empt
ex·emp·tion
ex·er·cise
ex·ert

ex·ha·la·tion
ex·haust
ex·hib·it
ex·hil·a·rate
ex·hort
ex·hume
ex·i·gen·cy (–cies)
ex·ig·u·ous
ex·ile
ex·is·tence
ex·is·ten·tial·ism
ex·it
ex·o·dus
ex·on·er·ate
ex·or·bi·tant
ex·or·cise
ex·o·ter·ic
ex·ot·ic
ex·pand
ex·panse
ex·pa·tri·ate
ex·pec·tan·cy (–cies)
ex·pec·to·rate
ex·pe·di·en·cy (–cies)
ex·pe·dite
ex·pe·di·tion
ex·pe·di·tious
ex·pel
ex·pend·able
ex·pen·di·ture
ex·pense
ex·pe·ri·ence
ex·per·i·ment
ex·pert
ex·per·tise
ex·pi·ate

ex·pi·ra·tion
ex·plain
ex·plan·a·tory
ex·ple·tive
ex·pli·ca·ble
ex·plic·it
ex·plode
ex·ploi·ta·tion
ex·plore
ex·plor·a·to·ry
ex·plo·sion
ex·po·nent
ex·port (noun), ex·port (verb)
ex·pose (to disclose; see *exposé*)
ex·po·sé (a statement; see *expose*)
ex·po·si·tion
ex post fac·to (Latin: after the fact)
ex·pos·tu·late
ex·po·sure
ex·pound
ex·press
ex·press·way
ex·pro·pri·ate
ex·pul·sion
ex·punge
ex·pur·gate
ex·qui·site
ex·tant
ex·tem·po·ra·ne·ous
ex·tem·po·rize
ex·tend
ex·ten·sion

ex·ten·sive
ex·tent
ex·ten·u·ate
ex·te·ri·or
ex·ter·mi·nate
ex·ter·nal
ex·tinct
ex·tin·guish
ex·tir·pate
ex·tol
ex·tort
ex·tra
ex·tract (noun), ex·tract (verb)
ex·tra·cur·ric·u·lar
ex·tra·dite
ex·tra·mar·i·tal
ex·tra·ne·ous
ex·traor·di·nary
ex·trap·o·late
ex·tra·sen·so·ry
ex·tra·ter·res·tri·al
ex·tra·ter·ri·to·ri·al
ex·trav·a·gance
ex·tra·vert, ex·tro·vert
ex·treme
ex·trem·i·ty (–ties)
ex·tri·cate
ex·trin·sic
ex·tru·sion
ex·u·ber·ant
ex·ude
ex·ult
ex·ul·tant
eye
eyre

**F**

fa·ble
fab·ric
fab·ri·cate
fab·u·lous
fa·cade, fa·çade
face
fac·et
fa·ce·tious
fa·cial
fac·ile
fa·cil·i·tate
fa·cil·i·ty (–ties)
fac·sim·i·le
fac·tion
fac·to·ry (–ries)
fac·tu·al
fac·ul·ty (–ties)
fad·dist
Fahr·en·heit
fail·ure
faint (lose consciousness; see *feint*)
fairy
fait ac·com·pli (French: accomplished fact)
faith·ful
fak·er
fal·con
fall
fal·la·cious
fal·la·cy (–cies)
fal·li·ble
fal·low
fal·set·to
fal·si·fy
fal·ter
fa·mil·iar
fam·i·ly (–lies)
fam·ine
fam·ish
fa·mous
fa·nat·ic
fan·ci·ful
fan·fare
fan·tasm, phan·tasm
fan·tas·tic
fan·ta·sy (–sies)
farce
far·away

far·ci·cal
fare·well
fa·ri·na
farm·er
far·ther
fas·ci·nate
fas·cism
fash·ion·able
fas·ten
fas·tid·i·ous
fa·tal
fate
fa·ther
fath·om
fa·tigue
fat·ten
fat·u·ous
fau·cet
fault·less
faun (mythological being; see *fawn*)
fau·na
faux pas (French: a social blunder)
fa·vor·able
fawn (young deer; see *faun*)
fear·ful
fea·si·ble
feast
feat (deed; see *feet*)
feath·er
fea·ture
fe·cund
fed·er·al
fee
fee·ble
feet (plural of foot; see *feat*)
feign
feint (something feigned; see *faint*)
fe·lic·i·tate
fe·line
fel·low·ship
fel·o·ny
fe·male
fem·i·nine
fence

fe·ral
fer·ment (noun), fer·ment (verb)
fe·ro·cious
fer·ret
fer·ry (–ries)
fer·tile
fer·til·ize
fer·vent
fer·vid
fer·vor
fes·ti·val
fes·toon
fe·tal
fet·id
fe·tus
feud
feu·dal
fe·ver
few
fi·an·cé (French: engaged man)
fi·an·cée (French: engaged woman)
fi·as·co
fi·ber·glass
fic·tion
fic·ti·tious
fid·dle
fi·del·i·ty (–ties)
fid·get
fi·du·cia·ry (–ries)
field
fiend
fierce
fi·ery
fi·es·ta
fifth
fif·ti·eth
fight
fig·ment
fig·ure
fig·u·rine
fil·a·ment
fil·ial
fil·i·bus·ter
fil·i·gree
fil·let, fi·let
fil·ly (fillies)

film
fil·ter
fi·nal
fi·na·le
fi·nance
fi·nan·cier
fine
fi·nesse
fin·ger·print
fi·nis
fin·ish
fi·nite
fire
fiord, fjord
fir·ma·ment
first
fis·cal
fis·sure
fix·ture
flac·cid
flag·el·late
flag·on
flag·pole
fla·grant
flair (natural aptitude; see *flare*)
flak
flam·boy·ant
fla·min·go
flam·ma·ble
flan·nel
flap·per
flare (unsteady glaring light; see *flair*)
flat·tery (–ter·ies)
flaunt
fla·vor
flaw·less
flax·en
flea (insect; see *flee*)
fledg·ling
flee (to run from; see *flea*)
fleece
fleur-de-lis, fleur-de-lys (fleurs-de-lis *or* fleur-de-lis, fleurs-de-lys *or* fleur-de-lys)
flew (past tense of fly; see *flue*)

flex·i·ble
fli·er
flight
flir·ta·tion
float·ing
floc·cu·lent
flock
flog
flood·light
floor·board
flor·al
flo·res·cence
flo·ri·cul·ture
flor·id
flo·rist
flo·ta·tion
flo·til·la
flot·sam
flounce
floun·der
flour (grain; see *flower*)
flow·chart
flow·er (blossom; see *flour*)
fluc·tu·ate
flue (air channel; see *flew*)
flu·ent
flu·id
flu·o·res·cent
flu·o·ri·date
flu·o·ri·nate
flu·o·ro·scope
flute
fly (flies)
fo·cal
fo·cus (–cus·es *or* –ci)
foe
foi·ble
fold·er
fo·liage
fo·lio
folk
fol·li·cle
fol·low
fol·ly (follies)
fo·ment
fon·dle
fon·due
food
fool·ish

foot·age
foot·note
for·age
for·ay
for·bear·ance
for·bid·den
force
for·ceps
forc·ible
fore·bear, for·bear
fore·cast
fore·clo·sure
for·eign
fore·man
fo·ren·sic
for·est·ry
fore·word (preface; see *forward*)
for·ev·er
for·feit
forg·ery (er·ies)
for·get·ful
for·giv·ing
for·go, fore·go
for·got·ten
fork
for·lorn
for·mal·i·ty (–ties)
for·mal·ly (following established custom; see *formerly*)
for·mat
for·ma·tive
for·mer·ly (at an earlier time; see *formally*)
for·mi·da·ble
for·mu·la (–las *or* –lae)
for·mu·late
for·syth·ia
fort (fortified place; see *forte*)
forte (one's strong point; see *fort*)
forth (forward; see *fourth*)
forth·right
for·ti·eth
for·ti·fi·ca·tion
for·tis·si·mo
for·ti·tude

fort·night
for·tress
for·tu·itous
for·tu·nate
fo·rum
for·ward (in front; see
    *foreword*)
fos·sil
fos·ter
foul (offensive to the
    senses; see *fowl*)
foun·da·tion
found·ry (–ries)
foun·tain
four
fourth (musical interval;
    see *forth*)
fowl (bird; see *foul*)
foy·er
fra·cas (–cas·es)
frac·tion
frac·ture
frag·ile
frag·ment
fra·grant
frail
fran·chise
frank·fur·ter
frank·in·cense
fran·tic
frap·pe, frap·pé
fra·ter·ni·ty (–ties)
fraud

fraud·u·lent
fraught
free·dom
freeze (turn into ice; see
    *frieze*)
freight
fre·net·ic, phre·net·ic
fren·zy (fren·zies)
fre·quent (adjective),
    fre·quent (verb)
fresh·man (–men)
Freud·ian
fri·ar (monk; see *fryer*)
fric·as·see
fric·tion
friend
frieze (architectural
    decoration; see *freeze*)
frig·ate
fright·en
fringe ben·e·fit
frisky
frit·ter
friv·o·lous
frol·ic
front·age
fron·tier
fron·tis·piece
fro·zen
fru·gal
fru·ition
fruit·ful
frus·trate

fry·er (something intended
    for frying; see *friar*)
fuch·sia
fu·el
fu·gi·tive
fugue
ful·crum
ful·fill, ful·fil
ful·some
fu·mi·gate
func·tion·al
fun·da·men·tal
fu·ner·al
fu·ne·re·al
fun·nel
fu·ri·ous
furl
fur·lough
fur·nace
fur·ni·ture
fu·ror
fur·ri·er
fur·row
fur·ther
fur·tive
fuse
fu·se·lage
fus·ible
fu·sil·lade
fu·sion
fu·tile
fu·til·i·ty (–ties)
fu·ture

gab·er·dine
gad·get
gai·ety (–eties)
gain·ful·ly
gait (manner of walking; see *gate*)
gal·axy (gal·ax·ies)
gal·lant
gal·le·on
gal·lery (–ler·ies)
gal·ley
gall·ing
gal·lon
gal·lop
ga·lore
ga·losh (–es)
gal·lows
gal·va·nize
gam·bit
gam·ble (bet on an uncertain outcome; see *gambol*)
gam·bol (skip about; see *gamble*)
game·keep·er
gam·ut
gan·der
gan·gli·on (gan·glia)
gan·grene
ga·rage
gar·bage
gar·ble
gar·den·er
gar·de·nia
gar·gan·tuan
gar·goyle
gar·ish
gar·land
gar·ment
gar·ner
gar·nish
gar·nish·ee
gar·ri·son
gar·ru·lous
gas·eous
gas·ket
gas·o·line
gas·tric
gas·tron·o·my

gate (opening in wall or fence; see *gait*)
gath·er·ing
gauche
gaudy
gauge
gaunt
gaunt·let
gauze
gav·el
ga·ze·bo
ga·zelle
ga·zette
gei·sha
gel·a·tin
gen·darme
gene
ge·ne·al·o·gy (–gies)
gen·er·al·i·ty (–ties)
gen·er·ate
gen·er·a·tion
gen·er·ic
gen·er·ous
gen·e·sis (–e·ses)
ge·net·ic
ge·nial
gen·i·tal
ge·nius (–nius·es *or* –nii)
gen·o·cide
genre
gen·teel
gen·tile
gen·til·i·ty (–ties)
gen·tle·man (–men)
gen·try
gen·u·flect
gen·u·ine
ge·og·ra·phy (–phies)
ge·ol·o·gy
ge·om·e·try (–tries)
ge·ra·ni·um
ge·ri·at·rics
ger·mane
ger·mi·cide
ger·mi·na·tion
ger·on·tol·o·gy
ger·ry·man·der
gest
ges·ta·tion

ges·tic·u·late
ges·ture
gey·ser
ghast·ly
gher·kin
ghet·to (ghettos *or* ghettoes)
ghoul·ish
gi·ant
gib·ber·ish
gibe
gib·lets
gi·gan·tic
gig·o·lo
gild (to overlay with a thin covering of gold or something similar; see *gilt*)
gift
gilt (covered with gold, or with something that resembles gold; see *gild*)
gim·mick
gin·ger
ging·ham
gi·raffe
gird·er
gir·dle
girth
gist
give
giz·zard
gla·cial
gla·cier
glad·i·a·tor
glad·i·o·la
glam·or·ous
glam·our, glam·or
glan·du·lar
glass·ware
glau·co·ma
gla·zier
glib
glim·mer
glimpse
glis·ten
glob·al
glob·u·lar
gloomy

glo·ri·ous
glos·sa·ry (–ries)
glossy (gloss·ies)
glove
glu·cose
glue
glut·ton
glyc·er·in
gnarl
gnash
gnat
gnaw
gnome
gnu (African antelope; see *knew* and *new*)
goal
gob·let
gog·gles
goi·ter
gold·en
golf (a game; see *gulf*)
gon·do·la
good·will
go·pher
gor·geous
go·ril·la (an ape; see *guerrilla*)
gos·sa·mer
gos·sip
gouge
gou·lash
gourd
gour·met
gout
gov·ern·ment
gov·er·nor
gra·cious
gra·da·tion
gra·di·ent
grad·u·al
grad·u·ate
grad·u·a·tion

grain
gram·mar
gra·na·ry (–ries)
gran·deur
grand·fa·ther
gran·di·ose
grand·mo·ther
gran·ite
grant
gran·u·late
graph·ic
graph·ite
grap·ple
grate (rasp noisily; see *great*)
grate·ful
grat·i·fy
grat·i·tude
gra·tu·ity (–i·ties)
grav·i·tate
grav·i·ty (–ties)
great (large; see *grate*)
greedy
gre·gar·i·ous
grem·lin
gre·nade
gren·a·dine
grey·hound
grid·dle
grid·iron
griev·ance
griev·ous
gri·mace
grime
grippe
gris·ly (inspiring horror; see *grizzly*)
griz·zly (bear; see *grisly*)
groan
gro·cery (–cer·ies)
gro·tesque
grot·to (–toes)

group
grouse (grouse *or* grouses)
grov·el
grudge
gru·el
grue·some
grum·ble
guar·an·tee (assurance of quality; see *guaranty*)
guaranty (something given as security; see *guarantee*)
guard·ian
gu·ber·na·to·ri·al
guer·ril·la (one who engages in irregular warfare; see *gorilla*)
guess
guest
guid·ance
guild
guile
guil·lo·tine
guilt
guise
gui·tar
gulf (part of an ocean, a chasm; see *golf*)
gul·li·ble
gul·ly (–lies)
gur·gle
gu·ru
gut·tur·al
guz·zle
gym·na·si·um
gym·nast
gy·ne·col·o·gy
gyp·sum
gyp·sy
gy·rate
gy·ro·scope

H

ha·be·as cor·pus (Latin: legal writ to bring a person before a court)
hab·er·dash·ery (–er·ies)
ha·bil·i·ment
hab·it·able
hab·i·tat
ha·bit·u·al
ha·bi·tué
hack·ney
had·dock
hag·gard
hag·gle
hail (greet; see *hale*)
hair (threadlike outgrowth on skin; see *hare*)
hal·cy·on
hale (free from disease; see *hail*)
half
hal·i·but
hal·i·to·sis
hal·le·lu·jah
hal·low
Hal·low·een
hal·lu·ci·na·tion
hal·lu·ci·no·gen
halve
hal·yard
ham·burg·er
ham·mer
ham·mock
ham·per
hand·i·cap
hand·i·craft
hand·ker·chief
han·dle
hand·some (pleasing appearance; see *hansom*)
handy
han·gar (place for housing aircraft; see *hanger*)
hang·er (device on which something is hung; see *hangar*)
han·som (cab; see *handsome*)
Ha·nuk·kah, Cha·nu·kah
hap·haz·ard
hap·pen

hap·pi·ness
hap·py
hara-kiri, hari-kari (Japanese: suicide by disembowelment)
ha·rangue
ha·rass
har·bin·ger
har·bor
hard·ly
hard·ship
har·dy
hare (animal resembling rabbit; see *hair*)
hare·brained
har·em
har·lot
harm·less
har·mon·ic
har·mo·ni·ous
har·mo·ny (–nies)
har·ness
har·poon
harp·si·chord
har·row·ing
har·ry
hart (male of red deer; see *heart*)
har·vest
hash·ish
has·sock
hatch·et
hate·ful
ha·tred
haugh·ty
haul
haunch
haunt
haute cou·ture (French: fashions created by famous designers)
haute cui·sine (French: elaborate style of cooking)
ha·ven
hav·oc
haw·thorn
haz·ard·ous
haze
ha·zel

head·ache
heal (restore to health; see *heel*)
health·ful
hear (listen; see *here*)
hear·ken
hearse
heart (bodily organ; see *hart*)
hearth
heart·i·ly
heat
heath
hea·then
heath·er
heav·en
heavy
heck·le
hec·tic
hedge
he·do·nism
heed·less
heel (part of foot; see *heal*)
hefty
he·ge·mo·ny
heif·er
height
hei·nous
heir
heist
he·li·cop·ter
he·li·um
help·ful
hemi·sphere
hem·lock
he·mo·phil·ia
hem·or·rhage
hem·or·rhoid
hence·forth
hen·na
hep·a·ti·tis
her·ald
herb
Her·cu·le·an
here (in this place; see *hear*)
he·red·i·tary
her·e·sy (–sies)
her·e·tic
her·i·tage

her·maph·ro·dite
her·met·ic
her·mit
her·nia
her·o·in (drug; see *heroine*)
her·o·ine (central figure in drama; see *heroin*)
her·on
her·ring·bone
hes·i·tate
het·ero·dox
het·er·o·ge·neous
het·ero·sex·u·al
heu·ris·tic
hew (to cut by blows; see *hue*)
hexa·gon
hex·am·e·ter
hi·a·tus
hi·ba·chi
hi·ber·nate
hi·bis·cus
hic·cough, hic·cup
hid·eous
hi·er·ar·chy (–chies)
hi·ero·glyph·ic
high·er (more elevated, taller; see *hire*)

hi·jack
hi·lar·i·ous
hin·drance
hinge
hip·po·drome
hip·po·pot·a·mus (–mus·es or –mi)
hire (employ, wage; see *higher*)
his·ta·mine
his·to·ri·an
his·tor·i·cal
his·to·ry (–ries)
his·tri·on·ic
hith·er·to
hives
hoar (frost; see *whore*)
hoard
hoarse
hoax
hob·ble
hock·ey
ho·cus-po·cus
hodge·podge
hoe
hoist
ho·li·ness
hol·lan·daise

hol·low
ho·lo·caust
ho·lo·gram
ho·lo·graph
hol·ster
hom·age
home·ly
ho·mi·cide
hom·i·ly (–lies)
ho·mo·ge·neous
ho·mog·e·nize
hom·onym
ho·mo·sex·u·al
hon·es·ty (–ties)
hon·ey
hon·or
hon·o·rar·i·um
hon·or·ary (–ar·ies)
hood·lum
hoo·li·gan
hope
hop·ing (longing for; see *hopping*)
hop·ping (jumping; see *hoping*)
horde
ho·ri·zon
hor·i·zon·tal

hor·mone

horo·scope

hor·ren·dous

hor·ri·ble

hor·rid

hor·ror

hors d'oeuvre (French: appetizers)

horse

hor·ti·cul·ture

ho·siery

hos·pi·tal

hos·tage

hos·tel

host·ess

hos·tile

ho·tel

hour (time; see *our*)

house·hold

hov·el

hov·er

howl

huck·le·ber·ry (–ries)

huck·ster

hue (complexion, see *hew*)

huge

hu·man·i·tar·i·an

hum·ble

hu·mid

hu·mi·dor

hu·mil·i·ate

hu·mil·i·ty

hu·mor

hu·mor·ous

hu·mus

hun·dredth

hun·ger

hur·dle

hur·dy-gur·dy (–dies)

hurl

hur·ri·cane

hur·ried

hur·tle

hus·band

hus·ky (–kies)

hus·tle

hy·a·cinth

hy·brid

hy·dran·gea

hy·drant

hy·drate

hy·drau·lic

hy·dro·chlo·ric

hy·dro·elec·tric

hy·dro·gen

hy·drom·e·ter

hy·dro·pho·bia

hy·drox·ide

hy·giene

hy·gien·ic

hy·men

hymn

hy·per·bo·la

hy·per·bo·le

hy·per·ten·sion

hy·phen

hyp·no·sis (–ses)

hyp·no·tism

hy·po·chon·dria

hy·poc·ri·sy (–sies)

hy·po·crite

hy·po·der·mic

hy·pot·e·nuse, hy·poth·e·nuse

hy·poth·e·sis (–ses)

hy·poth·e·size

hy·po·thet·i·cal

hys·ter·ec·to·my (–mies)

hys·te·ria

**I**

ice·berg
ice floe
ici·cle
ic·ing
icy
icon, ikon
icon·o·clast
idea
ide·al
iden·ti·cal
iden·ti·fi·ca·tion
iden·ti·fy
ide·ol·o·gy, ide·al·o·gy
  (–gies)
id·i·o·cy (–cies)
id·i·om
id·i·om·at·ic
id·io·syn·cra·sy (–sies)
id·i·ot
idle (not occupied; see *idol,*
  *idyll*)
idol (false god; see *idle,*
  *idyll*)
idol·a·try (–tries)
idol·ize
idyll, idyl (narrative poem;
  see *idle, idol*)
ig·loo
ig·ne·ous
ig·nite
ig·ni·tion
ig·no·ble
ig·no·min·i·ous
ig·no·rance
ig·nore
igua·na
ikon, icon
il·le·gal
il·leg·i·ble
il·le·git·i·mate
ill-got·ten
il·lib·er·al
il·lic·it (not permitted; see
  *elicit*)
il·lim·it·able
il·lit·er·ate
ill·ness
il·lu·mi·na·tion
il·lu·sion (misleading
  image; see *allusion*)

il·lu·so·ry
il·lus·trate
il·lus·tra·tion
il·lus·tri·ous
im·age
imag·in·able
imag·i·na·tive
imag·ine
im·bal·ance
im·be·cile
im·bibe
im·bro·glio
im·bue
im·i·ta·tion
im·i·ta·tive
im·mac·u·late
im·ma·nent (inherent; see
  *imminent*)
im·ma·te·ri·al
im·ma·ture
im·mea·sur·able
im·me·di·ate
im·me·mo·ri·al
im·mense
im·merse
im·mer·sion
im·mi·grate (to come into a
  country; see *emigrate*)
im·mi·nent (ready to take
  place; see *immanent*)
im·mo·bile
im·mod·er·ate
im·mod·est
im·mo·late
im·mor·al
im·mor·tal
im·mov·able
im·mune
im·mu·ni·ty (–ties)
im·pact (noun), im·pact
  (verb)
im·pair
im·pale
im·pal·pa·ble
im·par·tial
im·pass·able
im·passe
im·pas·sioned
im·pas·sive
im·pa·tience

im·peach
im·pec·ca·ble
im·pe·cu·nious
im·pede
im·ped·i·ment
im·pel
im·pend·ing
im·pen·e·tra·ble
im·pen·i·tence
im·per·a·tive
im·per·cep·ti·ble
im·per·fect
im·pe·ri·al
im·pe·ri·ous
im·per·ish·able
im·per·ma·nence
im·per·me·able
im·per·mis·si·ble
im·per·son·al
im·per·son·ate
im·per·ti·nent
im·per·turb·able
im·per·vi·ous
im·pet·u·ous
im·pe·tus
im·pi·ety (–eties)
im·pinge
im·pi·ous
imp·ish
im·pla·ca·ble
im·plau·si·ble
im·ple·ment
im·pli·cate
im·plic·it
im·plore
im·ply
im·po·lite
im·pol·i·tic
im·pon·der·a·ble
im·port (noun), im·port
  (verb)
im·por·tance
im·por·tu·nate
im·pose
im·po·si·tion
im·pos·si·bil·i·ty (–ties)
im·pos·si·ble
im·pos·tor, im·pos·ter
im·pos·ture
im·po·tent

im·pound
im·pov·er·ish
im·prac·ti·ca·ble
im·prac·ti·cal
im·pre·cate
im·pre·cise
im·preg·na·ble
im·pre·sa·rio
im·press
im·pres·sive
im·pri·ma·tur
im·print
im·pris·on·ment
im·prob·a·ble
im·promp·tu
im·prop·er
im·pro·pri·ety (–eties)
im·prove·ment
im·prov·i·dent
im·pro·vise
im·pru·dent
im·pu·dent
im·pugn
im·pulse
im·pu·ni·ty (–ties)
im·pu·ri·ty (–ties)
im·pute
in·abil·i·ty (–ties)
in ab·sen·tia
in·ac·ces·si·ble
in·ac·cu·ra·cy (–cies)
in·ac·tive
in·ad·e·qua·cy (–cies)
in·ad·e·quate
in·ad·mis·si·ble
in·ad·ver·tent
in·ad·vis·able
in·alien·able
in·al·ter·able
in·amo·ra·ta
inane
in·an·i·mate
in·ap·pli·ca·ble
in·ap·pre·cia·tive
in·ap·proach·able
in·ap·pro·pri·ate
in·ar·tic·u·late
in·ar·tis·tic
in·as·much
in·at·ten·tive

in·au·di·ble
in·au·gu·ral
in·au·gu·rate
in·aus·pi·cious
in·born
in·cal·cu·la·ble
in·can·des·cent
in·can·ta·tion
in·ca·pa·ble
in·ca·pac·i·tate
in·car·cer·ate
in·car·nate
in·cau·tious
in·cen·di·ary (–ar·ies)
in·cense (noun), in·cense
  (verb)
in·cen·tive
in·cep·tion
in·ces·sant
in·cho·ate
in·ci·den·tal·ly
in·cin·er·ate
in·cip·i·ent
in·cise
in·ci·sion
in·ci·sive
in·cite (to stir up; see
  *insight*)
in·clem·ent
in·cli·na·tion
in·cline
in·close, en·close
in·clude
in·cog·ni·to
in·co·her·ent
in·com·bus·ti·ble
in·come
in·com·men·su·ra·ble
in·com·pa·ra·ble
in·com·pat·i·ble
in·com·pe·tence
in·com·plete
in·com·pre·hen·si·ble
in·con·ceiv·able
in·con·clu·sive
in·con·gru·ous
in·con·se·quen·tial
in·con·sid·er·ate
in·con·sis·tent
in·con·sol·able

in·con·spic·u·ous
in·con·stant
in·con·test·able
in·con·tro·vert·ible
in·con·ve·nient
in·cor·por·ate
in·cor·rect
in·cor·ri·gi·ble
in·cor·rupt·ible
in·crease (noun), in·crease
  (verb)
in·creas·ing·ly
in·cred·i·ble
in·cred·i·bly
in·cre·du·li·ty
in·cred·u·lous
in·cre·ment
in·crim·i·nate
in·cu·bate
in·cu·ba·tor
in·cu·bus (–bus·es *or* –bi)
in·cul·cate
in·cum·bent
in·cur
in·cur·able
in·debt·ed
in·de·cent
in·de·ci·pher·able
in·de·ci·sion
in·de·fat·i·ga·ble
in·de·fen·si·ble
in·de·fin·able
in·def·i·nite
in·del·i·ble
in·del·i·cate
in·dem·ni·fy
in·den·ta·tion
in·den·ture
in·de·pen·dent
in·de·scrib·able
in·de·struc·ti·ble
in·de·ter·min·able
in·dex (in·dex·es *or*
  in·di·ces)
In·di·an
in·di·cate
in·dict (charge with
  offence; see *indite*)
in·dif·fer·ent
in·dig·e·nous

in·di·gent
in·di·gest·ible
in·di·ges·tion
in·dig·nant
in·dig·ni·ty (–ties)
in·di·go (–gos *or* –goes)
in·di·rect
in·dis·creet
in·dis·cre·tion
in·dis·crim·i·nate
in·dis·pens·able
in·dis·pose
in·dis·put·able
in·dis·sol·u·ble
in·dis·tinct
in·dis·tin·guish·able
in·dite (to put down in
   writing; see *indict*)
in·di·vid·u·al
in·di·vid·u·al·i·ty
in·di·vis·i·ble
in·doc·tri·nate
in·do·lence
in·dom·i·ta·ble
in·du·bi·ta·ble
in·duce
in·duct
in·dulge
in·dul·gence
in·dus·tri·al·ist
in·dus·try (–tries)
ine·bri·ate
in·ed·i·ble
in·ef·fa·ble
in·ef·fec·tive
in·ef·fec·tu·al
in·ef·fi·cien·cy (–cies)
in·elas·tic
in·el·i·gi·ble
in·eluc·ta·ble
in·ept
in·ep·ti·tude
in·equal·i·ty (–ties)
in·eq·ui·ta·ble
in·eq·ui·ty
in·ert
in·er·tia
in·es·cap·able
in·es·ti·ma·ble
in·ev·i·ta·ble

in·ex·cus·able
in·ex·haust·ible
in·ex·o·ra·ble
in·ex·pe·di·ent
in·ex·pen·sive
in·ex·pe·ri·enced
in·ex·pert
in·ex·pli·ca·ble
in·ex·press·ible
in·ex·tin·guish·able
in·ex·tri·ca·ble
in·fal·li·ble
in·fa·mous
in·fan·cy (–cies)
in·fan·ti·cide
in·fan·tile
in·fan·try (–tries)
in·fat·u·a·tion
in·fec·tion
in·fec·tious
in·fer
in·fer·ence
in·fe·ri·or·i·ty (–ties)
in·fer·nal
in·fer·no
in·fer·tile
in·fi·del·i·ty (–ties)
in·field
in·fil·trate
in·fi·nite
in·fin·i·tes·i·mal
in·fin·i·tive
in·fin·i·ty (–ties)
in·fir·ma·ry (–ries)
in·fir·mi·ty (–ties)
in·flame
in·flam·ma·ble
in·flam·ma·tion
in·flate
in·fla·tion
in·flec·tion
in·flex·i·ble
in·flict
in·flu·ence
in·flu·en·za
in·flux
in·for·mal
in·for·ma·tion
in·form·er
in·frac·tion

in·fra·red
in·fre·quent
in·fringe
in·fu·ri·ate
in·fuse
in·fu·sion
in·ge·nious (clever; see
   *ingenuous*)
in·ge·nu·i·ty (–ities)
in·gen·u·ous (showing
   childlike simplicity; see
   *ingenious*)
in·gest
in·glo·ri·ous
in·got
in·grained
in·grate
in·gra·ti·ate
in·grat·i·tude
in·gre·di·ent
in·gress
in·hab·it
in·hab·it·ant
in·ha·la·tion
in·hale
in·her·ent
in·her·i·tance
in·hib·it
in·hos·pi·ta·ble
in·hu·man
in·hu·mane
in·im·i·cal
in·im·i·ta·ble
in·iq·ui·ty (–ties)
ini·tial
ini·tiate
ini·tia·tive
in·jec·tion
in·ju·di·cious
in·junc·tion
in·jure
in·ju·ri·ous
in·ju·ry (–ries)
in·jus·tice
in·kling
in·land
in·let
in·mate
in me·mo·ri·am
in·nate

in·ning
in·no·cent
in·noc·u·ous
in·no·vate
in·no·va·tor
in·nu·en·do (−dos *or* −does)
in·nu·mer·able
in·oc·u·late
in·of·fen·sive
in·op·er·a·ble
in·op·er·a·tive
in·op·por·tune
in·or·di·nate
in·or·gan·ic
in per·so·nam (Latin:
    against a person)
in·quest
in·quire
in·qui·si·tion
in·quis·i·tive
in·road
in·sane
in·san·i·ty (−ties)
in·sa·tia·ble
in·scribe
in·scrip·tion
in·scru·ta·ble
in·sec·ti·cide
in·se·cure
in·sem·i·na·tion
in·sen·sate
in·sen·si·ble
in·sen·si·tive
in·sep·a·ra·ble
in·sert (noun), in·sert (verb)
in·side
in·sid·i·ous
in·sight (act of
    apprehending inner
    nature of things; see
    *incite*)
in·sig·nia, in·sig·ne (−nia *or*
    −ni·as)
in·sig·nif·i·cant
in·sin·cere
in·sin·u·ate
in·sip·id
in·sist
in·sis·tence
in·sole

in·so·lent
in·sol·u·ble
in·solv·able
in·sol·vent
in·som·nia
in·sou·ci·ance
in·spec·tor
in·spi·ra·tion
in·sta·bil·i·ty
in·stall, in·stal
in·stant
in·stan·ta·neous
in·stead
in·step
in·sti·gate
in·stinct
in·sti·tute
in·struct
in·stru·ment
in·sub·or·di·nate
in·sub·stan·tial
in·suf·fer·able
in·suf·fi·cient
in·su·lar
in·su·late
in·su·lin
in·sult (noun), in·sult (verb)
in·su·per·a·ble
in·sup·port·able
in·sup·press·ible
in·sur·ance
in·sur·gent
in·sur·mount·able
in·sur·rec·tion
in·tact
in·tan·gi·ble
in·te·ger
in·te·gral
in·te·grate
in·teg·ri·ty
in·tel·lect
in·tel·li·gence
in·tel·li·gen·tsia
in·tel·li·gi·ble
in·tem·per·ate
in·tend
in·tense
in·ten·tion·al
in·ter
in·ter·ac·tion

in·ter·cede
in·ter·cept
in·ter·ces·sion
in·ter·change·able
in·ter·com·mu·ni·ca·tion
in·ter·con·nect
in·ter·course
in·ter·de·part·men·tal
in·ter·dict
in·ter·est
in·ter·fere
in·ter·fer·ence
in·ter·im
in·te·ri·or
in·ter·ject
in·ter·lard
in·ter·line
in·ter·lin·ear
in·ter·lock
in·ter·lop·er
in·ter·lude
in·ter·mar·ry
in·ter·me·di·ary (−ar·ies)
in·ter·me·di·ate
in·ter·mez·zo (−zi *or* −zos)
in·ter·mi·na·ble
in·ter·mis·sion
in·ter·mit·tent
in·ter·mix
in·tern (noun), in·tern
    (verb)
in·ter·nal
in·ter·nal·ize
in·ter·na·tion·al
in·ter··ne·cine
in·tern·ee
in·tern·ment
in·ter·po·late
in·ter·pose
in·ter·pret
in·ter·ra·cial
in·ter·ro·gate
in·ter·rupt
in·ter·sect
in·ter·ses·sion
in·ter·sperse
in·ter·state
in·ter·stel·lar
in·ter·stice
in·ter·val

in·ter·vene
in·ter·view
in·tes·tate
in·tes·tine
in·ti·ma·cy (–cies)
in·ti·mate
in·tim·i·date
in·tol·er·a·ble
in·tol·er·ant
in·to·na·tion
in·tox·i·cate
in·trac·ta·ble
in·tra·mu·ral
in·tran·si·gent
in·tran·si·tive
in·tra·ve·nous
in·trep·id
in·tri·ca·cy (–cies)
in·tri·cate
in·trigue
in·trin·sic
in·tro·duce
in·tro·spec·tion
in·tro·ver·sion
in·tro·vert
in·tru·sion
in·tu·ition
in·tu·itive
in·un·date
in·val·id (adjective), invalid
    (noun)
in·valu·able
in·vari·able
in·va·sion
in·vec·tive

in·veigh
in·ven·tion
in·ven·to·ry (–ries)
in·verse
in·ver·te·brate
in·ves·ti·ga·tor
in·ves·ti·ture
in·ves·tor
in·vet·er·ate
in·vid·i·ous
in·vig·o·rate
in·vin·ci·ble
in·vi·o·la·ble
in·vis·i·ble
in·vi·ta·tion
in·vo·ca·tion
in·voice
in·voke
in·vol·un·tary
in·volve
in·vul·ner·a·ble
in·ward
io·dine
ion
io·ta
iras·ci·ble
irate
ire
ir·i·des·cence
iris (iris·es or iri·des)
irk·some
iron
ir·ra·di·a·tion
ir·ra·tio·nal
ir·rec·on·cil·able

ir·re·cov·er·able
ir·re·deem·able
ir·re·duc·ible
ir·re·fut·able
ir·reg·u·lar
ir·rel·e·van·cy (–cies)
ir·rel·e·vant
ir·re·li·gious
ir·re·me·di·a·ble
ir·rep·a·ra·ble
ir·re·place·able
ir·re·proach·able
ir·re·sist·ible
ir·res·o·lute
ir·re·spec·tive
ir·re·spon·si·ble
ir·re·triev·able
ir·rev·er·ent
ir·re·vers·ible
ir·rev·o·ca·ble
ir·ri·gate
ir·ri·ta·ble
ir·ri·tate
is·land
isle
iso·late
isos·ce·les
iso·tope
is·sue
isth·mus
ital·ic
item·ize
itin·er·ary (–ar·ies)
ivo·ry (–ries)
ivy (ivies)

J

jab·ber
jack·et
jade
jag·ged
jag·uar
jail·er, jail·or
ja·lopy (jalopies)
jam·bo·ree
jan·gle
jan·i·tor
jar·gon
jas·mine
jaun·dice
jaunt
jav·e·lin
jeal·ous
jeans
jeer
jel·ly (jel·lies)
jeop·ar·dize
jer·sey
jest
jet-pro·pelled
jet·ti·son
jet·ty (jetties)
jew·el·ry)

jibe, gibe
jig·ger
jit·ney
jock·ey
jo·cose
joc·u·lar
jo·cund
jodh·pur
jog·ging
join·ing
joint
jos·tle
jounce
jour·nal
jour·ney
joust
jo·vial
joy·ful
joy·ous
ju·bi·lant
ju·bi·lee
judge
judg·ment, judge·ment
ju·di·ca·ture
ju·di·cial
ju·di·cia·ry
ju·di·cious

jug·gler
juicy
ju·jit·su, ju·jut·su
juke·box
ju·lep
ju·li·enne
jum·ble
jum·bo
jump
junc·tion
junc·ture
jun·gle
ju·nior
ju·ni·per
jun·ket
jun·ta
ju·ris·dic·tion
ju·ris·pru·dence
ju·rist
ju·ror
jus·tice
jus·ti·fi·able
jus·ti·fi·ca·tion
jute
ju·ve·nile
jux·ta·pose

**K**

ka·lei·do·scope
kan·ga·roo
ka·pok
kar·a·kul
kar·at, car·at
ka·ra·te
ka·ty·did
kay·ak
kayo
keel
keen
keen·ness
keep·sake
kelp
ken·nel
kept
ker·chief
ker·nel (inner part of a
    seed; see *colonel*)
ker·o·sene, ker·o·sine
ketch
ketch·up, cat·sup
ket·tle
kha·ki
kib·butz
ki·bitz·er

ki·bosh
kid·nap
kid·nap·per, kid·nap·er
kid·ney
kiln
kilo·cy·cle
ki·lo·gram
kilo·li·ter
ki·lo·me·ter
kilo·watt
kil·ter
ki·mo·no
kin·der·gar·ten
kin·dle
kind·li·ness
kin·dling
kin·dred
kin·e·scope
kin·es·thet·ic
ki·net·ic
ki·osk
kitch·en·ette
kit·ty-cor·ner, cat·er-
    cor·ner
klep·to·ma·ni·ac

knack
knap·sack
knave (tricky fellow; see
    *nave*)
knead (press into a mass;
    see *need*)
knee
kneel
knell
knew (past tense of know;
    see *gnu, new*)
knick·knack
knife (knives)
knight (feudal nobleman;
    see *night*)
knob
knoll
knot
knowl·edge
knowl·edge·able
knuck·le
ko·ala
kohl·ra·bi (–bies)
ko·sher
ku·dos
kum·quat

L

la·bel
la·bor
lab·o·ra·to·ry (–ries)
la·bo·ri·ous
lab·y·rinth
lac·er·ate
lach·ry·mose
lack·ey
lack·lus·ter
la·con·ic
lac·quer
la·cu·na (–nae *or* –nas)
lad·der
la·den
lad·ing
la·dle
la·dy·ship
la·ger
lag·gard
la·gniappe
la·goon
la·icize
lair
lais·sez-faire (French:
    doctrine of individual
    freedom)
la·ity
lam·baste, lam·bast
lame (cripple; see *lamé*)
lamé (fabric; see *lame*)
la·men·ta·ble
lam·i·nate
lamp·light
lam·poon
lance
lan·dau
land·lord
lan·guage
lan·guid
lan·guish
lan·guor
lan·o·lin
lan·tern
lan·yard
la·pel
lap·i·dary (–dar·ies)
lapse
lar·ce·ny (–nies)
lar·der
large

lar·gess, lar·gesse
lar·i·at
lar·va (–vae)
lar·yn·gi·tis
lar·ynx (lar·ynxes)
la·sa·gna
las·civ·i·ous
la·ser
las·si·tude
las·so (las·sos *or* las·soes)
la·tent
lat·er·al
la·tex (la·ti·ces *or* la·tex·es)
lath (thin strip of wood; see
    *lathe*)
lathe (shaping machine; see
    *lath*)
lat·i·tude
la·trine
lat·ter
laud
lau·da·to·ry
laugh
laugh·able
launch
laun·der
laun·dry (–dries)
lau·re·ate
lau·rel
la·va·liere, la·val·liere
    (French: type of pendant
    worn as a necklace)
lav·a·to·ry (–ries)
lav·en·der
lav·ish
law·ful
law·ful·ly
lawn
law·yer
lax·a·tive
lax·ity
lay·ette
lay·man (–men)
la·zy
leach (to dissolve out; see
    *leech*)
lead
lead·er
leaf·let
league

leak (to escape through an
    opening; see *leek*)
lean (to incline; see *lien*)
learn
lease
leash
least
leath·er
leave
leav·en
lech·er
lech·er·ous
lec·tern
lec·ture
led·ger
leech (bloodsucking worm;
    see *leach*)
leek (herb; see *leak*)
leer
leery
lee·ward
lee·way
left
leg·a·cy (–cies)
le·gal
le·gal·i·ty (–ties)
leg·ate
le·ga·to
leg·end
leg·end·ary
leg·er·de·main
leg·gings, leg·gins
leg·gy
leg·horn
leg·i·ble
le·gion
le·gion·naire
leg·is·late
leg·is·la·tive
leg·is·la·ture
le·git·i·ma·cy
le·git·i·mate
le·gume
lei·sure
lem·ming
length
length·en
le·nient
len·i·ty
len·til

leop·ard
le·o·tard
lep·er
lep·re·chaun
lep·ro·sy
les·bi·an
le·sion
les·see
les·son
les·sor
le·thal
le·thar·gic
let·ter
let·tuce
leu·ke·mia
lev·ee (embankment; see *levy*)
lev·el
lev·i·ty
levy (assessment; see *levee*)
lewd
lex·i·cog·ra·phy
lex·i·con
li·a·ble
li·ai·son
li·ar
li·ba·tion
li·bel
lib·er·al
lib·er·ate
lib·er·tar·i·an
lib·er·tine
lib·er·ty (–ties)
li·bid·i·nous
li·brar·i·an
li·brary (–brar·ies)
li·bret·to (–tos *or* –ti)
li·cense, li·cence
li·cen·tious
li·chen
lic·it
lic·o·rice
lie (untruth; see *lye*)
lien (payment of debt; see *lean*)
lieu
lieu·ten·ant
life (lives)
lig·a·ment

lig·a·ture
light·ning
like·li·hood
li·lac
lily (lil·ies)
limb
lim·bo
lime·light
lim·er·ick
lim·i·ta·tion
limn
lim·ou·sine
lim·pid
lin·eal
lin·ear
lines·man (linesmen)
lin·ge·rie
lin·go (lingoes)
lin·gual
lin·guis·tic
lin·i·ment
lin·ing
li·no·leum
lin·seed
lin·tel
li·on·ize
liq·ue·fac·tion
liq·ue·fy
li·queur
liq·ui·date
li·quor
lisle
lis·some
lis·ten
lit·a·ny (–nies)
li·ter
lit·er·a·cy
lit·er·al
lit·er·ary
lit·er·ate
lit·er·a·ture
lithe
litho·graph
lit·i·gant
lit·i·gate
lit·mus
lit·tle
li·tur·gi·cal
lit·ur·gy (–gies)
liv·able

live·li·hood
live·li·ness
live·ly
liv·er
liv·er·wurst
live·stock
liv·id
liz·ard
lla·ma
loan
loath (unwilling, reluctant; see *loathe*)
loathe (dislike greatly; see *loath*)
lob·by (lobbies)
lob·ster
lo·cal (not general or widespread; see *locale*)
lo·cale (place related to a particular event; see *local*)
lo·cate
lock·et
lo·co·mo·tion
lo·cust
lodge
log·a·rithm
log·i·cal
lo·gis·tics
lo·gy, log·gy
loi·ter
lol·li·pop, lol·ly·pop
lone·li·ness
lone·ly
lon·gev·i·ty
lon·gi·tude
lore
loose
loot (something taken by force; see *lute*)
lop·sid·ed
lo·qua·cious
lo·tion
lot·tery (–ter·ies)
ló·tus, lo·tos
loud
lounge
lou·ver, lou·vre
lov·able, love·able
loy·al

loz·enge
lu·bri·cate
lu·cid
luck·i·ly
lu·cra·tive
lu·cre
lu·di·crous
lug·gage
lum·ba·go
lum·ber
lu·mi·nary (–nar·ies)

lum·mox
lu·na·cy (–cies)
lu·nar
lu·na·tic
lun·cheon
lun·cheon·ette
lunge
lurch
lu·rid
lurk
lus·cious
lus·trous

lute (musical instrument;
    see *loot*)
lux·u·ri·ous
lux·u·ry (–ries)
ly·ce·um
lymph
lynch
lynx (lynx *or* lynx·es)
ly·on·naise
lyre
lyr·ic

ma·ca·bre
mac·ad·am
mac·a·ro·ni
mac·a·roon
mac·er·ate
ma·chete
mach·i·na·tion
ma·chine
ma·chin·ist
mack·er·el
mack·i·naw
mack·in·tosh, mac·in·tosh
mac·ro·cosm
mac·ro·scop·ic
mad·am, ma·dame
mad·den·ing
ma·de·moi·selle
  (ma·de·moi·selles *or*
  mes·de·moi·selles)
ma·dras
mad·ri·gal
mael·strom
mae·stro (mae·stros *or*
  mae·stri)
mag·a·zine
ma·gen·ta
mag·got
mag·i·cal
ma·gi·cian
mag·is·trate
mag·nan·i·mous
mag·nate (person of rank
  and power; see *magnet*)
mag·ne·sia
mag·ne·sium
mag·net (something that
  attracts; see *magnate*)
mag·nif·i·cent
mag·ni·fy
mag·ni·tude
mag·no·lia
mag·pie
ma·ha·ra·ja, ma·ha·ra·jah
ma·hog·a·ny (–nies)
maid·en
mail (letters; see *male*)
maim
main (chief; see *mane*)
main·tain

maî·tre d'hô·tel (maî·tres
  d'hô·tel)
maize (Indian corn; see
  *maze*)
ma·jes·tic
ma·jor·i·ty (–ties)
mal·ad·just·ment
mal·a·dy (–dies)
mal·aise (French: indefinite
  feeling of ill health)
ma·lar·ia
mal·con·tent
mal de mer (French:
  seasickness)
male (masculine; see *mail*)
male·fac·tor
ma·lev·o·lent
mal·fea·sance
mal·formed
mal·func·tion
mal·ice
ma·li·cious
ma·lign
ma·lig·nan·cy (–cies)
ma·lin·ger
ma·lin·ger·er
mall
mal·lard
mal·lea·ble
mal·let
mal·nour·ished
mal·nu·tri·tion
mal·prac·tice
malt
mam·mal
mam·moth
man·age·ment
man·da·mus
man·da·rin
man·date
man·da·to·ry
man·di·ble
man·do·lin, man·do·line
mane (long, heavy hair on
  neck of horses; see *main*)
ma·neu·ver
man·gle
man·go (man·gos *or*
  man·goes)

mangy
ma·nia
ma·ni·ac
man·ic
ma·ni·cot·ti (plural also
  ma·ni·cot·ti)
man·i·cure
man·i·fest
man·i·fes·to
man·i·fold
ma·nip·u·late
man·li·ness
man·ne·quin
man·ner
man·or
man·sion
man·tel (shelf; see *mantle*)
man·tle (cloak; see *mantel*)
man·u·al
man·u·fac·ture
man·u·mit
ma·nure
manu·script
mar·a·schi·no
mar·a·thon
ma·raud·er
Mar·di Gras (French:
  Shrove Tuesday,
  celebration prior to Lent)
mar·ble
mare
mar·ga·rine
mar·gin
mar·gin·al
mari·gold
mar·i·jua·na, mar·i·hua·na
ma·rim·ba
mar·i·nate
ma·rine
mar·i·o·nette
mar·i·tal
mar·i·time
mar·jo·ram
mar·ket·able
mar·lin
mar·ma·lade
ma·roon
mar·quee
mar·quise

mar·qui·sette
mar·riage
mar·row
mar·shal, mar·shall (officer;
  see *martial*)
marsh·mal·low
mar·su·pi·al
mar·tial (relating to war;
  see *marshall*)
mar·ti·net
mar·tyr
mar·vel
marl·vel·ous, mar·vel·lous
mar·zi·pan
mas·cara
mas·cot
mas·cu·line
mas·och·ism
mas·och·ist
ma·son·ry (–ries)
mas·quer·ade
mas·sa·cre
mas·sage
mas·seur
mas·seuse
mas·sive
mas·ter·piece
mast·head
mas·ti·cate
mas·tiff
mas·toid
mat·a·dor
ma·te·ri·al (substance; see
  *matériel*)
ma·te·ri·al·ism
ma·té·ri·el, ma·te·ri·el
  (equipment and supplies;
  see *material*)
ma·ter·nal
ma·ter·ni·ty (–ties)
math·e·mat·ics
mat·i·nee
ma·tri·arch
ma·tric·u·late
mat·ri·mo·ny
ma·trix (ma·tri·ces *or*
  ma·trix·es)
ma·tron·ly
mat·ter

mat·tress
ma·ture
ma·tu·ri·ty
maud·lin
maul
mau·so·le·um
  (mau·so·le·ums *or*
  mau·so·lea)
mauve
mav·er·ick
max·i·mum (–ma *or*
  –mums)
may·hem
may·on·naise
may·or·al·ty
maze (network of passages;
  see *maize*)
mead·ow
mea·ger, mea·gre
me·an·der
mean·ing·ful
mea·sles
mea·sure
meat (flesh of domestic
  animals; see *mete*)
me·chan·ic
mech·a·nism
med·al (metal disk; see
  *meddle*)
med·dle (interfere; see
  *medal*)
me·dia (–di·ae)
me·di·an
me·di·ate
med·i·cal
med·i·ca·tion
me·dic·i·nal
med·i·cine
me·di·eval, me·di·ae·val
me·di·o·cre
me·di·oc·ri·ty (–ties)
med·i·tate
me·di·um (me·di·ums *or*
  me·dia)
med·ley
mega·cy·cle
mega·phone
mega·ton
mel·an·choly (–chol·ies)

mé·lange (French:
  incongruous elements)
me·lee (French: fight)
mel·lif·lu·ent
mel·lif·lu·ous
mel·low
me·lo·di·ous
melo·dra·ma
mel·o·dy (–dies)
mem·ber·ship
mem·brane
me·men·to
mem·oir
mem·o·ra·bil·ia
mem·o·ra·ble
mem·o·ran·dum
me·mo·ri·al
mem·o·ry (–ries)
men·ace
mé·nage (French:
  household)
me·nag·er·ie
men·da·cious
men·di·cant
me·nial
meno·pause
me·no·rah
men·stru·ate
men·su·ra·tion
men·tal
men·thol
men·tion
men·tor
menu
mer·can·tile
mer·ce·nary (–nar·ies)
mer·chan·dise
mer·chant
mer·cy (mer·cies)
mer·e·tri·cious
merge
merg·er
me·rid·i·an
me·ringue
mer·i·to·ri·ous
mer·maid
mes·dames
mes·mer·ize
mes·sage

mes·sen·ger
me·tab·o·lism
me·tal·ic
met·al·lur·gy
meta·mor·pho·sis (–ses)
met·a·phor
meta·phys·ics
mete (allot; see *meat*)
me·te·or·ic
me·ter
meth·a·done, meth·a·don
meth·od
meth·od·ol·o·gy (–gies)
me·tic·u·lous
mé·tier (French: an area of expertise)
met·ric
met·ro·nome
me·trop·o·lis
met·ro·pol·i·tan
met·tle
mez·za·nine
mez·zo·so·pra·no
mi·as·ma (–mas *or* –ma·ta)
mi·ca
mi·cro·anal·y·sis
mi·crobe
mi·cro·cosm
mi·crom·e·ter
mi·cro·phone
mi·cro·scope
mid·dle
midg·et
mid·night
mid·riff
midst
mien
might (power; see *mite*)
mi·graine
mi·grate
mi·gra·to·ry
mi·ka·do
mil·dew
mile·age
mi·lieu (mi·lieus *or* mi·lieux)
mil·i·tan·cy
mil·i·ta·rist
mil·i·tary
mil·i·tate

mi·li·tia
mil·len·ni·um
mil·li·gram
mil·li·li·ter
mil·li·me·ter
mil·li·nery
mil·lion·aire
mim·eo·graph
mi·met·ic
mim·ic
min·a·ret
mi·na·to·ry
minc·ing·ly
mind·less
min·er (mine worker; see *minor*)
min·er·al·o·gy
min·gle
min·ia·ture
min·i·mum
min·i·mize
min·ion
min·is·cule, mi·nus·cule
min·is·te·ri·al
mi·nor (comparatively unimportant; see *miner*)
mi·nor·i·ty (–ties)
min·strel
min·u·et
mi·nus·cule, min·is·cule
min·ute (space of time)
mi·nute (of small importance)
minx
mi·rac·u·lous
mi·rage
mire
mir·ror
mirth·ful
mis·al·li·ance
mis·an·thrope
mis·car·riage
mis·ce·ge·na·tion
mis·cel·la·neous
mis·cel·la·ny (–nies)
mis·chie·vous
mis·con·ceive
mis·con·strue
mis·de·mean·or
mis·er·a·ble

mi·ser·ly
mis·fea·sance
mis·han·dle
mis·in·ter·pret
mis·judge
mis·man·age
mis·no·mer
mi·sog·y·nist
mis·rep·re·sent
mis·sal (prayer book; see *missile*)
mis·shap·en
mis·sile (object or weapon thrown; see *missal*)
mis·sion·ary (–ar·ies)
mis·sive
mis·spell
mis·state
mis·take
mis·tle·toe
mis·tress
mis·tri·al
mite (small object or creature; see *might*)
mit·i·gate
mix·ture
mne·mon·ic
moat (trench; see *mote*)
mo·bile
mo·bi·li·za·tion
moc·ca·sin
mod·el
mod·er·ate
mod·er·a·tor
mod·ern·iza·tion
mod·es·ty
mod·i·fi·er
mod·ish
mod·u·late
mo·gul
mo·hair
moist·en
mo·lar
mo·las·ses
mo·lec·u·lar
mol·e·cule
mo·les·ta·tion
mol·li·fy
mol·ten
mo·men·tary

mo·men·tum
mon·arch
mon·as·tery (–ter·ies)
mon·e·tary
mon·ey (moneys or
    mon·ies)
Mon·gol·oid
mon·grel
mon·i·tor
mon·key
mono·chro·mat·ic
mon·o·cle
mo·nog·a·my
mono·gram
mono·logue, mono·log
mono·logu·ist,
    mo·no·lo·gist
mo·nop·o·ly (–lies)
mono·the·ism
mono·tone
mo·not·o·nous
mon·si·gnor (–gnors or
    –gno·ri)
mon·soon
mon·stros·i·ty (–ties)
mon·tage
mon·u·men·tal
moon·light
mo·raine
mor·al
mo·rale
mo·rass
mor·a·to·ri·um
    (mor·a·to·ri·ums or
    mor·a·to·ria)
mor·bid
mor·dant
mo·res
morgue
mor·i·bund
morn·ing (time from sunrise
    to noon; see mourning)
mo·ron·ic
mor·phine

mor·sel
mor·tal·i·ty
mort·gage
mor·ti·cian
mor·ti·fy
mor·tu·ary (–ar·ies)
mo·sa·ic
mosque
mos·qui·to (–tos or –toes)
mote (speck; see moat)
moth·er
mo·tif
mo·tion
mo·ti·va·tion
mo·tor
mot·tled
mot·to (mot·tos or
    mot·toes)
moun·tain·ous
mourn
mourn·ing (act of
    sorrowing; see morning)
mousse
mouth·ful
mou·ton
mov·able, move·able
mov·ie
moz·za·rel·la
mu·ci·lage
mu·cous
mug·ger
mug·gy
mu·lat·to (–toes or –tos)
mul·ber·ry (–ries)
mulct
mul·ti·eth·nic
mul·ti·fac·et·ed
mul·ti·far·i·ous
mul·ti·lat·er·al
mul·ti·me·dia
mul·ti·mil·lion·aire
mul·ti·na·tion·al
mul·ti·ple
mul·ti·tude

mum·ble
mum·bo jum·bo
mum·my (mummies)
mun·dane
mu·nic·i·pal
mu·nif·i·cent
mu·ni·tion
mu·ral
mur·der·ous
mus·cle (body tissue; see
    mussel)
mus·cu·lar
muse
mu·se·um
mu·si·cal
mu·si·cian
mus·ke·teer
musk·rat
mus·lin
mus·sel (mollusk; see
    muscle)
mus·tache
mus·tard
mu·ta·ble
mu·ta·tion
mu·ti·late
mu·ti·neer
mut·ter
mut·ton
mu·tu·al
muz·zle
my·o·pic
myr·i·ad
myrrh
myr·tle
mys·te·ri·ous
mys·tery (–ter·ies)
mys·tic
mys·ti·cism
mys·tique
myth·i·cal
my·thol·o·gy (–gies)

# N

na·ive (naïve)
na·ive·té (naïve·té)
na·ked·ness
na·palm
naph·tha
nap·kin
nar·cis·sism
nar·cis·sus
nar·cot·ic
nar·rate
nar·ra·tor
nar·row
na·sal·i·ty (–ties)
na·scent
nas·tur·tium
nas·ty
na·ta·to·ri·um
na·tion·al·i·ty (–ties)
na·tive
na·tiv·i·ty (–ties)
nat·u·ral·ize
naugh·ti·ness
nau·se·ate
nau·seous
nau·ti·cal
na·val (relating to ships;
    see *navel*)
nave (church aisle; see
    *knave*)
na·vel (depression in
    abdomen; see *naval*)
nav·i·gate
nav·i·ga·tor
near·by
neb·u·lous
nec·es·sary (–saries)
ne·ces·si·tate
neck·lace
nec·tar·ine
nee·dle·work
ne'er-do-well
ne·far·i·ous
ne·gate
neg·a·tive
ne·glect
neg·li·gee, neg·li·gé
neg·li·gent
neg·li·gi·ble
ne·go·ti·a·tion
neigh

neigh·bor·hood
nei·ther
nem·e·sis (–ses)
ne·on
neo·phyte
neph·ew
nep·o·tism
ner·vous·ness
nes·tle
net·ting
net·tle
net·work
neu·ral·gia
neu·ro·sis (–ses)
neu·rot·ic
neu·ter
neu·tral·ize
neu·tron
new (recent; see *gnu* and
    *knew*)
news·stand
nib·ble
nice·ty (–ties)
niche
nick·el, nick·le
nick·nack, knick·knack
nic·o·tine
niece
night (time from dusk to
    dawn; see *knight*)
night·in·gale
night·mare
nim·ble
nine·teen
nine·ty (nineties)
ninth
nip·ple
ni·trate
ni·tro·gen
ni·tro·glyc·er·in,
    ni·tro·glyc·er·ine
no·bil·i·ty
no·ble
noc·tur·nal
noc·turne
nod·ule
noi·some
noisy
no·mad

nom de plume (French: pen
    name, pseudonym)
no·men·cla·ture
nom·i·nal
nom·i·na·tion
nom·i·nee
non·al·co·hol·ic
non·be·liev·er
non·bel·lig·er·ent
non·cha·lance
non·com·ba·tant
non·com·mis·sioned
non·com·mit·tal
non·com·pli·ance
non·con·duc·tor
non·con·form·ist
non·de·script
non·en·ti·ty (–ties)
non·es·sen·tial
non·fic·tion
non·in·ter·ven·tion
non·pa·reil (French: having
    no equal)
non·par·ti·san
non·poi·son·ous
non·pro·duc·tive
non·prof·it
non·re·new·able
non·sec·tar·i·an
non·sense
non se·qui·tur
non·tax·able
non·vi·o·lence
noo·dle
noose
nor·mal
north·ern
nose
nos·tal·gia
nos·tril
nos·trum
no·ta·bly
no·ta·rize
no·ta·ry public (no·ta·ries
    public *or* no·ta·ry
    publics)
no·ta·tion
notch
note·wor·thy
no·tice·able

no·ti·fy
no·tion
no·to·ri·ety (–eties)
no·to·ri·ous
nou·gat
nought
noun
nour·ish·ment
nov·el·lette
nov·el·ty (–ties)
no·ve·na
nov·ice
no·vi·tiate

nox·ious
noz·zle
nu·ance
nu·bile
nu·cle·us (–clei or
    –cle·us·es)
nu·di·ty
nug·get
nui·sance
nul·li·fy
numb
number
nu·mer·al

nu·mer·a·tor
nu·mer·ous
nu·mis·mat·ic
nup·tial
nurse
nurs·ery (–er·ies)
nur·ture
nu·tri·tion
nu·tri·tious
nuz·zle
ny·lon
nymph
nym·pho·ma·ni·ac

oak·en
oa·sis (–ses)
oath
oat·meal
ob·bli·ga·to
ob·du·rate
obe·di·ence
obei·sance
obe·lisk
obese
obe·si·ty
obey
ob·fus·cate
obit·u·ary (–ar·ries)
ob·jec·tion
ob·jec·tor
ob·jet d'art (ob·jets d'art)
ob·li·gate
ob·li·ga·tion
oblig·a·to·ry
oblige
oblique
oblit·er·ate
obliv·i·on
obliv·i·ous
ob·long
ob·lo·quy (–quies)
ob·nox·ious
oboe
obo·ist
ob·scene
ob·scen·i·ty (–ties)
ob·scure
ob·scu·ri·ty (–ties)
ob·se·qui·ous
ob·se·quy (–quies)
ob·ser·vant
ob·ser·va·to·ry (–ries)
ob·ses·sion
ob·so·les·cence
ob·so·lete
ob·sta·cle
ob·ste·tri·cian
ob·stet·rics
ob·sti·nate
ob·strep·er·ous
ob·struc·tion
ob·tain
ob·trude
ob·tru·sive

ob·tuse
ob·vi·ate
ob·vi·ous
oc·ca·sion
oc·cip·i·tal
oc·clu·sion
oc·cult
oc·cu·pan·cy (–cies)
oc·cu·pant
oc·cu·pa·tion
oc·cu·py
oc·cur
oc·curred
oc·cur·rence
ocean
ocean·og·ra·phy
oce·lot
ocher, ochre
oc·ta·gon
oc·tag·o·nal
oc·tane
oc·tave
oc·tet
oc·to·ge·nar·i·an
oc·to·pus (–pus·es or –pi)
oc·u·list
odd·i·ty (–ties)
odd·ly
odi·ous
odi·um
odom·e·ter
odor·ant
odor·ous
od·ys·sey
of·fend·er
of·fense, of·fence
of·fer·to·ry (–ries)
off·hand
of·fi·cer
of·fi·cial
of·fi·ci·ate
of·fi·cious
off·set
off·spring (off·spring or
    off·springs)
ohm
oil·er
oily
oint·ment
okra

old-fash·ioned
old·ster
ole·ag·i·nous
ol·fac·to·ry
oli·gar·chy (–chies)
ol·ive
olym·pi·ad
om·elet, om·elette
om·i·nous
omis·sion
omit
om·ni·bus
om·nip·o·tence
om·ni·science
om·niv·o·rous
on·com·ing
one-night stand
oner·ous
on·ion
on·o·mato·poe·ia
on·set
on·shore
on·side
on·slaught
on·tol·o·gy
onus
on·ward, on·wards
on·yx
oo·long
opal·es·cent
opaque
open
op·er·a·ble
op·er·ate
op·er·at·ic
op·er·a·tion
op·er·et·ta
oph·thal·mol·o·gist
opi·ate
opin·ion
opin·ion·at·ed
opi·um
opos·sum
op·po·nent
op·por·tune
op·por·tu·nis·tic
op·por·tu·ni·ty (–ties)
op·po·site
op·pres·sion
op·pro·bri·ous

op·pro·bri·um
op·ti·cal
op·ti·cian
op·ti·mism
op·ti·mum (−ma or −mums)
op·tion
op·tom·e·trist
op·tom·e·try
op·u·lent
opus (opera or opus·es)
or·a·cle
oral (relating to the mouth;
    see *aural*)
or·ange
orate
or·a·to·rio (−ri·os)
or·a·to·ry (−ries)
or·bit·al
or·chard
or·ches·tra
or·chid
or·dain
or·deal
or·der
or·di·nance
or·di·nary (-nar·ies)
or·di·nari·ly
or·di·na·tion
ord·nance
or·dure
ore
oreg·a·no
or·gan
or·gan·ic
or·gan·ism
or·ga·ni·za·tion
or·ga·niz·er
or·gasm
or·gi·as·tic

or·gy (or·gies)
ori·en·tal
ori·en·ta·tion
or·i·fice
orig·i·nal·i·ty
orig·i·na·tor
ori·ole
or·i·son
or·na·men·tal
or·na·men·ta·tion
or·nate
or·nery
or·ni·thol·o·gy (−gies)
or·phan·age
orth·odon·tist
or·tho·dox
or·tho·pe·dic,
    or·tho·pae·dic
os·cil·late
os·mo·sis
os·prey
os·si·fi·ca·tion
os·si·fy
os·ten·si·ble
os·ten·ta·tious
os·teo·path
os·tra·cize
os·trich
oti·ose
ot·to·man
ought
ounce
our (relating to us; see
    *hour*)
oust
out·age
out·break
out·dis·tance
out·fit·ter

out·land·ish
out·pour·ing
out·ra·geous
ou·tré (French: bizarre)
out·ward
out·weigh
out·wit
oval
ova·ry (−ries)
ova·tion
over·alls
over·bear·ing
over·board
over·cast
over·con·fi·dent
over·dose
over·draft
over·ex·pose
over·haul
over·joyed
over·lap
over·rate
over·seas
over·seer
over·sight
overt
over·ture
over·whelm
over·wrought
ovu·late
ow·ing
own·er
ox·i·da·tion
ox·ide
ox·i·dize
ox·tail
ox·y·gen
oys·ter
ozone

**P**

pab·u·lum
pace·mak·er
pac·er
pachy·derm
pa·cif·ic
pac·i·fi·er
pack·age
pack·et
pact
pad·ding
pad·dle
pad·dock
pad·lock
pae·an (hymn; see *paeon, peon*)
pae·on (metrical foot; see *paean, peon*)
pa·gan
page
pag·eant·ry
pag·i·nate
pa·go·da
paid
pail (container; see *pale*)
pain (suffering; see *pane*)
pains·tak·ing
paint
pair (two; see *pare, pear*)
pa·ja·mas
pal·ace
pal·at·able
pal·ate (roof or mouth; see *palette, pallet*)
pa·la·tial
pa·la·ver
pale (deficient in color; see *pail*)
Pa·leo·lith·ic
pal·ette (painter's board; see *palate, pallet*)
pal·frey
pal·in·drome
pal·i·sade
pal·la·di·um (–la·dia)
pall·bear·er
pal·let (straw mattress; see *palate, palette*)
pal·li·ate
pal·lid
pal·lor

pal·met·to
palm·ist
pal·o·mi·no
pal·pa·ble
pal·pi·tate
pal·sy (palsies)
pal·try
pam·pa
pam·per
pam·phle·teer
pan·a·cea
pan·cre·as
pan·da
pan·de·mo·ni·um
pan·der
pane (sheet of glass; see *pain*)
pan·e·gy·ric
pan·el
pan·han·dle
pan·ic
pan·icked
pan·o·ply (–plies)
pan·ora·ma
pan·sy (pansies)
pan·the·ism
pan·ther
pan·ties
pant·ing
pan·to·mime
pan·try (pantries)
panty·waist
pa·pa·cy (–cies)
pa·pal
pa·pa·ya
pa·pier-mâ·ché
pa·poose
pa·pri·ka
pa·py·rus (pa·py·rus·es *or* pa·py·ri)
par·a·ble
pa·rab·o·la
para·chute
pa·rade
par·a·digm
par·a·dise
par·a·dox
par·af·fin
par·a·gon
para·graph

par·a·keet
par·al·lax
par·al·lel
par·al·lel·o·gram
pa·ral·y·sis
par·a·lyt·ic
par·a·lyze
pa·ram·e·ter
par·a·mount
par·amour
para·noia
para·noid
par·a·pet
par·a·pher·na·lia
para·phrase
para·ple·gic
par·a·site
para·sol
para·troop·er
par·boil
par·cel
parch
Par·chee·si
parch·ment
par·don·able
pare (shave off; see *pear, pair*)
pa·ren·tal
pa·ren·the·sis (–ses)
par·en·thet·i·cal·ly
pa·ri·etal
pa·rish·io·ner
par·i·ty (–ties)
par·ka
park·way
par·lay (two or more bets in advance; see *parley*)
par·ley (conference; see *parlay*)
par·lia·ment
par·lia·men·ta·ry
par·lor
par·mi·gia·na, par·mi·gia·no
pa·ro·chi·al
par·o·dy (–dies)
pa·role
par·ox·ysm
par·quet (French: type of flooring)
par·ri·cide

par·rot
par·ry
parse
par·si·mo·ni·ous
pars·ley
pars·nip
par·son·age
par·terre
par·tial
par·tic·i·pate
par·ti·cip·i·al
par·ti·ci·ple
par·ti·cle
par·tic·u·lar·ly
par·ti·san, par·ti·zan
par·ti·tion
par·ti·tive
part·ner
par·tridge
par·ve·nu (French: one
   with new wealth, lacking
   social standing)
pas·chal
pass·able
pas·sage
pas·sé (French: behind the
   times)
pas·sen·ger
pass·er·by (pass·ers·by)
pas·sion·ate
pas·sive
pass·port
past
paste
pas·tel
pas·teur·ize
pas·tille, pas·til
pas·time
pas·to·ral
past·ry (pastries)
pas·tur·age
pas·ty (pasties)
patch·work
patchy
pâ·té de foie gras (pâ·tés de
   foie gras)
pat·en
pat·ent
pa·ter·nal·ism
pa·ter·ni·ty

pa·ter·nos·ter
pa·thet·ic
pa·thol·o·gy (–gies)
pa·thos
path·way
pa·tience
pa·tient
pa·ti·na (–nas or –nae)
pa·tio
pa·tois (plural also pa·tois)
pa·tri·arch
pa·tri·cian
pat·ri·cide
pat·ri·mo·ny
pa·tri·ot·ic
pa·trol
pa·tron
pa·tron·age
pat·ro·nym·ic
pat·ter
pat·tern
pau·ci·ty
paunch
pau·per
pause
pave·ment
pa·vil·ion
pawn
pay·able
peace (state of tranquillity;
   see piece)
peace·ful
peachy
pea·cock
peak (sharp or pointed end;
   see peek, pique)
peal (loud ringing of bells;
   see peel)
pea·nut
pear (fruit; see pair, pare)
pearl
peas·ant·ry
peb·ble
pe·can
pec·ca·dil·lo
pec·to·ral
pe·cu·liar·i·ty (–ties)
pe·cu·ni·ary
ped·a·gogue, ped·a·gog
ped·a·go·gy

ped·al (foot lever; see
   peddle)
pe·dan·tic
ped·dle (travel with wares
   to sell; see pedal)
ped·es·tal
pe·des·tri·an
pe·di·a·tri·cian
pe·di·at·rics
ped·i·cure
ped·i·gree
ped·i·ment
pe·dom·e·ter
peek (look furtively; see
   peak, pique)
peel (strip off; see peal)
peer (equal; see pier)
peer·age
pee·vish
pei·gnoir
pe·jo·ra·tive
pe·koe
pe·lag·ic
pel·i·can
pel·let
pell-mell
pel·vic
pel·vis (pel·vis·es or
   pel·ves)
pe·nal·ize
pen·al·ty (–ties)
pen·ance
pen·chant
pen·ciled
pen·dant, pen·dent
pen·du·lous
pen·du·lum
pen·e·trate
pen·guin
pen·i·cil·lin
pen·in·su·la
pen·i·tence
pen·i·ten·tial
pen·i·ten·tia·ry (–ries)
pen·man·ship
pen·nant
pen·ni·less
pe·nol·o·gy
pen·sion
pen·ta·gon

pen·tam·e·ter
Pen·ta·teuch
pen·tath·lon
pent·house
pen·ul·ti·mate
pe·nu·ri·ous
pe·on (landless laborer; see
   *paean, paeon*)
pe·on·age
pe·o·ny (–nies)
peo·ple (peo·ple *or*
   peo·ples)
pep·per
per·ad·ven·ture
per·am·bu·late
per an·num
per·cale
per cap·i·ta
per·ceive
per·cent
per·cent·age
per·cen·tile
per·cept
per·cep·ti·ble
per·cep·tive
per·cep·tu·al
perch
per·chance
per·cip·i·ent
per·co·late
per·co·la·tor
per·cus·sion
per di·em
per·di·tion
per·e·gri·nate
pe·remp·to·ry
pe·ren·ni·al
per·fect (adjective),
   per·fect (verb)
per·fec·ta
per·fid·i·ous
per·fi·dy
per·fo·rate
per·force
per·for·mance
per·fume (noun), per·fume
   (verb)
per·func·to·ry
per·go·la
per·haps

per·i·gee
per·il·ous
pe·rim·e·ter
pe·ri·od·ic
peri·pa·tet·ic
pe·riph·ery (–er·ies)
peri·scope
per·ish·able
peri·to·ni·tis
per·i·win·kle
per·jure
per·ju·ry
per·ma·frost
per·ma·nent
per·me·able
per·me·ate
per·mis·si·ble
per·mis·sion
per·mit·ted
per·mu·ta·tion
per·ni·cious
per·ora·tion
per·ox·ide
per·pen·dic·u·lar
per·pe·tra·tor
per·pet·u·al
per·pe·tu·ity (–ities)
per·plex
per·qui·site
per·se·cu·tion
per·se·ver·ance
per·sis·tence
per·snick·e·ty
per·son·able
per·son·age
per·son·al (private, relating
   to a person; see
   *personnel*)
per·son·al·i·ty (–ties)
per·so·na non gra·ta (Latin:
   being unwelcome)
per·son·i·fi·ca·tion
per·son·nel (body of
   employees; see *personal*)
per·spec·tive
per·spi·ca·cious
per·spic·u·ous
per·spi·ra·tion
per·sua·sion
per·tain

per·ti·na·cious
per·ti·nent
per·tur·ba·tion
pe·ruse
per·vade
per·verse
per·vert (noun), per·vert
   (verb)
pes·si·mism
pes·ter
pes·tif·er·ous
pes·ti·lence
pes·tle
pet·al
pe·tard
pet·cock
pe·tit four (pe·tits fours *or*
   pe·tit fours) (French:
   small cake)
pe·ti·tion
pet·it jury
pe·tit mal
pet·it point
pe·trel (sea bird; se *petrol*)
pet·ri·fy
pet·rol (gasoline; see
   *petrel*)
pe·tro·leum
pet·ti·coat
pet·ti·fog·ger
pet·ti·ness (–ness·es)
pet·ty
pet·u·lant
pe·tu·nia
pew·ter
pha·lanx (pha·lanx·es *or*
   pha·lan·ges)
phan·tasm, fan·tasm
phan·tas·ma·go·ria
phan·tom
phar·i·sa·ical
phar·ma·ceu·ti·cal
phar·ma·cist
phar·ma·cy (–cies)
phar·ynx (pha·rynx·es *or*
   pha·ryn·ges)
phase
pheas·ant
phe·nom·e·nal
phi·lan·der·er

phi·lan·thro·py (–pies)
phi·lat·e·list
phi·lip·pic
philo·den·dron
phi·lol·o·gy
phi·los·o·pher
phlegm
phleg·mat·ic
pho·bia
phoe·be
phoe·nix
pho·nate
pho·net·ics
pho·nics
pho·no·graph
phony, phoney (phonies)
phos·phate
phos·pho·res·cent
pho·to·copy (–cop·ies)
pho·to·elec·tric
pho·to·graph·ic
pho·to·stat
phot·to·syn·the·sis
phrase
phrase·ol·o·gy (–gies)
phre·net·ic, fre·net·ic
phre·nol·o·gy
phys·i·cal
phy·si·cian
phys·i·cist
phys·ics
phys·i·ol·o·gy
phys·io·ther·a·py
phy·sique
pi·a·nist
pi·az·za
pi·ca
pic·a·dor (picadors *or* –es)
pic·ca·resque
pic·ca·lil·li
pic·co·lo
pick·a·back, pig·gy·back
pick·er·el
pick·et
pick·le
pic·nic
pic·nicked
pic·to·graph
pic·to·ri·al
pic·ture (painting, drawing

or photograph; see
*pitcher*)
pic·tur·esque
pid·dle
pid·gin (simplified speech;
see *pigeon*)
pie·bald
piece (part of a whole; see
*peace*)
pièce de ré·sis·tance
(pièces de ré·sis·tance)
(French: outstanding
item)
pier (dock; see *peer*)
pierce
pi·ety (pi·eties)
pi·geon (bird; see *pidgin*)
pig·ment
pil·fer
pil·grim·age
pil·ing
pil·lage
pil·lar
pil·low
pi·lot
pi·men·to
pim·ple
pin·afore
pince-nez (plural also
pince-nez) (French:
eyeglasses without
sidepieces, clipped to
nose)
pin·cer
pin·cush·ion
pine·ap·ple
pin·na·cle
pi·noch·le
pi·o·neer
pi·ous
pipe
pip·ing
pi·quant (French:
charming)
pique (to wound vanity; see
*peak, peek*)
pi·ra·cy (–cies)
pir·ou·ette (French: ballet
turn)
pis·ca·to·ry

pis·ta·chio
pis·til (plant organ; see
*pistol*)
pis·tol (gun; see *pistil*)
pitch·er (container for
liquids; see *picture*)
pitch·fork
pit·e·ous
pit·fall
pithy
piti·able
piti·ful
piti·less
pi·ton
pit·tance
piv·ot·al
pix·ie, pixy (pix·ies)
pix·i·lat·ed
piz·ze·ria
plac·ard
pla·cate
pla·ce·bo
place·ment
plac·id
plack·et
pla·gia·rize
plague
plaid
plain (level country;
lacking ornament; see
*plane*)
plain·tiff
plait
plane (tool; geometric
surface; see *plain*)
plan·et
plan·e·tar·i·um
plan·tain
plan·ta·tion
plaque
plas·ma
plas·ter
plas·tic
plas·ti·cize
pla·teau
plat·en
plat·form
plat·i·num
plat·i·tude
pla·ton·ic

pla·toon
plat·ter
plau·dit
plau·si·ble
play·go·er
play·mate
play·wright
pla·za
plead
pleas·ant·ry (–ries)
plea·sure
pleat
plebe
ple·be·ian
pleb·i·scite
pledge
ple·na·ry
pleni·po·ten·tia·ry (–ries)
plen·te·ous
plen·ti·ful
ple·o·nas·tic
pleu·ri·sy
pli·able
pli·ers
plight
plim·soll
plo·ver
plow, plough
plow·share
plum·age
plumb·er
plume
plum·met
plump
plun·der
plunge
plu·per·fect
plu·ral
plu·ral·i·ty (–ties)
plu·toc·ra·cy (–cies)
plu·to·ni·um
ply·wood
pneu·mat·ic
pneu·mo·nia
poach·er
pock·et·book
po·di·a·trist
po·di·um
po·em
po·et·i·cal

po·grom
poi·gnan·cy (–cies)
poi·gnant
poin·set·tia
point
poi·son·ous
po·lar·i·ty (–ties)
po·lar·ize
pole (long slender object;
    see *poll*)
po·lem·ic
po·lice (plural also po·lice)
pol·i·cy (–cies)
po·lio
pol·ish
po·lit·bu·ro
po·lit·i·cal
pol·i·ti·cian
pol·i·tics
pol·ka
poll (receive and record
    votes; see *pole*)
pol·len
pol·li·nate
pol·lu·tion
pol·troon
poly·clin·ic
poly·es·ter
po·lyg·a·my
poly·glot
poly·gon
pol·yp
poly·tech·nic
pome·gran·ate
pom·mel
pom·pon
pom·pos·i·ty (–ties)
pomp·ous
pon·cho
pon·der
pon·gee
pon·tiff
pon·tif·i·cal
pon·toon
po·ny·tail
poo·dle
pop·corn
pop·lar (tree; see *popular*)
pop·lin
pop·py (pop·pies)

pop·u·lace
pop·u·lar (commonly liked;
    see *poplar*)
pop·u·la·tion
pop·u·list
por·ce·lain
por·cu·pine
por·nog·ra·phy
po·ros·i·ty (–ties)
po·rous
por·poise
por·ridge
por·ta·ble
por·tend
por·tent
por·ten·tous
por·ter·house
port·fo·lio
por·ti·co (–coes *or* –cos)
por·tiere
por·tion
por·trait
por·tray
pos·it
po·si·tion
pos·i·tive·ly
pos·se
pos·sess·or
pos·ses·sion
pos·si·bil·i·ty (–ties)
post·age
pos·te·ri·or
pos·ter·i·ty
post·hu·mous
post·mor·tem
post·pone
post·script
pos·tu·late
pos·tur·ing
po·ta·ble
po·tage, pot·tage
po·ta·to (–toes)
po·ten·cy (–cies)
po·tent
po·ten·tate
po·ten·tial
po·tion
pot·pour·ri
pot·shot
pot·tery (–ter·ies)

poul·tice
poul·try
pounce
pound
pov·er·ty
pow·der
pow·er·ful
prac·ti·ca·ble
prac·ti·cal
prac·tice, prac·tise
prac·ti·tio·ner
prag·mat·ic
prai·rie
prate
prat·tle
prax·is (prax·es)
prayer·ful
preach
preachy
pre·am·ble
pre·ar·range
pre·car·i·ous
pre·cau·tion
pre·cede
pre·ce·dence
pre·ce·dent (noun),
    pre·ce·dent (adjective)
pre·cept
pre·cinct
pre·ci·os·i·ty (–ties)
pre·cious
prec·i·pice
pre·cip·i·tate
pré·cis
pre·cise
pre·ci·sion
pre·clude
pre·co·cious
pre·con·ceive
pre·con·cep·tion
pre·con·di·tion
pre·cur·sor
pred·a·tor
pre·dawn
pre·de·cease
pre·des·ti·na·tion
pre·de·ter·mine
pre·dic·a·ment
pred·i·cate
pre·dict

pre·di·lec·tion
pre·dis·pose
pre·doc·tor·al
pre·dom·i·nant
pre·em·i·nence
pre·empt
preen
pre·ex·is·tence
pre·fab·ri·cate
pref·ace
pref·a·to·ry
pre·fect
pre·fec·ture
pre·fer
pref·er·a·ble
pref·er·ence
pre·fig·ure
preg·na·ble
preg·nan·cy (–cies)
preg·nant
pre·heat
pre·hen·sile
pre·his·tor·ic
pre·in·duc·tion
prej·u·dice
prel·ate
pre·lim·i·nary (–nar·ies)
pre·lude
pre·mar·i·tal
pre·ma·ture
pre·med·i·cal
pre·med·i·tate
pre·mier (prime minister;
    see *premiere*)
pre·miere (first public
    performance; see
    *premier*)
pre·mise
pre·mi·um
pre·mo·ni·tion
pre·mon·i·to·ry
pre·oc·cu·pa·tion
prep·a·ra·tion
pre·pa·ra·to·ry
pre·pared·ness
pre·pon·der·ance
prep·o·si·tion
pre·pos·sess
pre·pos·ter·ous
pre·po·tent

pre·pran·di·al
pre·req·ui·site
pre·rog·a·tive
pres·age
pre·sanc·ti·fied
pres·by·ter
pre·scind
pre·scribe
pre·scrip·tion
pre·sent·able
pre·sen·ta·tion
pre·sent·ly
pres·er·va·tion·ist
pre·ser·va·tive
pre·shrunk
pres·i·den·cy (–cies)
pre·sid·i·um
pres·sure
pres·sur·ize
pres·tige
pres·ti·gious
pre·sume
pre·sump·tion
pre·sump·tu·ous
pre·tend·er
pre·ten·sion
pre·ten·tious
pre·ter·nat·u·ral
pre·test
pre·text
pret·ti·fy
pret·ti·ness
pret·ty
pret·zel
pre·vail
prev·a·lent
pre·var·i·cate
pre·vent·able
pre·view
pre·vi·ous
prey
prick·ly
priest·ly
prig·gish
pri·ma ballerina
pri·ma·cy
pri·ma don·na
pri·ma fa·cie
pri·mar·i·ly
pri·mate

prime
prim·er
pri·me·val
prim·ing
prim·i·tive
pri·mo·gen·i·ture
pri·mor·di·al
prim·rose
prince·ly
prin·ci·pal (head of school;
    see *principle*)
prin·ci·ple (fundamental
    law; see *principal*)
print·able
pri·or
prism
pris·mat·ic
pris·on·er
pris·tine
pri·va·cy (–cies)
pri·vate
pri·va·tion
priv·et
priv·i·lege
prize
prob·a·bil·i·ty (–ties)
prob·a·ble
pro·bate
pro·ba·tion·er
pro·ba·tive
pro·bi·ty
prob·lem·at·ic
pro·bos·cis (pro·bos·cises
    *or* pro·bos·ci·des)
pro·ca·the·dral
pro·ce·dur·al
pro·ce·dure
pro·ceed
pro·cess (pro·cess·es)
pro·ces·sion
pro·claim
proc·la·ma·tion
pro·cliv·i·ty (–ties)
pro·cras·ti·nate
pro·cre·ate
pro·crus·te·an
proc·tor
proc·u·ra·tor
pro·cure·ment
prod·i·gal

pro·di·gious
prod·i·gy (–gies)
pro·duce (noun), pro·duce
    (verb)
pro·duc·tion
pro·fan·i·ty (–ties)
pro·fes·sion
pro·fes·sor
pro·fi·cien·cy (–cies)
pro·file
prof·it (gain; see *prophet*)
prof·li·ga·cy (–cies)
pro·found
pro·fun·di·ty (–ties)
pro·fuse·ly
pro·gen·i·tor
prog·e·ny (–nies)
prog·no·sis
prog·nos·tic
prog·nos·ti·cate
pro·gram, pro·gramme
pro·gres·sion
pro·gres·sive
pro·hib·it
pro·hi·bi·tion
proj·ect (noun), pro·ject
    (verb)
pro·jec·tile
pro·jec·tion
pro·le·gom·e·non (–na)
pro·le·tar·i·at
pro·lif·er·ate
pro·lif·ic
pro·lix
pro·logue, pro·log
pro·long
prom·e·nade
prom·i·nence
pro·mis·cu·ity (–ities)
prom·is·ing
prom·is·so·ry (–ries)
prom·on·to·ry (–ries)
pro·mot·er
pro·mo·tion
prompt·ness
pro·mul·gate
pro·nate
pro·noun
pro·nounce·ment
pro·nun·ci·a·tion

pro·pae·deu·tic
pro·pa·gan·da
prop·a·gate
pro·pane
pro·pel
pro·pen·si·ty (–ties)
prop·er·ly
prop·er·ty (–ties)
proph·e·cy (–cies) (inspired
    declaration; see
    *prophesy*)
proph·e·sy (to predict; see
    *prophecy*)
prophet (one who foretells
    the future; see *profit*)
pro·phet·ic
pro·phy·lac·tic
pro·pin·qui·ty
pro·pi·ti·ate
pro·pi·tious
pro·por·tion
pro·pose
prop·o·si·tion
pro·pri·etary (–etar·ies)
pro·pri·etor
pro·pul·sion
pro·rate
pro·sa·ic
pro·sce·ni·um
pro·scribe
pro·scrip·tion
pros·e·cute
pros·e·cu·tor
pros·e·lyte
pros·e·ly·tize
pro·sit, prost
pros·o·dy (–dies)
pro·spec·tive
pro·spec·tus
pros·tate (gland; see
    *prostrate*)
pros·ti·tute
pros·trate (prone; see
    *prostate*)
pro·tag·o·nist
pro·te·an
pro·tec·tive·ly
pro·tec·tion
pro·té·gé
pro·tein

pro tem·po·re (Latin: for
  the present)
pro·test·er, pro·test·or
prot·es·tant
pro·tes·ta·tion
pro·tho·no·ta·ry (–ries)
pro·to·col
pro·ton
pro·to·type
pro·to·zo·an
pro·trac·tor
pro·trude
pro·tru·sion
pro·tu·ber·ant
prove
prov·en·der
pro·ver·bi·al
prov·i·dence
prov·i·den·tial
pro·vin·cial
pro·vi·sion·al
pro·vi·so
prov·o·ca·tion
pro·voc·a·tive
pro·vo·lo·ne (Italian: a kind
  of cheese)
pro·vost
prow·ess
prowl
prox·i·mate
prox·im·i·ty
proxy (prox·ies)
pru·dence
pru·ri·ence
pry·ing
psalm·ist
psal·tery, psal·try
  (psal·ter·ies *or* psal·tries)
pseud·onym
psy·che·del·ic
psy·chi·a·try
psy·chic
psy·cho·anal·y·sis
psy·cho·log·i·cal
psy·chol·o·gist
psy·cho·path
psy·cho·so·mat·ics
psy·cho·ther·a·py
ptar·mi·gan

pto·maine
pu·ber·ty
pu·bes·cent
pu·bic
pub·lic
pub·li·can
pub·lic·i·ty
pub·lic·ly
pub·lish·er
puck·er
pud·ding
pud·dle
pueb·lo (Spanish: village)
pu·er·ile
pu·gi·lism
pu·gi·list
pug·na·cious
puis·sance
pul·chri·tude
pul·let
pul·ley
pul·mo·nary
pul·mo·tor
pulp
pul·pit
pul·sar
pul·sate
pulse
pul·ver·ize
pu·ma
pum·ice
pum·mel
pump·er
pum·per·nick·el
pump·kin
punch
punc·til·io
punc·til·i·ous
punc·tu·al
punc·tu·ate
punc·tu·a·tion
punc·ture
pun·dit
pun·gen·cy
pun·gent
pun·ish·able
pu·ni·tive
pun·ster
punt·er

pup·pet
pup·pe·teer
pup·py·ish
pur·chase
pur·dah
pu·rée (French: to strain
  cooked food)
pur·ga·tive
pur·ga·to·ri·al
pur·ga·to·ry (–ries)
purge
pu·ri·fi·ca·tion
pu·ri·fy
pur·ist
pu·ri·tan·i·cal
pur·lieu (French:
  neighborhood)
pur·loin
pur·ple
pur·port
pur·pose
pur·pose·ly
pur·su·ance
pur·sue
pur·suit
pur·vey·or
pur·view
pushy
pu·sil·lan·i·mous
pussy·foot
pus·tu·lar
pus·tule
pu·ta·tive
pu·tre·fac·tion
pu·tre·fy
pu·trid
put·ter
put·ty (putties)
puz·zling
pyg·my (pygmies)
py·lon
py·or·rhea
pyr·a·mid
pyre
py·ro·tech·nics
pyr·rhic
py·thon
pyx
pyx·ie

quack·ery
quad·ran·gle
quad·rant
qua·dren·ni·al
quad·ri·lat·er·al
qua·drille (French: a type
   of square dance)
qua·driv·i·um
qua·droon
quad·ru·ped
qua·dru·ple
quaff
quag·mire
quail
quaint·ly
quake
qual·i·fi·ca·tion
qual·i·fied
qual·i·fy
qual·i·ta·tive
qual·i·ty (–ties)
qualm
qualm·ish
quan·da·ry (–ries)
quan·ti·fy
quan·ti·ta·tive
quan·ti·ty (–ties)
quan·tum (–ta)
quar·an·tine
quar·rel
quar·rel·some

quar·ry (quar·ries)
quar·ter
quar·ter·back
quar·tet, quar·tette
quar·to
quartz
qua·sar
quash
qua·train
qua·ver
quay
quea·sy, quea·zy
queen
queen-size
queer
quell
quench
quer·u·lous
que·ry (que·ries)
quest
ques·tion
ques·tion·able
ques·tion·naire
queue
quib·ble
quick·en
qui·es·cence
qui·et (free from noise; see
   *quite*)
qui·etude

qui·etus
quilt
quince
qui·nine
quin·tes·sence
quin·tet, quin·tette
quin·tile
quin·tu·plet
quip
quire (24 sheets of paper;
   variation of *choir*; see
   *choir*)
quirk
quirky
quis·ling
quit
quite (completely; see
   *quiet*)
quit·tance
quit·ter
quiv·er
quix·ot·ic
quiz (quiz·zes)
quiz·zi·cal
Quon·set
quo·rum
quo·ta
quot·able
quo·ta·tion
quote
quo·tient

R

rab·bi
rab·bin·ate
rab·bin·i·cal, rab·bin·ic
rab·bit (rab·bit *or* rab·bits)
rabble
ra·bid
ra·bies (plural also ra·bies)
rac·coon (rac·coon *or*
    rac·coons)
race·way
ra·cial
rac·ism
rack·et, rac·quet
ra·con·teur (French:
    storyteller)
racy
ra·dar
ra·di·al
ra·di·ance
ra·di·ate
ra·di·a·tor
rad·i·cal
rad·i·cal·ly
ra·dio·ac·tive
rad·ish
ra·di·um
ra·di·us (ra·di·us·es *or*
    ra·dii)
raff·ish
raf·fle
raf·ter
rag·a·muf·fin
rag·ged
rag·gle-tag·gle
rag·ing
rag·lan
ra·gout
raid·er
rail·lery (–ler·ies)
rail·road
rai·ment
rain (water falling in drops
    from the atmosphere; see
    *reign, rein*)
rain·bow
rainy
raise (to lift; see *raze*)
rai·sin
rai·son d'être (French:
    reason for existence)

ra·ja, ra·jah (Sanskrit: type
    of nobility)
rak·ish
ral·ly (rallies)
ram·ble
ram·bunc·tious
ram·i·fi·ca·tion
ram·i·fy
ram·page
ram·pant
ram·part
ram·rod
ram·shack·le
ran·cor·ous
ran·dom
rang·er
ran·kle
ran·sack
ran·som
ra·pa·cious
ra·pac·i·ty
ra·pid
ra·pi·er
rap·ine
rap·port
rar·efy
rar·i·ty (–ties)
ras·cal·i·ty (–ties)
rasp·ber·ry
raspy
ratch·et
rate
rat·i·fy
ra·tio
ra·tion
ra·tio·nal (relating to
    reason; see *rationale*)
ra·tio·nale (underlying
    reason; see *rational*)
ra·tio·nal·ize
rat·tan
rat·tle
rau·cous
raun·chy
rav·age
rav·en·ous
ra·vine
rav·i·o·li
ray·on

raze (destroy to the
    ground; see *raise*)
raz·zle-daz·zle
razz·ma·tazz
reach·able
re·ac·tion
re·ac·tion·ary
re·ac·ti·vate
re·ac·tor
read·able
readi·ly
ready-to-wear
re·align
re·al·is·tic
re·al·iza·tion
re·al·ly
realm
re·al·ty
ream
re·ap·por·tion
re·arm
rea·son·able
re·as·sur·ance
re·bate
re·bel·lious
re·bound
re·buff
re·buke
re·bus
re·but·tal
re·cal·ci·trance
re·ca·pit·u·late
re·cede
re·ceipt
re·ceiv·able
re·ceiv·er
re·cent·ly
re·cep·ta·cle
re·cep·tion·ist
re·cep·tive
re·cess
re·ces·sion
re·cid·i·vist
re·cip·ro·cate
rec·i·proc·i·ty (–ties)
re·cit·al
rec·i·ta·tive
reck·oned
rec·la·ma·tion
re·cluse

rec·og·ni·tion
re·cog·ni·zance
re·col·lect
rec·om·men·da·tion
rec·om·pense
rec·on·cil·able
re·con·dite
re·con·nais·sance
re·con·noi·ter
re·con·sti·tute
re·con·struc·tion
re·con·vert
re·cord·er
re·coup
re·course
re·cov·er·able
rec·re·ant
rec·re·ation
re·crim·i·nate
re·cru·des·cence
re·cruit
rect·an·gu·lar
rec·ti·fy
rec·ti·lin·ear
rec·ti·tude
rec·tor
re·cum·bent
re·cu·per·ate
re·cur·rent
re·cy·cle
re·dac·tion
red·den
re·deem·er
re·demp·tive
re·de·sign
re·dis·trict
red·o·lent
re·dou·ble
re·dound
red tape
re·duc·ible
re·duc·tion
re·dun·dan·cy (–cies)
re·elec·tion
re·en·act
re·en·try
re·fec·to·ry (–ries)
re·fer·able
ref·er·ee
ref·er·ence

ref·er·en·dum
re·fer·ral
re·fi·nance
re·fine·ment
re·flec·tion
re·flec·tor
re·flex
ref·or·ma·tion
re·for·ma·to·ry (–ries)
re·frac·to·ry (–ries)
re·frain
re·fresh·ment
re·frig·er·a·tor
ref·u·gee
re·fund (noun), re·fund
　(verb)
re·fur·bish
re·fus·al
ref·u·ta·tion
re·gal (royal; see *regale*)
re·gale (to give pleasure;
　see *regal*)
re·ga·lia
re·gard·less
re·gat·ta
re·gen·cy (–cies)
re·gen·er·ate
re·gent
re·gime, ré·gime
reg·i·men (systematic plan;
　see *regiment*)
reg·i·ment (military unit;
　see *regimen*)
re·gion·al
reg·is·ter (to enroll
　formally; see *registrar*)
reg·is·trar (keeper of
　records; see *register*)
reg·is·try (–tries)
re·gres·sion
re·gres·sive
re·gret·ta·bly
reg·u·lar·i·ty (–ties)
reg·u·la·to·ry
re·gur·gi·tate
re·ha·bil·i·tate
re·hears·al
reign (sovereignty; see
　*rain, rein*)
re·im·burse

rein (part of a bridle; stop
　or check; see *rain, reign*)
rein·deer
re·in·force
re·in·vest·ment
re·is·sue
re·it·er·ate
re·jec·tion
re·join·der
re·ju·ve·nate
re·lapse
re·la·tion
rel·a·tive
rel·a·tiv·i·ty (–ties)
re·lax·ation
re·lease
rel·e·gate
re·lent·less
rel·e·van·cy
re·li·abil·i·ty
re·li·ance
rel·ic
re·lief
re·lieve
re·luc·tant
re·lied
re·lo·cate
re·main·der
re·mark·able
re·me·di·a·ble
re·me·di·al
rem·e·dy (–dies)
re·mem·brance
rem·i·nis·cence
re·mis·sion
re·mit·tance
rem·nant
re·mon·strate
re·morse·ful
re·mote
re·mov·able
re·mu·ner·ate
re·nais·sance, re·na·scence
ren·der
ren·dez·vous
ren·di·tion
ren·e·gade
re·nege
re·ne·go·ti·ate
re·new·al

re·nounce
ren·o·vate
rent·al
re·nun·ci·a·tion
re·open
re·or·ga·ni·za·tion
re·pair·able
rep·a·ra·tion
rep·ar·tee
re·pa·tri·ate
re·peal
re·peat·ed·ly
re·pel·lent, re·pel·lant
re·pen·tance
re·per·cus·sion
rep·er·toire
rep·er·to·ry (–ries)
rep·e·ti·tious
re·place·able
re·plen·ish
re·plete
rep·li·ca
rep·li·cate
re·port·able
re·pose
re·pos·i·to·ry (–ries)
re·pos·sess
rep·re·hend
rep·re·hen·si·ble
rep·re·sen·ta·tive
re·pres·sion
re·prieve
re·pri·sal
re·prise
re·proach
rep·ro·bate
re·pro·duc·tion
rep·tile
re·pub·lic
re·pu·di·ate
re·pug·nance
re·pul·sive
rep·u·ta·ble
re·pute
re·quest
re·qui·em
re·quire·ment
req·ui·site
req·ui·si·tion
re·scind

res·cue
re·search
re·sem·blance
re·sent·ful
res·er·va·tion
res·er·voir
re·shuf·fle
res·i·dence
res·i·den·tial
re·sid·u·al
res·i·due
res·ig·na·tion
re·sil·ience
res·in·ous
re·sis·tance
re·sist·er (one who
    opposes; see *resistor*)
re·sis·tor (electrical device;
    see *resister*)
res·o·lute
re·solve
res·o·nance
res·o·na·tor
re·sound
re·source·ful
re·spect·abil·i·ty (–ties)
re·spec·tive·ly
res·pi·ra·tion
res·pi·ra·tor
re·splen·dent
re·spon·dent
re·spon·si·bil·i·ty (–ties)
re·spon·sive
re·spon·so·ry (–ries)
re·state·ment
res·tau·rant
res·ti·tu·tion
res·tive
res·to·ra·tion
re·strain
re·stric·tion
re·struc·ture
re·sult
re·sume (to begin again;
    see *resumé*)
re·su·mé (short account of
    career; see *resume*)
re·sump·tion
re·sur·gence
res·ur·rec·tion

re·sus·ci·tate
re·tail·ing
re·tain·er
re·tal·i·ate
re·tar·da·tion
re·ten·tive
ret·i·cence
ret·i·cule
ret·i·nue
re·tire·ment
re·tract
re·trench
ret·ri·bu·tion
re·triev·al
ret·ro·ac·tive
ret·ro·grade
ret·ro·gress
re·tro·spect
re·turn·able
re·unite
re·us·able
re·veal
rev·eil·le
rev·e·la·tion
rev·el·er, rev·el·ler
rev·el·ry (–ries)
re·venge·ful
rev·e·nue
re·ver·ber·ate
rev·er·ence
rev·er·en·tial
rev·er·ie, rev·ery
    (rev·er·ies)
re·ver·sal
re·vers·ible
re·vert·ible
re·view (to see again; see
    *revue*)
re·vile
re·vi·sion
re·vi·tal·ize
re·viv·al
re·vive
re·vo·ca·ble
re·voke
re·volt
rev·o·lu·tion
rev·o·lu·tion·ize
re·volv·er

re·vue (theatrical
production; see *review*)
re·vul·sion
re·ward
re·write
rhap·so·dy (–dies)
rheo·stat
rhet·o·ric
rheu·mat·ic
rhi·noc·er·os
(rhi·noc·er·os·es *or*
rhi·noc·eros *or*
rhi·noc·eri)
rhu·barb
rhyme
rhythm
rib·ald
rib·bon
rice
rick·ety
rid·dance
rid·dle
ridge
ri·dic·u·lous
ri·fle
rift
rig·ging
right (correct; see *rite*)
righ·teous
ri·gid·i·ty (–ties)
rig·ma·role
rig·or·ous
ring·er
rins·ing
ri·ot·ous
ri·par·i·an
rip·ple
ris·i·ble
risky
ris·qué (French: off-color)
rite (a ceremonial act; see
*right*)
rit·u·al

ri·val·ry (–ries)
riv·er·side
riv·et
roach
road
roam
roan
roast
rob·bery (rob·ber·ies)
ro·bot
ro·bust
rock·et
ro·co·co
ro·dent
ro·deo (ro·de·os)
rogue
rogu·ish
rol·lick·ing
ro·man·ti·cize
ron·deau (ron·deaux)
rook·ery (rook·er·ies)
roomy
roost·er
root·less·ness
ro·sa·ry (–ries)
ro·se·ate
ro·sette
Rosh Ha·sha·nah
ros·i·ly
ros·ter
ros·trum
ro·ta·ry (–ries)
ro·ta·tion
rote
ro·tund
ro·tun·da
roué (French: man devoted
to sensual pleasures)
rouge
rough
rou·lette
round·about

rouse
roust·about
rout (disorderly retreat; see
*route*)
route (line of travel; see
*rout*)
rou·tine
rou·tin·ize
rov·ing
row·dy
roy·al·ist
roy·al·ty (–ties)
rub·bery
rub·bish
rub·ble
ru·bi·cund
ru·bric
ruck·sack
rud·der
ru·di·men·ta·ry
ruf·fi·an
ruf·fle
rug·by
rug·ged
ru·in·ous
rul·ing
rum·ba
rum·ble
ru·mi·nate
rum·mage
ru·mor
run·ner
rup·ture
ru·ral
ruse
rus·set
rus·tic
rus·ti·cate
rust·i·ness
rus·tle
ru·ta·ba·ga
ruth·less
rye

**S**

sab·bat·i·cal
sa·ber, sa·bre
sa·ble
sab·o·tage
sab·o·teur
sac·cha·rine
sac·er·do·tal
sa·chem
sa·chet
sac·ra·ment
sa·cred
sac·ri·fice
sac·ri·fi·cial
sac·ri·lege
sac·ris·tan
sac·ris·ty (–ties)
sa·cro·il·i·ac
sac·ro·sanct
sad·den
sad·dle
sa·dism
sa·fa·ri
safe·ty (safeties)
saf·flow·er
sa·ga
sa·ga·cious
sage
sail (canvas used to propel
    ship; see *sale*)
sail·or
sal·able, sale·able
sal·ad
sal·a·ry (–ries)
sale (act of selling; see *sail*)
sales check
sales·clerk
sales tax
sa·lient
sa·line
sa·li·va
sal·i·vate
sal·low
salm·on (sal·mon *or*
    sal·mons)
sa·lon (elegant living room;
    see *saloon*)
sa·loon (place selling
    alcoholic drinks; see
    *salon*)
sal·ta·to·ry

sa·lu·bri·ous
sal·u·tary
sa·lu·ta·to·ri·an
sa·lute
sal·vage
sal·va·tion
salve
sam·o·var (Russian: an urn
    used to boil water for
    tea)
sam·ple
san·a·to·ri·um
sanc·ti·fi·ca·tion
sanc·ti·mo·nious
sanc·tion
sanc·tu·ary (–ar·ies)
san·dal
sand·wich (–es)
sane
san·guine
san·i·tary
san·i·ta·tion
sap·ling
sap·phire
sar·casm
sar·coph·a·gous,
    sar·co·phag·ic
sar·dine (sar·dines *or*
    sar·dine)
sar·don·ic
sard·onyx
sa·ri, sa·ree (Sanskrit:
    woman's Hindu garment)
sar·sa·pa·ril·la
sar·to·ri·al
sas·sa·fras
sa·tan·ic
satch·el
sate
sa·teen
sat·el·lite
sa·ti·ate
sa·ti·ety
sat·in
sat·ire
sat·is·fac·tion
sat·u·rate
sat·ur·nine
sa·tyr
saucy

sau·er·kraut
sau·na
saun·ter
sau·sage
sau·té
sau·terne
sav·age·ly
sa·van·na, sa·van·nah
sa·vant
sav·able, save·able
sav·ior, sav·iour
sa·voir faire (French:
    sureness in social
    behavior)
sa·vory, sa·voury
sax·o·phone
scab·bard
sca·brous
scaf·fold
scald·ing
scal·lion
scal·lop
scalp·er
scan·dal
scan·dal·ous
scanty
scape·goat
scap·u·lar
scar·ci·ty (–ties)
scarf
scary, scar·ey
scath·ing
scat·o·log·i·cal
scat·ter
scav·enge
sce·nar·io
sce·nar·ist
scen·ery (–er·ies)
sce·nic
scent·ed
scep·ter, scep·tre
sched·ule
sche·mat·ic
scheme
scher·zo (scher·zos *or*
    scher·zi)
schism
schis·mat·ic
schiz·oid
schizo·phre·nia

schnau·zer
schol·ar·ly
scho·las·tic
school
schoo·ner
schwa
sci·at·ic
sci·en·tif·ic
scin·til·late
sci·on
scis·sors
scle·ro·sis
scoff·law
scone
scope
scorch
scor·ing
scorn·ful
scor·pi·on
scoun·drel
scour
scourge
scram·ble
scrap·ing (grate harshly;
    see *scrapping*)
scrap·ping (quarreling,
    converting to scrap; see
    *scraping*)
scratch
scraw·ny
scream
screech
screen
screen·play
screen test
screw
scrib·ble
scrim·mage
scrim·shaw
script
scrip·ture
scrof·u·lous
scrounge
scruff
scru·ple
scru·pu·lous
scru·ti·nize
scu·ba
scuff
scuf·fle

sculp·tor
sculp·ture
scur·ri·lous
scut·tle
scythe
sea (body of water; see
    *see*)
seamy
sé·ance (French: a session
    to receive spirit
    communications)
search
sea·shore
sea·son·al
seat
se·cede
se·ces·sion
se·clu·sion
sec·ond·ary
se·cre·cy (–cies)
sec·re·tar·i·at
sec·re·tary (–tar·ies)
se·crete
se·cre·tive
sect
sec·tar·i·an
sec·tion·al
sec·tor
sec·u·lar
se·cu·ri·ty (–ties)
se·dan
se·date
sed·a·tive
sed·en·tary
se·der
sedge
sed·i·ment
se·di·tion
se·duce
se·duc·tive
sed·u·lous
see (perceive by eye; see
    *sea*)
seed·ling
seem·ing·ly
seep·age
seer·suck·er
see·saw
seethe
seg·ment

seg·re·gate
seg·re·ga·tion
se·gue
seine
seis·mic
seis·mo·graph
seize
sei·zure
sel·dom
se·lec·tion
se·lec·tive
self-con·scious
self-de·fense
self-por·trait
sell (to exact a price for;
    see *cell*)
sell·er (one who offers for
    sale; see *cellar*)
se·man·tics
sema·phore
sem·blance
se·mes·ter
semi·an·nu·al
sem·i·nal
sem·i·nar
sem·i·nary (–nar·ies)
semi·pro·fes·sion·al
sem·pi·ter·nal
sen·a·to·ri·al
se·nes·cence
se·nile
se·nil·i·ty
se·nior·i·ty
sen·sa·tion
sense
sense·less
sen·si·bil·i·ty (–ties)
sen·si·tive
sen·so·ry
sen·su·al
sen·su·ous
sent (past of *send*; see
    *cent*)
sen·tence
sen·ten·tious
sen·tient
sen·ti·men·tal
sen·ti·nel
sen·try (sentries)
sep·a·ra·ble

sep·a·rate
sep·a·ra·tion
sep·ten·ni·al
sep·tu·a·ge·nar·i·an
sep·ul·cher, sep·ul·chre
se·quel
se·quence
se·quen·tial
se·ques·ter
se·quoia
se·ra·pe (Mexican Spanish:
   type of men's woolen
   shawl)
ser·aph, ser·a·phim
   (ser·aphs *or* ser·a·phim)
ser·e·nade
se·ren·i·ty
serge
ser·geant
se·ri·al (arranged in series;
   see *cereal*)
se·ri·a·tim
se·ries (plural also series)
se·ri·ous
ser·mon
ser·pent
ser·rat·ed
se·rum
ser·vant
ser·vice
ser·vice·able
ser·vi·tude
ses·a·me
ses·qui·cen·ten·ni·al
ses·qui·pe·da·lian
ses·sion
ses·tet
set·tle
set·tle·ment
sev·enth
sev·er·al
sev·er·ance
se·ver·i·ty
sew·age
sew·ing
sex·ism
sex·tant
sex·ton
sex·u·al
sexy

shab·by
schack·le
shad·ing
shad·owy
shaft
shag·gy
shaky
shale
shal·low
sham·ble
shame·ful
sham·poo
sham·rock
shank
shan·ty (shanties)
shape
shard
share·crop·per
shark
sharp·en
shat·ter
shav·ing
sheaf (sheaves)
shear (cut off; see *sheer*)
sheath (case for a blade;
     see *sheathe*)
sheathe (to put into a
     sheath; see *sheath*)
sheer (transparent; see
     *shear*)
sheet
sheikh, sheik
shelf (shelves)
shel·lac
shel·ter
she·nan·i·gan
shep·herd
sher·bet
sher·iff
sher·ry (sherries)
shib·bo·leth
shield
shifty
shin·gle
shin·ing
shiny
ship·ment
shirk·er
shirr
shirt·sleeve

shish ke·bab
shiv·er
shoal
shock
shoe
shop
shor·ing
short·age
short·en·ing
short·hand
short-term
should
shoul·der
shout
shove
shov·el
show·case
show·er
showy
shrap·nel
shrewd
shriek
shrine
shrink
shriv·el
shroud
shrub·bery
shrug
shud·der
shuf·fle
shut·ter
shut·tle
shy
sib·i·lant
sick·le
sick·ly
sick·ness
side·line
si·de·re·al
siege
sieve
sigh
sight·ly
sign
sig·nal
sig·na·to·ry (−ries)
sig·na·ture
sig·nif·i·cant
si·lent
sil·hou·ette

sil·i·con
silky
silver·ware
sil·very
sim·i·an
sim·i·lar
sim·i·lar·i·ty (–ties)
sim·i·le
si·mil·i·tude
si·mo·ny
sim·per
sim·ple
sim·pli·fy
sim·u·la·tion
si·mul·ta·neous
sin·cere·ly
si·ne·cure
sin·ew
singe
singe·ing
sin·gle
sin·gly
sin·gu·lar·i·ty (–ties)
sin·is·ter
sin·u·ous
si·nus
si·phon
si·ren
sis·ter·ly
site (place; see *cite*)
sit·u·at·ed
sit·u·a·tion
six·ty (sixties)
size
siz·zle
skein, skean, skeane
skel·e·ton
skep·ti·cal
sketchy
skied
ski·ing
skil·let
skill·ful, skil·ful
skim·ming
skimpy
skip·per
skirl
skir·mish
skit·tish

skul·dug·gery, skull
  dug·gery (–ger·ies)
skulk
sky
slack·en
sla·lom
slan·der·ous
slaugh·ter
slav·ery
slea·zy
sledge
sledge·ham·mer
sleek
sleeve
sleigh
slen·der·ize
sleuth
slic·ing
slick·er
slide
slight·ing·ly
slime
slip·pery
slip·shod
slith·er
sliv·er
slob·ber
sloe (fruit; see *slow*)
slo·gan
sloop
slope
slop·ing
slop·py
sloth·ful
slouch
slough
slov·en·ly
slow (not hasty; see *sloe*)
sludge
slug·gish
sluice
slum·ber
slushy
sly
small
smart
smat·ter·ing
smear
smelly

smid·gen, smid·geon,
  smid·gin
smile
smirk
smith·er·eens
smoke
smol·der, smoul·der
smooth
smor·gas·bord
smudge
snail
snake
sneak·er
sneer
sneeze
snif·ter
snip·er
snob·bery
snor·kel
snow·flake
snow·mo·bile
snug·gle
soap opera
soapy
soar·ing
so·ber·ly
so·bri·ety
so·bri·quet
soc·cer
so·cia·bil·i·ty (–ties)
so·cial·ism
so·cial·ize
so·ci·etal
so·ci·ety (–et·ies)
so·cio·eco·nom·ic
so·ci·ol·o·gy
so·da·list
so·dal·i·ty (–ties)
sod·den
soft·ware
sog·gy
soil
soi·rée, soi·ree (French:
  evening party)
so·journ
so·lace
so·lar
sol·der
sol·dier

sole (fish *or* bottom of foot;
   see *soul*)
so·le·cism
sol·emn
so·lem·ni·ty (–ties)
so·le·noid
so·lic·it
so·lic·i·tor
so·lic·i·tous
so·lic·i·tude
sol·i·dar·i·ty
so·lid·i·fy
so·lil·o·quize
sol·i·taire
sol·i·tary
sol·i·tude
so·lo·ist
sol·u·ble
so·lu·tion
solv·able
sol·ven·cy
som·ber, som·bre
som·nam·bu·list
som·no·lent
son (male child; see *sun*)
so·nar
son·ic
son·net
so·no·rous
soothe
sooty
so·phis·ti·cat·ed
soph·ist·ry
soph·o·more
so·po·rif·ic
so·pra·no (–nos)
sor·cer·er
sor·did
so·ror·i·ty (–ties)
sor·row·ful
sor·tie (French: type of
   attack)
soul (spiritual essence; see
   *sole*)
sought
sound
soup du jour (French: soup
   of the day)
sour

source
south·ern
sou·ve·nir
sov·er·eign, sov·ran
so·vi·et
soy·bean
space
spa·cial
spa·cious
spa·ghet·ti
span·gled
span·iel
spar·ing·ly
spar·kle
spar·row
sparse
spasm
spas·mod·ic
spas·tic
spa·tial
spat·u·la
spay
speak·er
spe·cial
spe·cial·ty (–ties)
spe·cies
spe·cif·ic
spec·i·fic·ca·tion
spec·i·fic·i·ty
spec·i·men
spec·ta·cle
spec·tac·u·lar
spec·ta·tor
spec·tral
spec·trum
spec·u·late
speech·less
spend·thrift
sperm
sphag·num
sphere
spher·i·cal
sphinx (sphinx·es *or*
   sphin·ges)
spice
spic·ing
spi·dery
spiel
spig·ot

spill·age
spin·ach
spin·dle
spin·dly
spin·et
spin·ster
spi·ral
spir·i·tu·al
spite·ful
splashy
splen·dor
sple·net·ic
splice
splin·ter
splut·ter
spoil·age
spokes·man
spo·li·a·tion
spon·dee
sponge
spongy
spon·sor
spon·ta·ne·ity
spon·ta·ne·ous
spooky
spoon·ful (spoon·fuls *or*
   spoons·ful)
spo·rad·ic
spore
sport·ive
sporty
spot·light
spot·ty
spouse
spright·ly
spring·time
springy
sprin·kling
sprock·et
sprout
spry
spunky
spu·ri·ous
spurred
spu·tum
spy (spies)
squab·ble
squad·ron
squal·id

squa·lor
squan·der
square
squash
squat·ted
squat·ter
squawk
squeaky
squeal
squea·mish
squeeze
squelch
squint
squire
squirm
squir·rel (squir·rels *or* squir·rel)
squirt
sta·bil·i·ty (–ties)
sta·ble
stac·ca·to
stacked
sta·di·um (sta·dia *or* sta·di·ums)
staff
stage
stag·ing
stag·nant
staid
stair·case
stake (pointed post; see *steak*)
sta·lac·tite
sta·lag·mite
stale·mate
stalk
stal·lion
stal·wart
stam·i·na
stam·mer
stam·pede
stance
stan·chion
stan·dard·ize
stand·by
stan·za
sta·ple
starchy
star·ry
star·tle

star·va·tion
stash
state
state·ment
stat·ic
sta·tion
sta·tion·ary (immobile; see *stationery*)
sta·tio·nery (materials for writing; see *stationary*)
stat·is·ti·cian
sta·tis·tics
stat·ue
stat·ure
sta·tus
stat·u·to·ry
staunch
stead·fast
steak (slice of meat; see *stake*)
steal (to take the property of another; see *steel*)
stealthy
steel (a metal; see *steal*)
stee·ple
steer·age
stein
stel·lar
sten·cil
ste·nog·ra·pher
sten·to·ri·an
step (an advance of a foot; see *steppe*)
steppe (treeless plain; see *step*)
ste·reo·type
ster·ile
ster·ling
ste·ve·dore
stew·ard
stick·ler
sticky
sti·fle
stig·ma·tize
sti·let·to
stim·u·late
stim·u·lus
stin·gy
sti·pend
stip·u·late

stir·rup
stitch
stock·ade
stock·bro·ker
stodgy
stol·id
stom·ach·ache
stop·page
stor·age
sto·ried
stow·age
strad·dle
strag·gle
straight (free from curves; see *strait*)
straight·en
strait (a narrow passageway between two bodies of water; see *straight*)
strang·er
stran·gle
stran·gu·late
strat·a·gem
stra·te·gic
strat·e·gy (–gies)
strat·i·fy
strato·sphere
stra·tum (stra·ta)
streaky
stream·line
strength
stren·u·ous
stress·ful
stretch·er
stri·at·ed
strick·en
stric·ture
stri·dent
strike
strin·gent
strobe
stroll
strong
struc·tu·ral
struc·ture
strug·gle
strum·pet
strych·nine
stub·ble
stub·by

stuc·co
stu·dent
stu·dio
stu·di·ous
study
stul·ti·fy
stum·bling
stu·pe·fy
stu·pen·dous
stur·dy
stur·geon
stut·ter
sty, stye (sties *or* styes)
style
styl·ish
styl·ized
sty·lus (sty·li *or* sty·lus·es)
suave
sub·com·mit·tee
sub·con·scious
sub·due
sub·ject (noun), sub·ject
  (verb)
sub·ju·gate
sub·lime
sub·lim·i·nal
sub·ma·rine
sub·merge
sub·mis·sion
sub·or·di·nate
sub·orn
sub·poe·na
sub·scribe
sub·scrip·tion
sub·se·quent
sub·ser·vi·ent
sub·side
sub·sid·iary
sub·si·dize
sub·si·dy (–dies)
sub·sis·tence
sub·stance
sub·stan·tial
sub·stan·tive
sub·sti·tute
sub·sume
sub·ter·fuge
sub·tle
sub·trac·tion
sub·ur·bia

sub·ver·sion
suc·ceed
suc·cess·ful
suc·ces·sion
suc·ces·sor
suc·cinct
suc·co·tash
suc·cu·lent
suc·cumb
suck·le
suc·tion
sud·den
sudsy
sue
suede, suède
suf·fer·ance
suf·fice
suf·fi·cient
suf·fo·cate
suf·frage
suf·fuse
sug·ges·tion
sui·cid·al
suit·able
suite
suit·or
sulky
sul·phur, sul·fur
sul·try
sum·ma·ry (abridgment of
  discourse; see *summery*)
sum·mer·time
sum·mery (like summer;
  see *summary*)
sum·mit
sum·mon
sump·tu·ous
sun (celestial body; see
  *son*)
su·per·an·nu·ate
su·perb
su·per·cil·ious
su·per·fi·cial
su·per·flu·ity (–ities)
su·per·flu·ous
su·per·in·ten·dent
su·pe·ri·or
su·per·la·tive
su·per·nat·u·ral
su·per·sede

su·per·sti·tious
su·per·vi·so·ry
su·pine
sup·plant
sup·ple
sup·ple·men·ta·ry
sup·pli·ant
sup·pli·cate
supply (supplies)
sup·port·ive
sup·po·si·tion
sup·pos·i·to·ry (–ries)
sup·pres·sion
sup·pu·rate
su·prem·a·cy (–cies)
sur·cease
sur·charge
sure·ty (–ties)
sur·face
sur·feit
surge
sur·geon
sur·gi·cal
sur·mise
sur·name
sur·plice
sur·plus
sur·re·al·ism
sur·ren·der
sur·ro·gate
sur·round·ings
sur·tax
sur·veil·lance
sur·vey (noun), sur·vey
  (verb)
sur·viv·al
sus·cep·ti·bil·i·ty (–ties)
sus·cep·ti·ble
sus·pect (noun), sus·pect
  (verb)
sus·pense
sus·pi·cious
sus·te·nance
su·ture
svelte
swad·dling
swag·ger
swampy
swank
swar·thy

swash·buck·ler
swas·ti·ka
swath, swathe
swear
sweaty
sweet·ened
swel·ter
swept
swerve
swin·dle
swing
swirl
swish
switch
swiv·el
swol·len
sword
syb·a·rite

syc·a·more
sy·co·phant
syl·lab·ic
syl·lab·i·fy
syl·la·bus (–bi *or* –bus·es)
syl·lo·gism
sylph
syl·van
sym·bol·ic
sym·met·ri·cal, sym·met·ric
sym·me·try (–tries)
sym·pa·thet·ic
sym·phon·ic
sym·po·sium
symp·tom
syn·a·gogue, syn·a·gog
syn·chro·nize
syn·co·pate

syn·di·cate
syn·ec·do·che
syn·od
syn·onym
syn·op·sis
syn·op·tic
syn·tax
syn·the·size
syn·thet·ic, syn·thet·i·cal
syph·i·lis
sy·ringe
syr·upy
sys·tem·at·ic,
   sys·tem·at·i·cal
sys·tem·atize
sys·tem·ic

T

Ta·bas·co
tab·by
tab·er·na·cle
tab·la·ture
ta·bling
tab·leau (tab·leaux *or*
     tab·leaus)
ta·ble·spoon·ful
     (ta·ble·spoon·fuls *or*
     ta·ble·spoons·ful)
tab·let
tab·loid
ta·boo, ta·bu
tab·o·ret, tab·ou·ret
     (French: type of seat or
     stand)
tab·u·lar
tab·u·late
tab·u·la·tor
ta·chom·e·ter
tac·it
tac·i·turn
tack·le
tacky
tact·ful
tac·tic·al
tac·tile
tad·pole
taf·fe·ta
taff·rail
taf·fy
tail (rear end; see *tale*)
tai·lored
taint
tak·ing
talc
tal·cum
tale (story: see *tail*)
tal·ent
tales·man (juror; see
     *talisman*)
tal·is·man (charm: see
     *talesman*)
talk·ative
talk·ie (sound motion
     picture; see *talky*)
talky (too much talk; see
     *talkie*)
tall·ish
tal·low

tal·ly (tal·lies)
tal·ly·ho
tal·on
ta·ma·le
tam·a·rack
tam·bou·rine
tam·ing
tam·per
tan·a·ger
tan·dem
tan·ge·lo
tan·gent
tan·gen·tial
tan·ger·ine
tan·gi·ble
tan·gling
tan·gled
tan·go (tan·gos)
tangy
tan·kard
tan·nery (–ner·ies)
tan·ning
tan·ta·lize
tan·ta·mount
tan·trum
tape
ta·per
tap·es·tried
tap·es·try (–tries)
tap·i·o·ca
tar·an·tel·la
ta·ran·tu·la
tar·di·ly
tar·dy
tare (weed; see *tear*)
tar·get
tar·iff
tar·mac
tar·nish
tar·ot
tar·pau·lin
tar·pon
tar·ra·gon
tar·ry
tar·tan
tar·tar
task
tas·sel
taste·ful
tasty

tat·tered
tat·too
tat·ty
taught
taunt
taupe
taut
tau·tol·o·gy (–gies)
tav·ern
taw·dry
taw·ny
tax·a·tion
tax-ex·empt
taxi·der·my
tax·ied
taxi·ing
tax·on·o·my (–mies)
tax·pay·er
teach·able
tea·ket·tle
teak·wood
team (group; see *teem*)
team·ster
tear (damage from being
     torn; see *tare*)
teas·ing
teat
tech·ni·cal
tech·ni·cian
tech·nique
tech·no·log·i·cal,
     tech·no·log·ic
te·dious
te·di·um
teem (filled to overflowing;
     see *team*)
teen·age
tee·ter
teethe
tee·to·tal·er, tee·to·tal·ler
tele·cast
tele·com·mu·ni·ca·tion
tele·gram
tele·graph
te·le·ol·o·gy
te·lep·a·thy
tele·phon·ing
tele·pho·to
tele·scope
tele·typ·ist

tele·vise
tel·ex
te·mer·i·ty (–ties)
tem·per·a·ment
tem·per·ate
tem·per·a·ture
tem·pered
tem·pes·tu·ous
tem·plate
tem·ple
tem·po (tem·pi or tem·pos)
tem·po·ral
tem·po·rar·i·ly
tem·po·rize
tempt
temp·ta·tion
tem·pu·ra
ten·a·ble
te·na·cious
te·nac·i·ty
ten·ant
ten·den·cy (–cies)
ten·den·tious, ten·den·cious
ten·der·ize
ten·der·loin
ten·der·ly
ten·don
ten·dril
ten·e·ment
te·net
ten·or
tense
ten·sile
ten·sion
ten·ta·cle
ten·ta·tive
ten·ter·hook
ten·u·ous
ten·ure
te·pee
tep·id
ter·gi·ver·sa·tion
ter·i·ya·ki (Japanese: spicy
    meat or shelfish dish)
ter·ma·gant
ter·mi·nal
ter·mi·nate
ter·mi·na·tion
ter·mi·nol·o·gy (–gies)
ter·mi·nus (–ni or –nuses)

ter·mite
terp·si·cho·re·an
ter·race
ter·ra·cot·ta
ter·rain, ter·rane
ter·rar·i·um (ter·rar·ia or
    ter·rar·i·ums)
ter·raz·zo
ter·res·tri·al
ter·ri·ble
ter·ri·er
ter·rif·ic
ter·ri·fy
ter·ri·to·ri·al
ter·ri·to·ry (–ries)
ter·ror·ize
ter·ry
terse
ter·tia·ry
tes·sel·late
tes·ta·ment
tes·ta·tor
test·ed
tes·ti·cle
tes·ti·fy
tes·ti·mo·ni·al
tes·ti·mo·ny (–nies)
tes·ty
tet·a·nus
tête-à-tête (French: private
    conversation between
    two people)
teth·er
tet·ra·chlo·ride
te·tram·e·ter
text·book
tex·tile
tex·ture
thank·ful
thatch
the·atre, the·ater
the·at·ri·cal
theft
their (relating to them; see
    there)
the·ism
the·mat·ic
theme
thence
the·oc·ra·cy (–cies)

theo·lo·gian
the·ol·o·gy (–gies)
the·o·rem
the·o·ret·i·cal
the·o·rist
the·o·ry (–ries)
the·os·o·phy
ther·a·peu·tic
ther·a·pist
ther·a·py (–pies)
there (in that place; see
    their)
ther·mal
ther·mom·e·ter
ther·mo·stat
the·sau·rus (the·sau·ri or
    the·sau·rus·es)
the·sis
thes·pi·an
thew
they
thick·en·ing
thick·et
thief
thiev·ery (–er·ies)
thigh
thim·ble·ful
think·able
thin·ner
third
thirsty
thir·teenth
this·tle
thith·er
thong
tho·rac·ic
thorny
thor·ough·bred
thor·ough·fare
though
thought
thought·ful
thou·sand
thrash
thread·bare
threat·en
three-di·men·sion·al
thren·o·dy (–dies)
thresh·old
thrift

thrive

throat

throe

throm·bo·sis (–bo·ses)

throne

thronged

throt·tle

through

through·out

thru·way

thug

thumb

thump

thun·der·ous

thwart

thyme

thy·roid

ti·ara

tick·et

tick·ing

tick·le

tid·al

tid·ings

ti·di·ness

tier

tight·rope

tile

till·age

tim·ber (wood; see *timbre*)

tim·bre (quality of sound; see *timber*)

time·ly

time·table

tim·id

tim·ing

tim·o·rous

tim·pa·nist

tinc·ture

tin·der

tinge

tin·gle

tin·kle

tin·ny

tin·sel

tint·ing

tip·sy

ti·rade

tire

tis·sue

tithe

tit·il·late

tit·i·vate, tit·ti·vate

ti·tled

tit·tle

toasty

to·bac·co

to·bog·gan

toc·sin

tod·dle

to·ga

to·geth·er·ness

tog·gle

toil

toile (French: type of fabric)

toil·worn

to·ken·ism

tole

tol·er·a·ble

tol·er·ance

toll

tom·a·hawk

to·ma·to (–toes)

tomb

to·mor·row

to·nal·i·ty (–ties)

tongue

tongu·ing

to·nic·i·ty

to·night

ton·nage

ton·sil·lec·to·my (–mies)

ton·sil·li·tis

ton·so·ri·al

ton·sure

tool·box

tooth·some

to·paz

top·i·cal

to·pog·ra·phy

to·pol·o·gy (–gies)

top·ple

top·sy-tur·vy

toque

to·re·ador (Spanish: bullfighter)

tor·men·tor

tor·na·do (–dos *or* –does)

tor·pe·do (–does)

tor·pid

tor·por

torque

tor·ren·tial

tor·rid·ly

tor·sion

tor·so (tor·sos *or* tor·si)

tor·ti·lla

tor·toise

tor·tu·ous

tor·ture

to·tal·i·tar·i·an

to·tal·i·ty (–ties)

to·tal·ly

to·tem

touch

touchy

tough·en

tou·pee (French: wig)

tour de force (French: a feat of strength, skill, or ingenuity)

tour·ism

tour·na·ment

tour·ney

tour·ni·quet

tou·sle

to·ward

tow·el·ing, tow·el·ling

tow·er·ing

tow·head

town house

tox·ic

toy

tra·chea (tra·che·ae *or* tra·che·as)

trac·ing

trac·ta·ble

trac·tion

trac·tor

trade·mark

tra·di·tion

tra·duce

traf·fic

traf·ficked

tra·ge·di·an (actor in tragic roles; see *tragedienne*)

tra·ge·di·enne (actress in tragic roles; see *tragedian*)

trag·e·dy (–dies)

trail
train·ing
trai·tor·ous
tra·jec·to·ry (–ries)
tram·mel
tram·ple
tram·po·line
trance
tran·quil
tran·quil·ize, tran·quil·lize
tran·quil·li·ty, tran·quil·i·ty
trans·ac·tion
trans·at·lan·tic
tran·scen·dence
trans·scen·den·tal
tran·con·ti·nen·tal
tran·scribe
trans·script
tran·sect
tran·sept
trans·fer·al
trans·fer·ence
trans·for·ma·tion
trans·fu·sion
trans·gres·sion
tran·sience
tran·sient
tran·sis·tor
tran·sit
tran·si·tion
tran·si·to·ry
trans·la·tion
trans·lu·cent
trans·mis·si·ble
trans·mit·tance
trans·mute
tran·som
trans·par·en·cy (–cies)
tran·spire
trans·port·able
trans·pose
trans·verse
tra·peze
trashy
trau·ma
tra·vail
trav·eled, trav·elled
trav·el·er, trav·el·ler
trav·el·ing trav·el·ling
trav·el·ogue, trav·el·og

tra·verse
trav·es·ty (–ties)
trawl·er
treach·er·ous
trea·cle
trea·dle
trea·son·able
trea·sur·er
trea·tise
trea·ty
treble
trek·king
trel·lis
trem·ble
tre·men·dous
trem·or
trem·u·lous
tren·chant
trep·i·da·tion
tres·pass
tres·tle
tri·an·gle
tri·bal
trib·u·la·tion
tri·bu·nal
trib·u·tary
trick·ery
tri·col·or
tri·cy·cle
tri·dent
tri·fling
trig·ger
tril·o·gy (–gies)
tri·mes·ter
trin·ket
trio
tri·ple
trip·let
trip·li·cate
trip·tych
trite
tri·umph
tri·um·vir·ate
triv·et
triv·i·al
trol·ley, trol·ly (trol·leys *or* trol·lies)
trom·bone
tro·phy (trophies)
trop·i·cal

trou·ba·dour
trou·bling
trough
troupe
trou·sers
trow·el
tru·an·cy (–cies)
tru·cu·lence
true
tru·ism
tru·ly
trum·pet·er
trun·cat·ed
trun·cheon
trun·dle
truss
trust·ee
truth·ful
try
tryst
tu·ba
tu·ber·cu·lar
tu·ber·cu·lo·sis
tu·ber·ous
tu·bu·lar
tu·ition
tum·brel, tum·bril
tu·mes·cent
tu·mor
tu·mul·tu·ous
tun·dra
tung·sten
tu·nic
tun·nel·ing, tun·nel·ling
tur·ban
tur·bid
tur·bine
tur·bo·jet
tur·bo·prop
tur·bot
tur·bu·lence
tu·reen
tur·gid
tur·moil
turn·key
tur·pen·tine
tur·pi·tude
tur·quoise, tur·quois
tur·ret·ed
tur·tle

tus·sle
tus·sock
tu·te·lage
tu·te·lary
tu·to·ri·al
tut·ti-frut·ti
tux·e·do (–dos *or* –does)
twain
tweak
tweedy
twee·zers
twelfth
twen·ti·eth
twi·light

twill
twine
twinge
twin·kling
twirl
twist
twitch
twit·ter
two·fer
ty·coon
ty·ing, tie·ing
tym·pa·num (–na *or*
   –nums)
type·script

type·writ·er
ty·phoid
ty·phoon
ty·phus
typ·i·cal
typ·i·fy
ty·pog·ra·phy
ty·ran·ni·cal, ty·ran·nic
tyr·an·nize
tyr·an·nous
tyr·an·ny (–nies)
ty·ro

ubiq·ui·tous
ubiq·ui·ty
ud·der
ug·li·ness
ukase
uku·le·le
ul·cer
ul·cer·ous
ul·na
ul·ster
ul·te·ri·or
ul·ti·mate
ul·ti·ma·tum (–tums *or* –ta)
ul·tra
ul·tra·vi·o·let
ul·u·late
um·ber
um·bil·i·cal
um·bra (um·bras *or* um·brae)
um·brage
um·brel·la
um·laut
um·pire
un·abat·ed
un·able
un·abridged
un·ac·cept·able
un·ac·com·pa·nied
un·ac·count·able
un·ac·cus·tomed
un·adorned
un·adul·ter·at·ed
un·af·fect·ed
un·aid·ed
un·alien·able
un·aligned
un·al·ter·able
un·am·big·u·ous
una·nim·i·ty
unan·i·mous
un·an·tic·i·pat·ed
un·ap·peal·ing
un·ap·pe·tiz·ing
un·ap·proach·able
un·armed
un·ashamed
un·asked

un·as·sail·able
un·as·sist·ed
un·at·trac·tive
un·avail·able
un·avoid·able
un·awares
un·bal·anced
un·be·com·ing
un·be·known
un·be·liev·able
un·bi·ased
un·bri·dled
un·budg·ing
un·can·ny
un·cer·tain·ty (–ties)
un·change·able
un·char·i·ta·ble
un·cle
un·com·fort·able
un·com·mu·ni·ca·tive
un·com·pli·men·ta·ry
un·con·di·tion·al
un·con·scio·na·ble
un·con·trol·la·ble
un·couth
unc·tion
unc·tu·ous
un·de·bat·able
un·dem·o·crat·ic
un·de·ni·able
un·der·achiev·er
un·der·gird
un·der·grad·u·ate
un·der·priv·i·leged
un·der·signed
un·der·stand
un·der·state·ment
un·der·tak·er
un·de·sir·able
un·de·vi·at·ing
un·due
un·du·lant
un·dy·ing
un·easy
un·em·ployed
un·en·dur·able
un·equiv·o·cal
un·err·ing

un·ex·cep·tion·able
un·fa·mil·iar
un·fash·ion·able
un·fa·vor·able
un·feigned
un·flag·ging
un·flat·ter·ing
un·flinch·ing
un·for·get·ta·ble
un·for·tu·nate·ly
un·fre·quent·ed
un·gain·ly
un·glued
un·gov·ern·able
un·gra·cious
un·gram·mat·i·cal
un·guard·ed
un·handy
un·hes·i·tat·ing
un·hinged
uni·corn
uni·di·rec·tion·al
uni·fi·ca·tion
uni·for·mi·ty (–ties)
uni·fy
uni·lat·er·al
un·imag·in·able
un·im·pas·sioned
un·im·peach·able
un·in·hib·it·ed
un·in·tel·li·gi·ble
un·in·ten·tion·al
un·in·ter·rupt·ed
union
unique
uni·sex
uni·son
unit
uni·tary
unite
uni·ver·sal
uni·ver·si·ty (–ties)
un·kempt
un·know·able
un·known
un·law·ful
un·less
un·lim·it·ed

un·man·ly
un·man·ner·ly
un·men·tion·able
un·mis·tak·able
un·mit·i·gat·ed
un·nec·es·sary
un·oc·cu·pied
un·of·fi·cial
un·or·ga·nized
un·or·tho·dox
un·pal·at·able
un·par·al·leled
un·par·lia·men·ta·ry
un·pleas·ant
un·plumbed
un·prec·e·dent·ed
un·pre·dict·able
un·prej·u·diced
un·pre·ten·tious
un·prof·it·able
un·qual·i·fied
un·ques·tion·ing
un·rav·el
un·re·al·is·tic
un·rea·son·able
un·re·gen·er·ate
un·re·lent·ing
un·re·spon·sive
un·re·strained
un·ri·valed, un·ri·valled
un·ruly
un·sad·dle
un·safe
un·sat·u·rat·ed
un·saved
un·sa·vory
un·scathed
un·sci·en·tif·ic
un·scram·ble
un·scru·pu·lous
un·sea·son·able
un·seat
un·seem·ly
un·seg·re·gat·ed
un·se·lect·ed
un·self·ish
un·set·tle
un·shack·le

un·sheathe
un·shod
un·sight·ly
un·skill·ful
un·snap
un·snarl
un·so·cia·ble
un·so·phis·ti·cat·ed
un·sought
un·sound
un·spar·ing
un·speak·able
un·sports·man·like
un·spot·ted
un·sta·ble
un·steady
un·stop·pa·ble
un·stressed
un·struc·tured
un·stud·ied
un·sub·stan·tial
un·suc·cess·ful
un·suit·able
un·swerv·ing
un·tan·gle
un·tapped
un·taught
un·ten·a·ble
un·think·able
un·ti·dy
un·tie
un·til
un·time·ly
un·ti·tled
un·touch·abil·i·ty
un·touch·able
un·trod·den
un·truth·ful
un·tu·tored
un·twine
un·used
un·usu·al
un·ut·ter·able
un·var·nished
un·veil
un·ver·bal·ized
un·voiced
un·war·rant·able

un·wary
un·whole·some
un·wieldy
un·wise
un·wit·ting
un·wont·ed
un·wor·thi·ness
un·wound
un·writ·ten
un·yield·ing
un·yoke
un·zip
up·beat
up·braid
up·bring·ing
up·com·ing
up·date
up·grade
up·heav·al
up·hol·ster
up·lift
up·on
up·pi·ty
up·right·ness
up·ris·ing
up·roar·i·ous
up·set
up·side down
up·stage
up·stand·ing
up·surge
up·swept
up·tight
up·turn
up·ward, up·wards
up·wind
ura·ni·um
ur·ban (relating to a city;
    see *urbane*)
ur·bane (suave; see *urban*)
ur·ban·ite
ur·chin
ure·mia
ure·ter
ure·thra
urging
ur·gen·cy (–cies)
uric

uri·nal

uri·nary

urine

urn

us·able, use·able

us·age

use·ful

use·ful·ness

ush·er

usu·al

usu·al·ly

usu·fruct

usu·rer

usu·ri·ous

usurp

usu·ry

uten·sil

uter·ine

uter·us (uteri *or* −us·es)

util·i·tar·i·an

util·i·ty (−ties)

ut·most

uto·pi·an

ut·ter·ance

ut·ter·most

uvu·la (−las *or* −lae)

ux·o·ri·al

ux·o·ri·ous

va·can·cy (–cies)
va·cant
va·cate
va·ca·tion·ing
vac·ci·nate
vac·cine
vac·il·late
vac·il·la·tion
va·cu·ity (–ities)
vac·u·ole
vac·u·ous
vac·u·um
va·de me·cum (Latin:
  something carried about
  regularly by a person)
va·ga·bond
va·ga·ry (–ries)
va·gi·na (–nae *or* –nas)
vag·i·ni·tis
va·gran·cy (–cies)
va·grant
vague
vain (worthless; see *vane*)
vain·glo·ri·ous
va·lance (drapery: see
  *valence*)
vale·dic·tion
vale·dic·to·ri·an
vale·dic·to·ry (–ries)
va·lence (combining power
  or chemical element; see
  *valance*)
val·en·tine
va·le·ri·an
va·let
val·e·tu·di·nar·i·an
val·iant
val·id
val·i·date
va·lid·i·ty
val·late
val·ley (valleys)
val·or
valse
valu·able
val·u·ate
val·u·a·tor
val·ue
val·ued
val·ue·less

va·lu·ta
valve
val·vu·lar
va·moose
vam·pire
va·na·di·um
van·dal·ism
van·dal·ize
vane (weathercock; see
  *vain*)
van·guard
va·nil·la
van·ish
van·i·ty (–ties)
van·quish
van·tage
va·pid·i·ty (–ties)
va·por
va·por·iza·tion
va·por·iz·er
va·por·ous
vari·abil·i·ty
vari·able
vari·ance
vari·ant
vari·a·tion
vari·col·ored
var·i·cose
var·i·cos·i·ty (–ties)
var·ied
var·ie·gate
va·ri·etal
va·ri·ety (–et·ies)
vari·form
var·i·ous
var·let
var·mint
var·nish
var·si·ty (–ties)
vary
vas·cu·lar
vase
va·sec·to·my (–mies)
Vas·e·line
va·so·mo·tor
vas·sal·age
vast·ly
va·tic·i·na·tion
vaude·ville
vaude·vil·lian

vault
vaunt
veal
vec·tor
veer
vee·ry (–ries)
veg·e·ta·ble
veg·e·tar·i·an
veg·e·tate
veg·e·ta·tive
ve·he·mence
ve·hi·cle
ve·hic·u·lar
veiled
veined
ve·lar
veld, veldt
vel·le·ity (–ities)
vel·lum (leather binding;
  see *velum*)
ve·loc·i·pede
ve·loc·i·ty (–ties)
ve·lo·drome
ve·lour, ve·lours (plural
  also ve·lours)
ve·lum (part of soft palate;
  see *vellum*)
vel·vet
vel·vety
ve·nal
vend
vend·ee
ven·der, ven·dor
ven·det·ta
ve·neer
ven·er·a·ble
ven·er·ate
ven·er·a·tor
ve·ne·re·al
ven·ery
ve·ne·tian blind
ven·geance
venge·ful
ve·nial
ve·ni·re
ve·ni·re·man (–men)
ven·i·son
ven·om
ven·om·ous
ve·nous

vent
ven·ti·late
ven·ti·la·tor
ven·tral
ven·tri·cle
ven·tril·o·quist
ven·ture
ven·ture·some
ven·tur·ous
ven·ue
ve·ra·cious
ve·rac·i·ty (–ties)
ve·ran·da, ve·ran·dah
ver·bal·ly
ver·ba·tim
ver·be·na
ver·biage
ver·bose
ver·dant (French: green)
ver·dict
ver·di·gris
ver·dure
verge
verg·er
verg·ing
ve·rid·i·cal
ver·i·fi·able
ver·i·fi·ca·tion
ver·i·fy
ver·i·ly
veri·si·mil·i·tude
ver·i·ta·ble
ver·i·ty (–ties)
ver·mi·cel·li
ver·mil·ion, ver·mil·lion
ver·min
ver·min·ous
ver·mouth
ver·nac·u·lar
ver·nal
ver·ni·er
ver·sa·til·i·ty
verse
ver·si·cle
ver·si·fi·ca·tion
ver·si·fi·er
ver·sion
ver·sus
ver·te·bra
ver·te·brate

ver·tex
ver·ti·cal
ver·tig·i·nous
ver·ti·go
verve
very
ves·i·cant
ves·i·cle
ves·pers
ves·sel
ves·tal
ves·ti·ary (–ar·ies)
ves·tib·u·lar
ves·ti·bule
ves·tige
vest·ment
ves·try (–tries)
ves·ture
vetch
vet·er·an
vet·er·i·nar·i·an
vet·er·i·nary
ve·to (–toes)
vex·a·tion
vex·a·tious
vi·a·ble
via·duct
vi·al
vi·and
vi·at·i·cum (–cums or –ca)
vibes
vi·brant
vi·brate
vi·bra·tor
vi·bur·num
vic·ar
vic·ar·age
vi·car·i·ate
vi·car·i·ous
vice·roy
vi·chys·soise
vic·i·nage
vi·cin·i·ty (–ties)
vi·cious
vi·cis·si·tude
vic·tim·ize
vic·to·ri·ous
vic·to·ry (–ries)
vict·ual
vict·ual·ler, vict·ual·er

vid·eo·tape
view·ing
vig·i·lance
vig·i·lan·te
vi·gnette
vig·or·ous
vil·i·fi·ca·tion
vil·i·fy
vil·lag·er
vil·lain
vil·lainy (–lain·ies)
vil·los·i·ty (–ties)
vin·ci·ble
vin·cu·lum (–lums or –la)
vin·di·cate
vin·dic·tive
vin·e·gar
vin·ery (–er·ies)
vin·tage
vi·nyl
vi·o·la
vi·o·la·ble
vi·o·late
vi·o·lence
vi·o·let
vi·o·lin
vi·per
vi·ra·go
vir·eo (–e·os)
vir·gin·al
vir·gin·i·ty (–ties)
vir·i·des·cent
vi·rid·i·ty
vir·tu·al·ly
vir·tue
vir·tu·os·i·ty (–ties)
vir·tu·o·so (–sos or –si)
vir·tu·ous
vir·u·lence
vi·rus
vis·age
vis-à-vis (French: face to
   face with)
vis·cer·al
vis·cid
vis·cos·i·ty (–ties)
vis·count
vis·cous
vis·i·bil·i·ty (-ties)
vis·i·ble

vi·sion·ary
vis·i·ta·tion
vis·i·tor
vi·sor
vis·ta
vi·su·al
vi·tal
vi·tal·i·ty (–ties)
vi·ta·min
vi·ti·ate
vit·re·ous
vit·ri·ol
vi·tu·per·a·tive
vi·va·cious
viv·id
viv·i·fy
vi·vip·a·rous
vivi·sec·tion
vix·en
vi·zier
vo·cab·u·lary (–lar·ies)
vo·cal·ist
vo·ca·tion

voc·a·tive
vo·cif·er·ate
vo·cif·er·ous
vod·ka
vogue
voice
void
vol·a·tile
vol·ca·nic
vol·ca·no (–noes or –nos)
vo·li·tion
vol·ley (vol·leys)
volt·age
vol·ta·ic
vol·u·ble
vol·u·bil·i·ty
vol·ume
vo·lu·mi·nous
vol·un·tary
vol·un·ta·rism
vol·un·teer
vo·lup·tu·ary (–ar·ies)
vo·lup·tuous

vom·it
voo·doo
vo·ra·cious
vo·rac·i·ty
vor·tex (vor·ti·ces or
    vor·tex·es)
vo·ta·ry (–ries)
vo·tive
vouch
vouch·safe
vow·el
voy·age
voy·eur
vul·gar
vul·gar·i·an
vul·gar·ism
vul·gate
vul·ner·a·ble
vul·pine
vul·ture
vy·ing

wacky
wad·ding (soft mass; see *wading*)
wad·dle
wad·ing (step through water; see *wadding*)
wa·fer
waf·fle
waft
wage
wag·ging (to be in motion; see *waging*)
wag·gle
wag·ing (to engage in; see *wagging*)
wag·on
waif
wail
wain
wain·scot·ing, wain·scot·ting
waist (narrowed part of body above hips; see *waste*)
wait·er
wait·ress
waive (relinquish voluntarily; see *wave*)
wak·ened
walk·ie-talk·ie
wal·let
wal·lop
wal·low
wall·pa·per
wal·nut
wal·rus
waltz
wam·pum
wan·dered
wan·der·lust
wan·ing
wan·ton
war·bled
war·den
ward·robe
ware·house
war·fare
wari·ly
war·mon·ger

warmth
warn
warp
war·rant
war·ran·tee (person to whom warranty is made; see *warranty*)
war·ran·tor
war·ran·ty (–ties) (written guarantee; see *warrantee*)
war·ren
war·ring
war·rior
wash·able
wasp·ish
was·sail
wast·age
waste (refuse from human habitations; see *waist*)
waste·land
wast·rel
watch·ful
wa·ter·proof
wa·tery
watt·age
wat·tle
wave (moving swell on sea surface; see *waive*)
wave·length
wavy
wax·en
waxy
way·far·er
way·lay
way·side
way·ward
weak·ened
weal
wealthy
wean
weap·on
wear·able
wea·ried
wea·sel (–sels)
weath·er (state of atmosphere; see *wether, whether*)
weath·er·cock

weave
web·bing
wed·ding
wedg·ing
wed·lock
weedy
weep·ing
wee·vil
weigh
weighty
weir
weird·ly
weirdo
wel·com·ing
weld·er
wel·fare
wel·kin
welsh
welt
wel·ter
wench
were·wolf
west·ern
west·ward
weth·er (castrated sheep; see *weather, whether*)
whack
whale
wham·my (–mies)
wharf (wharves *or* wharfs)
what·so·ev·er
wheat·en
whee·dle
wheel·ing
wheeze
whelp
whence
when·ev·er
where·abouts
where·as
where·fore
where·so·ev·er
wher·ev·er
wher·ry (–ries)
whet
wheth·er (alternative condition; see *weather, wether*)
whey

which·ev·er
whiff
while
whim·per
whim·si·cal
whim·sy, whim·sey
  (whim·sies *or* whim·seys)
whine
whin·ny
whip·pet
whirl·wind
whis·ker
whis·key, whis·ky
  (whis·keys *or* whis·kies)
whis·pered
whis·tle
whis·tling
whit
whit·en·er
whith·er
whit·tle
whoa
whole·sal·er
whole·some
whol·ly
whoop
whore (prostitute; see *hoar*)
whose
why
wick·er
wide·awake
wid·ow·er
width
wield
wie·ner
wife (wives)
wig·gle
wig·wam
wil·der·ness
wile
will·ful
wil·lies
wil·lowy
wim·ple
wince
winch

wind·ing
wind·lass
win·dow
wind·swept
windy
wined
wing·span
win·ner
win·now
win·some
win·ter·rize
win·ter·time
win·try
winy
wip·ing
wire·less
wir·ing
wiry
wis·dom
wise
wish·ful
wishy-washy
wispy
wist·ful
witch·ery (–er·ies)
with·al
with·drawn
withe
with·er
with·hold
with·out
wit·less
wit·ness
wit·ti·cism
wit·ty
wiz·ard
wiz·ened
wob·ble
woe·be·gone
woe·ful, wo·ful
wold
wolf (wolves)
wolf·ish
wom·an·ish
womb
won·der·ful

won·drous
wont (habit; see *won't*)
won't (will not; see *wont*)
wood·en
woody
woof·er
wool·en, wool·len
woo·zy
wordy
work·able
work·a·day
work·man·ship
world·ly
world·wide
wormy
wor·ri·some
wor·ry (wor·ries)
wors·en
wor·ship·ful
worst
wor·sted
wor·thy
would
wound·ed
wrack
wran·gle
wrap·per
wrath·ful
wreak
wreath (wreaths)
wreathe
wreck·age
wrench
wres·tle
wretch·ed
wrig·gle
wrist·watch
wring
wrin·kle
writ
writhe
writ·ing
wronged
wrought
wry
wurst

**X**

x-ax·is
xe·non
xe·no·phile

xe·no·pho·bia
xe·rox

Xmas
X-ray
xy·lo·phone


**Y**

yacht
yachts·man (–men)
ya·hoo
yak
yak·king
yam
Yan·kee
yap·ping
yard·age
yar·mul·ke, yar·mel·ke
yar·row
yawl
yawn·ing
yawp, yaup
year·ling
year·ly
yearn
yeasty
yegg
yel·low·ish
yelp·er

yeo·man (–men)
ye·shi·va, ye·shi·vah
   (ye·shi·vas or
   ye·shi·voth) (Hebrew:
   type of Jewish school)
yes·ter·day
yield
yip·pee
yo·del
yo·ga
yo·gurt, yo·ghurt
y-ax·is
yoke (wooden bar; see
   *yolk*)
yo·kel
yolk (yellow portion of egg;
   see *yoke*)
Yom Kip·pur
yon·der
yoo-hoo
yore

you
young
young·ster
your (relating to you; see
   *you're*)
you're (you are; see *your*)
your·self (your·selves)
youth·ful
you've
yowl
yo-yo
yuc·ca
yule
yule·tide
yum·my
yum-yum
yurt
YMCA
YMHA
YWCA
YWHA


**Z**

za·ba·glio·ne
zag·ging
za·ny (–nies)
zapped
zeal·ot
zeal·ous
ze·bra
zeit·geist (German: cultural
   climate of an era)
ze·nith
zeph·yr
zep·pe·lin
ze·ro (ze·ros or ze·roes)

zesty
zigged
zig·zag
zilch
zil·lion
zinc
zin·nia
Zi·on·ism
zip code
zip·per
zir·con
zith·er
zo·di·ac

zom·bie, zom·bi
zon·al
zone
zonked
zoo (zoos)
zoo·log·i·cal, zoo·log·ic
zo·ol·o·gy
zoom
zoy·sia
zuc·chet·to (–tos)
zuc·chi·ni (–ni or –nis)
zwie·back
zy·gote

# The Importance of Spelling

# Why Bother to Spell Correctly?

**Your spelling can show a great deal about you.**

# Why Bother to Spell Correctly

We have all made mistakes in spelling, but that is no reason for giving up the attempt to perfect our spelling until we write each word we use correctly. Who would deny that a bad speller reveals his or her mental inefficiency as surely as does the dull or ungrammatical conversationalist? We all know that our futures are often determined by the impressions we make upon important people. We may lose that job, or that raise, or that official position because of something we have said that was not good English usage. Sometimes a slip into bad English may pass unnoticed or be forgotten, with no harm to us. A mistake in spelling, however, is always there to confront the reader. And that error becomes magnified with each reading until all the merits of our letter or article are forgotten and only the misspelling remains to point a forbidding finger at us.

Graphologists are able to deduce many things about your character merely by noting the shape of the letters, the placing of the words, or the slant of the writing. But your misspelled words reveal to the trained observer even more about you; and the revelations are usually unfavorable. Thus, by misspelling certain types of words you can show yourself to be:

- Hard of hearing
- Suffering from weak eyesight
- Inclined to too rapid reading
- Careless in your speech
- Lacking in exactness in thought
- Deficient in the power to associate similar things
- Unable or unwilling to refer to the dictionary

These are pretty serious deficiencies to reveal in your letter of application or invitation before its receiver even sees you. Do you realize the handicap you must overcome if you are ever given a personal interview on the strength of the letter?

There is absolutely no excuse for habitual bad spelling today. Spelling has been studied scientifically by specialists, who have discovered not only the cause for bad spelling, but its cure. You can become an almost perfect speller by applying the proper remedies to your own particular spelling malady. We each suffer from a certain kind of spelling disorder. Having discovered your own particular variety of the disease, you can cure yourself; and you will never suffer from a recurrence of the same indisposition.

When you can spell correctly every word you employ without thinking twice about it, then your life, as far as your writing is concerned, will be much happier. Think of all the time saved in trips to the dictionary or in pondering over this or that spelling! Consider the saving in nervous energy; for you will no longer be uncertain of yourself, and no longer be angry because you realize your weakness and feel that you will never get out of it. You can get out of it! Thousands have discovered that correct spelling can be learned as easily as adding figures or planting flowers. If you will try to discover your special weakness and take the recommended cure you will surely improve and finally recover. But first let us discover why the English language is so difficult to spell.

# Why Is Spelling So Difficult?

**The _k_ in _knave_ was not always silent. English pronunciation changed; spelling didn't.**

# Why Is Spelling So Difficult?

Nearly everybody has difficulty with spelling. Foreign-born speakers have trouble learning English because they see no relationship between the way words are spelled and the way they are pronounced. Native-born speakers of English have trouble for the same reason.

In other languages words are spelled as they are pronounced. If you did not know Italian and came across the Italian word, *inglese*, meaning English, you might pronounce it *ing-gleez*. In Italian, however, the word is pronounced *een-glay-say* because in that language there are no silent vowels such as the silent *e* in English.

There are thousands of English words in which some vowels and consonants are not pronounced. English spelling and pronunciation are often unrelated.

Why?

## Linguistic Change

To find the answer we must take a brief look at the development of the English language.

About the middle of the fifth century, three tribes, the Angles, Saxons, and Jutes, who inhabited a section of the North Sea shore which is now Germany and Denmark, invaded Britain, drove the inhabitants into Wales, and established their own kingdoms. They spoke a language which was basically German. Today it is referred to as Old English or Anglo-Saxon.

In 1066 A.D. the Normans, who lived in northwestern France, invaded and conquered Britain. They imposed their language and culture on the conquered land. The common people began to speak a dialect which was a mixture of Anglo-Saxon and Norman French. This dialect is called Middle English.

The most important author to write in this new dialect was Geoffrey Chaucer whose famous book, *The Canterbury Tales*, written about 1387, is still read with enjoyment today.

Chaucer and his contemporaries spelled words as they were pronounced. A final *e* was pronounced like the *a* in *about*; for instance, *nonne* (nun) was pronounced *non-nuh*. All consonants and vowels were pronounced.

Pronunciation began to change about Chaucer's time and continued to change for almost two hundred years, until about 1550. One reason for the change was the French influence because England held large possessions in France. There were other reasons for the shift in pronunciation which we do not fully understand.

At this time printing was introduced into England. The most famous printer of the period, William Caxton, preserved Chaucer's Middle English spelling. Those who came after him followed his example even though most words were no longer pronounced as they had been in Chaucer's time. Pronunciation changed but spelling remained the same. English spelling was no longer phonetic.

The Modern English period began about 1550. From that time until today pronunciation has continued to change, but spelling has remained relatively fixed. There have been spelling changes, of course, but the rate of change has slowed down.

Does this mean that there are no spelling rules? Not at all. There are basic rules, each with exceptions to be sure, but the exceptions are not so numerous as you might think. You can learn these rules with a little effort. By learning them you will greatly improve your spelling ability. In succeeding chapters these rules are stated and explained.

# Our Confusing Alphabet

Our alphabet is another cause of spelling difficulties.

A single letter may stand for several different sounds. For example, the letter *a* represents six different sounds and the letter *s* four.

**Single Letters with Several Sounds**

| *A* | *S* |
|---|---|
| p*a*t (ă) | *s*ea (s) |
| b*a*ke (ā) | no*s*e (z) |
| c*a*re (â) | *s*ure (sh) |
| f*a*ther (ä) | plea*s*ure (zh) |
| *a*ll (a) | |
| *a*bout (ə) | |

At the same time one sound may be represented by several different letters or combinations of letters. For example, the sound of *ā* may be spelled

## Single Sounds Represented by Several Letters

### *ā Sound*

ay — *as in* say

a — *as in* page

ai — *as in* maid

au — *as in* gauge

e — *as in* fete

ey — *as in* obey

ei — *as in* weigh

The *-ough* words show how many different pronunciations may result from identical spelling.

## -OUGH Has Many Sounds

| Word | Sound |
|------|-------|
| thr*ough* | (oo) |
| r*ough* | (uff) |
| c*ough* | (awf) |
| pl*ough* | (ow) |
| thor*ough* | (oh) |
| hicc*ough* | (up) |

To show to what extremes one may go in the strangeness of English spelling, consider the word *potato*. Using some of the unusual combinations in English it is possible to spell the word thus: *ghoughpteighbteau*.

Here is the key:

| | | |
|------|------|------|
| *gh* | as pronounced in hiccou*gh* | |
| *ough* | as pronounced in th*ough* | |
| *pt* | as pronounced in *pt*omaine | gh/ough/pt/eigh/bt/eau |
| *eigh* | as pronounced in w*eigh* | (potato) |
| *bt* | as pronounced in de*bt* | |
| *eau* | as pronounced in b*eau* | |

Try to discover why the word *fish* can be spelled *ghoti*.

# Homonyms and Homophones

Words spelled and pronounced alike but differing in meaning are called *homonyms*.

## Homonyms

### Same Spelling, Same Pronunciation, Different Meaning

| | |
|---|---|
| pool (a body of water) | pool (a game) |
| dear (beloved) | dear (high-priced) |
| fair (light-colored) | fair (a market) |

Words pronounced alike but differing in spelling, derivation, and meaning are called *homophones*.

## Homophones

### Different Spelling, Same Pronunciation, Different Meaning

| | |
|---|---|
| air | heir |
| ate | eight |
| be | bee |
| beat | beet |
| berth | birth |
| compliment (praise) | complement (that which completes) |
| sum | some |
| their | there |

The abundance of homonyms and homophones in English is a source of difficulty especially to foreign-born students.

# Regional Pronunciations

In some regions of our country some words are pronounced differently from common usage. For example, creek is pronounced *crik*; sauce, *sass*; film, *filum*; and draw, *drawr*.

Since we tend to spell words as we hear them pronounced, these and similar regional pronunciations cause spelling difficulties. We must be able to discern dialectal pronunciations to avoid spelling errors.

> ### Remember!
>
> - **Pronunciation has changed rapidly since Modern English began, but spelling has remained relatively stable. As a result, spelling and pronunciation do not always correspond.**
> - **A single alphabetic symbol may stand for several different sounds, and one sound may be represented by more than one symbol.**
> - **There are hundreds of homonyms and homophones in our language. They have brought many a person to despair.**
> - **Local pronunciations may be a source of spelling errors.**

These characteristics of English do not sufficiently explain why misspelling is so widespread. Other factors enter which will be discussed in subsequent pages.

# 3

# Why
# You
# Misspell

*Reed·ing kan bee in·tres·ting.* **And it often improves spelling!**

# Why You Misspell

We betray our characteristics and feelings in many ways: for example, by the way we behave, speak, sit, and listen. A keen observer like the fictional Sherlock Holmes can learn much about a person by noticing little things.

Your mistakes in spelling tell people many things about yourself. Some of them you may not want people to know. But once the misspelled word is on paper, there is no recall. You have to suffer the consequences, be they social ostracism, failure to get that position or raise, or loss of respect from your reader.

Consider the fate of the secretary in Arnold Bennet's delightful comedy, "The Stepmother."

Christine: Dismiss me, madam?
Gardner: Cora, can you be so cruel?
Mrs. Prout: Alas, yes! She has committed the secretarial sin which is beyond forgiveness. She has misspelt.
Gardner: Impossible!

## Mispronunciation

We have a tendency to spell words as we hear them. If a word is not pronounced correctly, it will be misspelled. Spelling errors may result from listening to the slovenly enunciation of others or they may result from our own mispronunciations.

*Learn to spell by syllables.* If you omit syllables when speaking, you are likely to omit them when writing. For example, if you omit a syllable in *incidentally* so that the word comes out as *incidently*, you are likely to write it that way.

Here are some words in which syllables or letters are commonly omitted. The correct number of syllables is indicated in parentheses.

## Words with Syllables Commonly Omitted

| Correct Word | Mispronounced Word |
|---|---|
| au·thor·i·ta·tive (5) | au·thor·i·tive (4) |
| in·ter·est·ing (4) | in·tres·ting (3) |
| priv·i·lege (3) | priv·lege (2) |
| lic·o·rice (3) | lick·rice (2) |
| di·a·mond (3) | di·mond (2) |
| mack·er·al (3) | mack·rel (2) |
| sar·sa·pa·ril·la (5) | sars·pa·ril·la (4) |
| lab·o·ra·to·ry (5) | la·bra·to·ry (4) |

When practicing spelling aloud, break the word into syllables. Spell by syllables. You will find this method helpful.

Sometimes when you pronounce a word incorrectly you add a syllable where it does not belong, omit a sound, or substitute one sound for another. The following is a list of words that are commonly mispronounced. The correct pronunciation and spelling is as shown. The common mispronunciation and subsequent misspelling is in parentheses. Do you make the mistakes shown in parentheses?

## Words Commonly Mispronounced

| Correct Word | Mispronounced Word |
|---|---|
| athletic | athaletic |
| asked | ast |
| February | Febuary |
| government | goverment |
| kindergarten | kindergarden |
| library | libery |
| piggyback, pickaback | pigaback |
| poinsettia | poinsietta |
| strictly | strickly |

If you have a habit of slurring consonants, omitting syllables, or running syllables together like a verbal accordion player, you make it difficult for your listeners to understand what you are saying. You create an unfavorable impression and raise a barrier to your social and professional success.

One way of improving your speech habits is by listening attentively to individuals who speak clearly. Most radio and television announcers use good American speech. So do most clergymen, statesmen, teachers, and actors and actresses, especially those associated with the legitimate stage. The best speakers speak unaffectedly, pleasantly, and distinctly.

# Emotional Disturbance

Everybody has a slip of the tongue now and then. We may be anxious to say something and the words rush out pell-mell. What a mess we make of it! That agitation is revealed when you misspell words whose correct spelling you know. You may not want the reader to think that you are easily aroused. You may be applying for a job where calmness and restraint are prerequisites. But your spelling will give you away.

These are words spelled in a way to reveal your emotional disturbances:

> complete (compelte)
> flies (files)
> applied (appiled)

---

**Suggestion!**

**After writing a letter or report, read it over carefully. You may find errors committed in haste or agitation. Correct them before your letter application or report leaves your hands.**

---

# Hasty Reading

About 10,000 books are published in America each year. If you wanted to read all of them you would have to read about twenty-one a day, every single day in the year. Of course that is impossible. We can't even get around to reading one book a day. This tremendous supply of reading matter (we have not mentioned the morning and evening newspaper, and half a dozen magazines each month) has caused the formation of the habit of hasty reading.

There is a limit to the speed with which you can read. If you go beyond that limit, words become indistinct, blurred, and meaningless. If you boast about finishing the latest novel in two hours, the chances are you misspell many words because you do not have a clear picture of them. You can rarely read more than fifty pages an hour and derive the full benefit of the reading.

Check up on yourself. You will discover that many words which you first met in print, you misspell in your personal writings because you raced over them instead of forming a clear picture of the words in your mind.

This is not to deny the value of rapid reading for a specific purpose which is called *skimming*. When you are not particularly interested in getting every idea and fact from the printed page but only some statistic or date or personal name, it would be a waste of time to read every word slowly. A rapid glance at the entire page will give you the answer you are seeking. However, to read for ideas, beauty of style, or for a detailed explanation requires slow careful reading.

# Infrequent Reading

Individuals who read extensively and carefully are usually good spellers. They have learned to spell by reading. Almost unconsciously they observe the spelling of the words they read.

On the other hand poor spellers usually do not have the reading habit. They limit their reading to newspaper headlines or an occasional magazine article.

Read widely, everyday if possible. Reading is an excellent means of improving your spelling.

# Faulty Observation

A story is told of Toscanini, the great conductor, that illustrates his phenomenal power of observation. Of course, the world knows that he conducted entirely from memory; that he committed to memory the entire score of Respighi's *Pines of Rome* in twenty-four hours. A certain bassoon-player wanted to be excused from a rehearsal because his bassoon needed some repairing. One of the keys would not play the note.

"What note doesn't play?" asked the maestro.
"B-flat," answered the bassoon-player.
"Never mind. Stay for the rehearsal. There are no B-flats for the bassoon parts in tonight's program."

That is careful observation. Infinite pains, hours of concentration and nerve-wracking study went into such perfect knowledge. How many of us will take those pains. How many of us care to observe.

The fault of poor observation is with most of us. The reason is our inertia. Careful observation is too much trouble. By failing to note the correct spelling at first, we fall into the habit of misspelling many words.

Many people, when they are doubtful about the spelling of a word, write it down two or three times. The incorrect forms do not *appear* right. They have a mental picture of the correct word. When they write the correct form, something clicks within them. They recognize they have it right.

You will notice that those who have observed carefully have formed such a vivid picture of the word that they can recall it when they want.

# Failure to Consult the Dictionary

There are more than 600,000 words in the English language. Probably no one knows how to spell all of them. Misspellings occur because some words are rare and unusual.

But the spelling of most words is easy because spelling follows established rules. If in doubt, don't guess. Consult the dictionary.

Keep a dictionary at hand when you write. Check on the spelling of unusual words or those words which give you trouble.

Develop the dictionary habit!

---

## Remember!

Misspellings occur because of:
- **Mispronunciations**
- **Emotional disturbance**
- **Hasty reading**
- **Infrequent reading**
- **Faulty observation**
- **Uncertainty or ignorance**

**Careful observation pays and pays well.**

---

# 4

# How To Become A Good Speller

Why is *stAnding* a good memory device for the word *stationAry*? Learn to devise your own spelling shortcuts.

# How To Become A Good Speller

Aristotle, the great Greek philosopher, was tutor to the future king, Alexander the Great. One day they were doing a lesson in mathematics which required many calculations. Alexander, always impatient, suddenly threw aside his work and exclaimed:

"Why must I go through all these little steps? Why can't I get the answer immediately? I'm the future king!"
"There is no royal road to knowledge," answered his tutor.

There is no royal road to knowledge. There is no short cut to any branch of learning, and that is especially true for spelling. We had trouble with spelling in America long before Noah Webster published his famous speller. Nobody was ever born a perfect speller. Spellers are *made*; not born. Everyone can become a good speller by following certain scientifically prepared steps. There are some who had to learn the spelling of every word they met painfully and slowly. That was a waste of nervous energy. Time and nerve-power will be conserved, and success will be assured if you will follow the steps enumerated below. This is a prescription for good spelling that has rarely failed. Why not give it a trial?

## Learn the Rules and Develop Memory Devices

1. Learn and apply the rules of spelling.
2. Try to discover little devices of your own that will help you to remember the spelling of words that have no rules.

EXAMPLE
PRINCIP*AL* VS. PRINCIP*LE*
*Principal:* the head of a school or the main thing.
*Principle:* a rule or a truth.

Much slaughter on the battlefield of spelling has been caused by these two enemies of peace of mind and soul. And yet one simple device will remove forever the confusion caused by them.

A princi*ple* is a ru*le*. Both of these end in -*le*. Now you have the whole secret. If it means a ru*le*, spell it with the -*le*.

The other meaning must be spelled princi*pal*. You may remember it another way. If your principal was a fine fellow, he was a *pal* to you. And there you have the second sure way of remembering these two spelling demons.

## EXAMPLE
STATION*ARY* VS. STATION*ERY*
*Stationary:* immobile.
*Stationery:* materials for writing.

These two have been fighting on our literary battleground ever since we can remember. You think you have the correct spelling when suddenly the other one butts in and then you're lost again.

How can you be certain? Easily. Take a lett*er*; yes, a lett*er*. That's what stationery is used for, and you'll notice that lett*er* ends in -*er*. Now station*ery* ends in -*ery*.

The other word means st*a*nding still. Think of the *a* in st*a*nding and you'll remember the -*ary* in station*ary*.

## EXAMPLE
SEP*AR*ATE

The word sep*ar*ate has long been a trouble spot.

Think of the word p*art*. When you sep-*ar*-ate, you take things ap-*art*. That will tell you to be sure to spell the word with *ar*.

## EXAMPLE
TH*EIR* VS. TH*ERE*

Here is a good way to prevent the confusion in spelling of *their* and *there*.

*There* is an adverb referring to place. Notice that it contains the word *here*, which also refers to place. For example, The books are *there*.

*Their* is a personal pronoun referring to ownership. For example, *Their* books.

You will never confuse *there* and *their* if you remember that (t)*here* referring to place always contains *here*. The following sentence uses both words correctly: *Their* possessions are over *there*.

These four devices you may use. But the best of these tricks are the ones you think up yourself. When you discover a way to spell a word that has always given you trouble, you will be so overjoyed at the discovery that you will never forget the spelling. All laws of psychology teach us that we seldom forget anything we learned with pleasure. Therefore, try to be a spelling discoverer; enjoy your latest discovery and one more spelling demon will be eliminated.

> **Remember!**
>
> **Form your own memory devices.**

# Consult the Dictionary

The dictionary is probably the most valuable book in one's library. You should form the habit of consulting it the moment you are confronted with any spelling difficulty. Don't delay. When a word bothers you, and no rule or device will help, look it up while the annoyance is fresh. This is good psychology. The sooner you remove the cause of the annoyance (the doubtful word) the more certain will you be of its disappearance as an annoyance.

A dictionary is more reliable than memory. It will provide the correct spelling of words, indicate the correct pronunciation, and supply the meaning of the words. It will show the difference between *capital* and *capitol*, *strait* and *straight*, and *formerly* and *formally*.

The recommendation made in the previous chapter about consulting the dictionary bears repetition. Keep a dictionary on your desk. You will find it an invaluable tool. If you do not already own a dictionary, purchase one. It will be a good investment.

> **Remember!**
>
> **Consult the Dictionary.**

# Make Your Own Spelling List

Make a list of your difficult words. Try to use these as often as the opportunity presents itself. Mark Twain, who has had no superior in American humor, and whose principles of writing deserve the respect of all who would learn, said, "Use a new word correctly three times, and it's yours." Use a word that has given *you* trouble three times correctly and you should not have any difficulty. The important thing is to use it *correctly*. Misspelling a word a number of times only fixes the misspelling more firmly. There is a popular expression to the effect that "Practice makes perfect." But that should really be "Practice makes permanent." If we always make the same mistake, no amount of practice will do anything to improve our knowledge. Remember to use it correctly the first time.

# Listen Attentively

Develop the art of listening carefully. Many people whose hearing shows no organic defect are poor listeners. They do not pay attention and consequently they don't really hear what is being said. The more cultured the topic, the more alert must the listener be. These days there is much talk in the field of economics. Terms like *government, security, conservation* are heard repeatedly. Do you hear *gover-n-ment* or *guvment*? *Scurity* or security? *Consivation* or *conservation*?

It is true that sometimes the speaker himself is at fault because his enunciation is not perfect. That does not excuse the listener, however. If a word does not seem quite clear to you, you owe it to yourself to consult the dictionary as soon as you are near one. Thus you will firmly establish that word in your mind.

---

**Remember!**

- **Learn the rules and the exceptions.**
- **Consult the dictionary if you are in doubt.**
- **Make your own spelling list.**
- **Listen attentively.**

---

What has just been said are general instructions. Below are the steps you are to follow in learning any particular word that has given you trouble. Don't take short cuts. Follow the instructions to the letter!

---

**Method for Learning to Spell Any Hard Word!**

1. *Look* at your word. *Pronounce* each syllable carefully. For example,

   *in·de·pen·dent.*

2. *Close your eyes* or turn away and form a picture of the word in your mind. If the letters are not clearly before you, look at the word again, until you see it with your eyes closed.

3. *Pronounce* the word and write it at the same time. If you are not sure, try to picture the word. Be certain that you write it correctly the first time.

4. *Write* the word a second time as used in a sentence.

5. The next day write the word as someone else reads it to you.

# Rules
# for
# Spelling

# Better Spelling by Ear

*Car·bu·ret·or* or
*Car·bur·e·tor*?
**Four simple rules will
take care of all such
words.**

# Better Spelling
# By Ear

## Know the Rules!

It is possible, of course, to consult your dictionary every time you are in doubt about the spelling of a word. The knowledge of a few helpful rules, however, will make it unnecessary for you to waste precious time in consulting the dictionary on every occasion when you are in doubt. As is true of almost all rules in English grammar, there are some exceptions to the rules in spelling, too. It is, therefore, necessary to master the exceptions as well as the rules. Study the rules, do the exercises, and try using some of the words you have studied as soon as possible. Remember that your ultimate aim in spelling is to be able to spell every word you want to use without wasting any time trying to figure out the spelling or wasting precious minutes looking up in the dictionary every word of more than two syllables.

## Spell by Pronunciation

It has been mentioned before that an impression conveyed by several senses will remain longer in the mind than one coming through only one sense organ. Most human beings are visual-minded. They form only an eye-impression of the things they learn. Some people (musicians especially) are ear-minded. You may discover that you are ear-minded by employing the following spelling devices.

Although English has been rightly accused of not being spelled exactly as it sounds, the fact remains that thousands of words *are spelled* precisely as they are pronounced. If you pronounce these words correctly when you are in doubt about them, you will find no difficulty in spelling them.

You must first understand something about *syllables* and *syllabication*. The late E. L. Thorndike of Columbia University in his *Century Junior Dictionary* defined a syllable as "part of a word pronounced as a unit consisting of a vowel alone or with one or more consonants."

do        — word of one syllable
dough·nut — word of two syllables
syl·la·ble — word of three syllables

# Divide a Word into Syllables

## Rule 1

*Begin* a syllable with a consonant when the consonant is between two vowels and the first vowel is *long*.

### EXAMPLE

ro·man·tic

The consonant *m* begins the second syllable because the vowel *o* is long.

The long vowels are pronounced exactly as they are pronounced when you recite the alphabet.

ā — *as in* hay
ē — *as in* bee
ī — *as in* kite
ō — *as in* note
ū — *as in* mute

Other examples of Rule 1 are:

Mo·hawk   ro·tate   na·ture

## Rule 2

*End* a syllable with a consonant when the consonant is between two vowels and the first vowel is *short*.

### EXAMPLE

hab·it

The consonant *b* ends the first syllable because it is between two vowels and the first vowel is short.

The short vowels are present in this line:

Patter, petter, pitter, potter, putter

Syllables with short vowels:

a — *as in* fash·ion, tap·es·try
e — *as in* nec·es·sa·ry
i — *as in* crit·i·cism
o — *as in* prom·i·nent
u — *as in* sub·urb

Other examples of rule 2 are:

proph·et   pun·ish   ex·ec·u·tive

## Rule 3

**Adjoining consonants most often separate into syllables.**

### EXAMPLES

mur·mur   can·dy   ex·pense

## Rule 4

**Double consonants are not divided when a suffix is added.**

### EXAMPLES

mill·er   hiss·ing

These rules should help you also in dividing words at the end of a line. Study the syllabication of the following words that are associated with the automobile:

per·for·mance
gas·o·line
man·u·fac·ture
pneu·mat·ic
se·dan

It was one of the principles of the government of Ancient Rome to "divide and conquer." The same rule might apply for long words. Divide them into their component syllables and you can conquer them.

# Spell as You Pronounce Syllable by Syllable

Many words appear difficult to spell until we pronounce them carefully. They fall naturally into simple syllables and their difficulty disappears.

---

**Method!**

1. **Pronounce the word slowly.**
2. **Spell it aloud** *by syllables*.
3. **Pronounce it slowly twice more, writing as you do so.**
4. **Pronounce it quickly in a sentence, writing the whole sentence.**

**Each of the following words will lose its terror if you use this method.**

| | |
|---|---|
| ac·com·mo·date | en·deav·or |
| mag·nif·i·cent | priv·i·lege |
| mag·a·zine | dis·ap·pear |

---

## Exercise 1

*Divide the following words into syllables.*

1. bonanza _____
2. repent _____
3. fatigue _____
4. punishment _____
5. ordeal _____
6. rummage _____
7. missing _____
8. gasoline _____
9. excavate _____
10. tyrannical _____

# Pay Attention to Troublesome Words

In this section are lists of words that have had their thousands of victims. Have someone dictate these words to you. Spell them. Then compare your spelling with those in the book. The ones you have spelled correctly, you need no longer bother with. Your misspelled words, you must examine. What errors did you make? There is an entire section for each error. Practice the words until you can spell them correctly without the need of thinking twice about them. These words may all be learned by accustoming your ear to hear them correctly.

## Difficult "A" Words

Each of the following words has *a* trouble. People forget the existence of *a* and substitute another letter:

| | | |
|---|---|---|
| captain | certain | calendar |
| finally | grammar | illegal |
| maintain | plain | criminal |
| preparations | probable | dictionary |
| separate | straight | liberal |
| usually | villain | justifiable |
| balance | equivalent | equally |
| performance | salary | congressional |
| actually | extravagant | professional |
| village | capital | temperature |
| partially | principal | similar |

## Difficult "E" Words

Each of the words below has an *e* difficulty. Writers frequently forget the *e* and use another letter incorrectly.

| | | |
|---|---|---|
| apparently | competent | conscience |
| dependent | coherent | audience |
| prominent | current | correspondence |
| machinery | efficient | existence |
| independent | experience | magnificent |
| stationery | opponent | patience |
| privileges | permanent | superintendent |
| luncheon | cafeteria | description |

## Difficult "I" Words

In the following words, the *i*'s have it:

| | | |
|---|---|---|
| acquainted | auxiliary | business |
| compliment | definite | exhibition |
| criticized | sympathized | until |
| participle | peculiar | principle |
| quantities | quiet | respectively |
| physical | individual | hosiery |
| articles | rime | anticipate |

## Difficult "O" Words

Do you omit these *o*'s? In the words below, the letter *o* comes in for much abuse and neglect. Be kind to these words:

| | | |
|---|---|---|
| attorney | authorize | competitors |
| conspicuous | conqueror | editor |
| favorable | memorial | minor |
| notorious | organization | senator |
| society | strenuously | tailor |
| odor | aviator | capitol |
| colonel | accustomed | authority |
| colors | favorite | interior |
| humorist | memory | motorist |
| precious | proprietor | successor |
| surgeon | | |

## Double Letter Problems

Concentrate on the double letters in these words. They are the cause of many common errors:

| | | |
|---|---|---|
| accommodate | agreed | agreeable |
| beginning | committee | guaranteed |
| embarrass | loose | proceed |
| necessary | parallel | succeed |
| recommend | speech | too |
| across | baggage | assistance |
| dissatisfaction | affirmative | appearance |
| disappeared | chauffeur | appropriate |
| disappointed | immigrant | disapproved |
| illegible | possession | interrupted |
| occasion | | Mediterranean |
| opposite | | professor |

## Letters Not "Seen"

It used to be said of children that they should be seen and not heard. These words have letters that are often not seen when writing. Don't omit them:

government       prom*p*tly       Feb*r*uary
inde*b*ted        pamp*h*let       ple*d*ged
                 condem*n*

---

## Exercise 2

*Some of the following words are spelled correctly and some are misspelled. Put a check on the blank if a word is spelled correctly. Rewrite it correctly if it is misspelled.*

1. grammar _____
2. seperate _____
3. usally _____
4. village _____
5. calender _____
6. existence _____
7. description _____
8. untill _____
9. attorney _____
10. senator _____
11. odor _____
12. accomodate _____
13. proffessor _____
14. goverment _____
15. promptly _____
16. accross _____
17. ilegible _____
18. equivelent _____
19. precious _____
20. accustomed _____

---

## Reversal Problems

A common type of misspelling occurs when letters are interchanged. For example, *l* and *v* are often reversed in *relevant* so that the word is misspelled *revelant*. This type of error is called *metathesis*. Observe the correct spelling of the following ten words:

| Correct | Incorrect |
| --- | --- |
| cava*l*ry | calvary |
| child*ren* | childern |
| hund*red* | hunderd |
| jewe*l*ry | jewlery |
| lary*n*x | larnyx |
| mod*ern* | modren |
| patt*ern* | pattren |
| *pers*piration | prespiration |
| re*lev*ant | revelant |
| west*ern* | westren |

---

> ### Notice!
>
> The mountain mentioned in the Bible is Calvary. It is spelled with a capital C and should not be confused with cavalry, a troop of horsemen.

## Exercise 3

*Fill in the missing letters:*

1. hund __ __ d
2. mod __ __ n
3. p __ __ spiration
4. west __ __ n
5. re __ e __ ant

6. ca __ a __ ry
7. child __ __ n
8. jew __ __ __ y
9. lar __ __ x
10. patt __ __ n

# 6

---

# Some Special Difficulties

**You too can succeed in handling**
***IE* vs. *EI***
***-CEED* vs. *-SEDE***
***vs. -CEDE***
**It's not hard!**

# Some Special Difficulties

## The *IE* And *EI* Difficulty

The *Saturday Review of Literature* once published the following story:

A neophyte copy editor in a large advertising agency was slowly going out of his mind because his copy chief was constantly taking a small slip of paper from his breast pocket, looking at it, leering, then putting it back. After watching this for months he managed one day, when the copy chief was taking a nap, to steal the secret paper from the jacket in back of the chief's chair. He opened the slip of paper with trembling hands.
It read.
"*I* before *E* except after *C*" [1]

You may be rel*ie*ved when you rec*ei*ve this information. Although a great deal of misch*ie*f has been caused by people who were confused about the use of *ie* or *ei*, there is a simple rule that will take care of all cases. Learn this rule!

### Rule

**Put i before e,
Except after c,
Or when sounded like *a*,
As in *neighbor* and *weigh*;
And except *seize* and *seizure*
And also *leisure*,
*Weird*, *height*, and *either*,
*Forfeit* and *neither*.**

[1] Reprinted by permission of *Saturday Review of Literature*.

> **Remember!**
>
> **When the two letters *IE* or *EI* are sounded like ē, then: It is *i* before *e* except after *c*.**

## *IE*

Examine the list below.

|  |  |
|---|---|
| bel*ie*f | p*ie*ce |
| f*ie*ld | pr*ie*st |
| misch*ie*f | rel*ie*ve |
| y*ie*ld |  |

Notice that in no case does a *c* precede the *ie*. It is always a letter other than *c*.

Now examine the additional list.

| | | | | |
|---|---|---|---|---|
| ach*ie*ve | befr*ie*nd | f*ie*f | fr*ie*ze | handkerch*ie*f |
| aggr*ie*ve | bel*ie*ve | f*ie*nd | front*ie*r | hyg*ie*ne |
| al*ie*n | bes*ie*ge | f*ie*rce | gr*ie*f | interv*ie*w |
| ch*ie*f | b*ie*r | f*ie*ry | gr*ie*vance | l*ie*f |
| l*ie*n | br*ie*f | fr*ie*nd | gr*ie*ve | l*ie*ge |
| n*ie*ce | l*ie*u | m*ie*n | misch*ie*f | misch*ie*vous |
| qu*ie*t | p*ie*bald | p*ie*d | p*ie*rce | p*ie*ty |
| rev*ie*w | rel*ie*f | rel*ie*ve | repr*ie*ve | retr*ie*ve |
| s*ie*ge | ser*ie*s | sh*ie*ld | shr*ie*k | th*ie*very |
| v*ie*w | w*ie*ld | s*ie*ve | th*ie*f | y*ie*ld |

## Exercise 1

*Study the list above carefully; notice that never does a* c *precede the ie. Any other letter in the alphabet may do so, but not the* c. *Write each word once, one word to a line; pronounce it; then write it once in a sentence; follow this scheme.*

| Word | Pronounce | Sentence |
|---|---|---|
| ach*ie*ve | a chē̄ v | I hope to ach*ie*ve my goal. |

## Exercise 2

*When you feel certain that you know the preceding words, copy and fill in the missing letters in the following:*

1. aggr _ _ ve    6. misch _ _ f    11. rel _ _ ve     16. perc _ _ ve
2. br _ _ f         7. sh _ _ ld     12. l _ _ sure    17. gr _ _ f
3. fr _ _ nd      8. shr _ _ k     13. handkerch _ _ f 18. n _ _ ce
4. gr _ _ ve      9. w _ _ ld      14. rec _ _ pt    19. conc _ _ ve
5. front _ _ r    10. spec _ _ s     15. s _ _ ze      20. v _ _ l

Sometimes it will help you to form words into certain groups. Thus if you associate the words with ch*ief* you will get

*chief*

handker*chief*   mis*chief*   mis*chie*vous

If you remember the spelling of *chief* (and few ever forget it), the spelling of the other three is easy for you. Think of:

| -ield | -ieve | -ief | -ier |
|-------|-------|------|------|
| f*ield* | rel*ieve* | rel*ief* | t*ier* |
| sh*ield* | repr*ieve* | br*ief* | front*ier* |
| | bel*ieve* | bel*ief* | |

## EI

Now we can master the other combinations. Study the following chart:

**Handling *EI***

| EI follows C | EI because the sound is ā as in HAY | special cases |
|--------------|-------------------------------------|---------------|
| dec*ei*t | fr*ei*ght | *ei*ther |
| perc*ei*ve | v*ei*l | h*ei*ght |
| rec*ei*ve | n*ei*gh | l*ei*sure |
| | | forf*ei*t |
| | | n*ei*ther |
| | | s*ei*ze |
| | | w*ei*rd |
| | | s*ei*zure |

## EXAMPLE
*EI follows C*
Read this list carefully and notice that in each case the *ei* follows *c*.

| | |
|---|---|
| c*ei*ling | dec*ei*tful |
| conc*ei*t | dec*ei*ve |
| conc*ei*ted | rec*ei*pt |
| conc*ei*ve | rec*ei*ve |

## EXAMPLE
*EI Sounds as Ā*
The following list has the *ei* because it sounds like *ā* in *bay*.

| | | |
|---|---|---|
| deign | rein | veil |
| inveigh | skein | vein |
| inveigle | sleigh | weigh |
| reign | surveillance | weight |

You have noticed that in *reign*, there is the sound of *ā*. In *foreign*, *sovereign* and *sovereignty* the *eign* is not sounded as ā, but spelled *ei*. This sentence will help you to associate these four words:

The *foreign sovereign* resigned when his *sovereignty* was disputed.

## EXAMPLES
*Special Cases*
1. The final *feit* is pronounced *fit*.

forfeit
counterfeit
surfeit

2. These are pronounced *ī* as *kite*. Be sure to put the *e* in.

height
sleight

3. A few words have *cie*, but in all cases the *c* is pronounced as *sh*.

| | | | |
|---|---|---|---|
| ancient | deficient | glacier | species |
| conscience | efficient | proficient | sufficient |

# Exercise 3

*As a final test of your skill, have someone dictate the following paragraph to you.*

A thief tried to deceive a priest. The priest was a friendly soul, but such mischief was beyond belief. Rather than forfeit the night's receipts, he feigned weakness. He waited for an opportunity to seize his attacker and because of his superior height was able to overpower his enemy.

# The -*SEDE*, -*CEED* and -*CEDE* Difficulty

Because various letters are pronounced alike in English, difficulties in spelling arise. Originally the letter *c* was pronounced as a *k*. We know that, because the old Romans of 2,000 years ago sounded it that way. They had a word *centum*, which means "one hundred." Today, when a student in high school studies Latin, he says *kentum* (like kennel). But this same word in Italian is pronounced *chento* (cento); in French it is *saunt* (cent). Because it came into English from the French back in the days of the Norman conquest of 1066, our word *cent* is really one-hundredth part of something and is pronounced *sent*. This similarity of pronunciation between *c* and *s* is responsible for the confusion in spelling words ending in -*cede, -ceed*, and -*sede*.

## -*SEDE*

You should never forget the single word ending in -*sede*. It is *supersede*.

## -*CEED*

You can easily remember all the words in -*ceed*. There are only three:

pro*ceed*  ex*ceed*  suc*ceed*

If you want a little device to aid your memory with these words, think of boxer. First, he is a *pro*-fessional. When he is past his prime, he is an *ex*-fighter; then he has a *suc*-cessor.

## -*CEDE*

All the other words in this class end in -*cede*. Some are:

| | |
|---|---|
| accede | recede |
| precede | secede |
| concede | |

---

**Remember!**

**The ending -CEDE is more common than -SEDE or -CEED. Memorize the few words that end in -SEDE or -CEED. All other words end in -CEDE.**

# Exercise 4

*Have the following passage read aloud to you as you spell the italicized words. If you misspell any, study the reason for the error. Follow the procedure outlined on page 111 for mastering difficult words until you have learned all the words in this group.*

Little countries no longer like to *accede* to the wishes of large countries. In many parts of the world the old type of imperialism has been *superseded*. Wars over natural resources are *receding* into history, to be *succeeded* by pacts of mutual interest. Although we cannot be *excessively* optimistic about hopes for permanent peace, we must *concede* that the outlook is bright. The *successor* to the old-time viceroy is the new representative of the former colonial power who *intercedes* in his country's interest, but is always willing to listen to the other side. Such mutual respect must *precede* any plan for world-wide disarmament and eventual peace.

# Prefixes

## One simple rule is the key in adding all prefixes.

# Prefixes

This chapter contains only one rule. The rule is simple and easily learned. It will help you avoid many misspellings. It has to do with prefixes.

*A prefix is one or more syllables attached to the beginning of a word.* Prefixes, as those below, change the meaning of words to which they are attached.

$$
\begin{array}{lll}
dis + \text{agree} & = \text{disagree} \\
il + \text{logical} & = \text{illogical} \\
un + \text{kind} & = \text{unkind} \\
mis + \text{spell} & = \text{misspell} \\
super + \text{vision} & = \text{supervision}
\end{array}
$$

## A List of Common Prefixes

Here is a list of some common prefixes. Become familiar with them to discover the meaning and spelling of words which are new to you.

**Common Prefixes**

| Prefix | Meaning | Examples |
|---|---|---|
| *a-* | on, in | abed |
| | | afire |
| | not, without | asexual |
| | | achromatic (without color) |
| *ab-* | away, from | abject |
| | | abduct |
| *ante-* | before | anteroom (a room before another) |
| | | antediluvian (before the flood) |
| | | antecedent (a preceding event) |
| *anti-* | against | antiseptic (against poisoning) |
| | | anti-noise (against noise) |
| *circum-* | around | circumscribe (to write around) |
| | | circumnavigate (to sail around) |
| | | circumlocution (act of talking around a topic rather than directly) |

| Prefix | Meaning | Examples |
|--------|---------|----------|
| com-, con- | with, together | concelebrate (to celebrate together) |
| | | commingle (to combine) |
| de- | down | descend |
| | | demote (to put down) |
| dis- | apart | dismember (to tear from limb to limb) |
| | | dissolve (to fall apart in a liquid) |
| | | disarm (to separate a soldier from his weapons) |
| hyper- | above, beyond | hyperactive |
| | | hypercritical |
| hypo- | under, beneath | hypothesis (an assumption under consideration) |
| il-, im-, in-, ir- | not | illogical |
| | | immoral |
| | | indisposed |
| | | irrelevant |
| inter- | among, between | interview |
| | | intercollegiate |
| | | international |
| intra- | within | intracoastal |
| | | intravenous (with a vein) |
| | | intramural (within the walls) |
| mis- | wrongly, unfavorably | misjudge |
| | | misunderstand |
| | | misappropriate |
| non- | not | nonsense |
| | | noncombatant |
| | | nonconformist |
| over- | excessive | overcharge |
| | | overcoat |
| per- | through | permeate (to penetrate) |
| | | perspire |
| | | persevere |
| post- | behind, after | post-mortem (after death) |
| | | postpone |
| | | postgraduate |
| pre- | before | precede |
| | | precipitate |
| | | predecessor |
| | | prevent |
| pro- | forward, instead of | procession |
| | | provide (to look forward) |
| | | promote |
| | | provisions |

| Prefix | Meaning | Examples |
|--------|---------|----------|
| re- | back, again, against | refer (to bring back to the previous question) |
| | | retaliate (to fight back) |
| | | retract (to take back) |
| | | repel (to hurl back) |
| sub- | under | subway |
| | | subtract |
| | | subscribe (to write under written material) |
| super- | above | superintendent |
| | | superficial |
| | | superstructure |
| trans- | across | transcontinental |
| | | transfer |
| | | transplant |
| | | translucent (permitting the passage of light) |
| un- | not | unnatural |
| | | unnoticeable |
| | | unoccupied |

# Adding a Prefix

Armed with a knowledge of these prefixes, you are now ready for the spelling rule relating to them.

## Rule

**When you add a prefix, do *not* change the spelling of either the prefix or the original word.**

### EXAMPLES

| | | |
|---|---|---|
| *dis* + appear | = | disappear |
| *inter* + action | = | interaction |
| *in* + eligible | = | ineligible |
| *trans* + mit | = | transmit |
| *hyper* + sensitive | = | hypersensitive |

Simple, isn't it? Yet with this easy rule, you can spell correctly thousands of words.

## Caution!

Most errors occur when a prefix ends with the same letter with which the word begins. For example:

*un* + natural  = unnatural (*not* unatural)
*dis* + satisfied = dissatisfied (*not* disatisfied)
*mis* + step    = misstep (*not* mistep)

Remember, when you add a prefix, do *not* change the spelling of either the prefix or the original word.

## Exercise 1

*How many s's in:*

1. di ___(?)___ olve
2. di ___(?)___ imilar
3. mi ___(?)___ pell
4. di ___(?)___ appear
5. mi ___(?)___ take

## Exercise 2

*Try your skill in building your own words. Take, for example,* scribe, *meaning a writer.*

circum
trans
sub
de
pro
pre
⟩scribe

*Give the meaning of each.*

## Exercise 3

*By adding the proper Latin prefixes to the following italicized words, spell the new formations correctly.*

**EXAMPLES:**
not *satisfied*     *dissatisfied*
not *legible*       *illegible*

1. A *step* wrongly taken                    _____
2. not to *understand*                       _____
3. not *similar*                             _____
4. to *echo* again and again                 _____
5. below the *standard*                      _____
6. above the speed of *sound*                _____
7. before the time of *Columbus*             _____
8. he is against *imperialism*               _____
9. one who *navigates* around the globe      _____
10. complications after an *operation*       _____

# Pay Attention to *PER-, PRE-, PRO-*

Some difficulties with the spelling of prefixes may be due to carelessness in pronunciation. Thus if you don't pronounce *prescription* properly, you may not spell the prefix with *pre*. The reverse error may come with a word like *pers*piration, in which the initial *per* may be misspelled.

Knowing the meaning of certain prefixes, as indicated earlier in this chapter, will help you to both know the meaning of the word and its spelling.

## *PER-, PRE-, PRO-*

**PER- means "through"**

| Word | Meaning |
|------|---------|
| permeate | to penetrate through and through |
| perforate | to pierce through |
| perpetual | through the years |
| persist | to continue through a project |
| persecute | to follow through |
| perspective | to see through |

## *PRE-* means "before"

| Word | Meaning |
|------|---------|
| precocious | to develop earlier |
| prefer | to place before |
| prepare | to make ready beforehand |
| prejudice | a judgment before the evidence is in |
| prescribe | to write before |

## *PRO-* means "forward"

| Word | Meaning |
|------|---------|
| propose | to place before a group |
| prophecy | something stated before it happens |
| proceed | to move forward |
| proclaim | to shout before |
| produce | to bring forth |
| prognosis | to forecast the probable outcome of a disease |

## Exercise 4

*Underline the correct spelling of the pairs of words in the following sentences.*

1. The secret police (persecuted, presecuted) the prisoner.
2. Let us (preceed, proceed) with the trial.
3. This young bright child was obviously (precocious, percocious).
4. We must look at world affairs in the proper (perspective, prospective).
5. The patient asked the doctor to (proscribe, prescribe) something for his cough.
6. The illness was diagnosed as a (perforated, proferated) ulcer.
7. It costs a great deal to (perduce, produce) a musical comedy.
8. We must (persist, presist) in our efforts to find ways to peace.
9. Searching for the truth requires (perpetual, prepetual) effort.
10. Let us (propose, perpose) a toast.

# Confusing Suffixes

**Some of the most common suffix problems are treated with simple guidelines.**

# Confusing Suffixes

A suffix is one or more syllables attached to the end of a word.

**EXAMPLES**

desire + *able* = desirable
move + *ing* = moving
kind + *ly* = kindly
mean + *ness* = meanness
fame + *ous* = famous

## Words Ending in -*ABLE*, -*IBLE*

These suffixes are troublesome. When you are able to add them correctly, you are well on your way to becoming a good speller.

### Rule 1

**The ending -ABLE is more common than -IBLE. If in doubt, use -ABLE and you have more than a fair chance of being correct.**

### -*ABLE*

1. Our most familiar words add -ABLE to form the adjective.

comfort + *able* = comfortable
drink + *able* = drinkable
eat + *able* = eatable
laugh + *able* = laughable
read + *able* = readable
talk + *able* = talkable
unthink + *able* = unthinkable

**139**

2. A noun ending in -ATION will have an adjective ending in -ABLE.

> abomination
> abomin*able*

# -IBLE

1. Words ending in *-ible* are often preceded by a double SS before the -IBLE.

> acce*ss*ible          permi*ss*ible
> admi*ss*ible          transmi*ss*ible
> compre*ss*ible

2. Words ending in *-ible* often have a noun form ending in *-ion*. Drop the -ION and add -IBLE.

> accession
> access*ible*

Examine the following words which are all formed the same way:

| | | |
|---|---|---|
| admission | expansion | extension |
| admiss*ible* | expans*ible* | extens*ible* |
| compression | reversion | corruption |
| compress*ible* | revers*ible* | corrupt*ible* |
| permission | coercion | division |
| permiss*ible* | coerc*ible* | divis*ible* |
| transmission | comprehension | perception |
| transmiss*ible* | comprehens*ible* | percept*ible* |
| combustion | digestion | reprehension |
| combust*ible* | digest*ible* | reprehens*ible* |
| destruction | | |
| destruct*ible* | | |

3. Use -IBLE to keep the soft sound of *g* or *c*. The word *tangent* has the adjective *tangible* because an *-able* would change the pronunciation of *g* from its present *j* sound to the sound of *g* in *gum*. Other words in this class are:

> deduc*ible*          produc*ible*          reduc*ible*
> conduc*ible*          corrig*ible*          incorrig*ible*
> elig*ible*          inelig*ible*          irasc*ible*
> intellig*ible*          invinc*ible*          leg*ible*

> **Remember!**
>
> **Be sure that you know all the reasons for adding -*ible*.**
> 1. **It follows double *ss* and comes from a noun ending in -*sion* (permission/permiss*ible*).**
> 2. **It comes from a noun ending in -*ion* (coercion/coerc*ible*).**
> 3. **It keeps the *c* or *g* soft (deduc*ible*, elig*ible*).**

## Exercise 1

*Here is a list of words. Add* -able *or* -ible.

| | | |
|---|---|---|
| account | depend | market |
| avoid | detest | perish |
| comfort | discount | return |
| companion | fashion | review |
| credit | favor | season |

*Did you add* -able *to each of these? Then you were 100% correct.*
*Now add* -able *or* -ible *to the roots of these words:*
HINT:               consol-*a*-tion               consol-*able*

> commendation
> admiration
> conformation
> appreciation
> consideration

*Did you add* -able *to the roots of each of these words? You were 100% correct.*
*Remember, a noun ending in* -ation *will have an adjective in* -able.
*As a final task, add the endings* -able, *or* -ible *to the roots of the following words.*
HINT:               demonstr-*ation*               demonstr-*able*

| | | |
|---|---|---|
| derivation | exportation | notation |
| duration | habitation | refutation |
| estimation | imagination | separation |
| execration | irritation | taxation |
| | lamentation | toleration |

*You should add* -able *to the roots of each of the words.*

## Exercise 2

*Have someone dictate the following passage which contains many words ending in the suffixes -ible or -able.*

The prosecuting attorney protested that the evidence by the defendant about his *taxable* income was *inadmissible*. In the first place, it was not easily *accessible*. In the second place, although the evidence was originally *acceptable* in a lower court, the decisions in such courts are *reversible*.

The defendant's attorney objected that such reasoning was *unsupportable* and *intolerable* and that it was *reprehensible* on his opponent's part to bring up such a claim. The tension was increasing *perceptibly*. If this continued, the defending attorney might have to be ejected *forcibly*, or be *eligible* for disbarment. However, it took some time for the atmosphere to be cleared and the case proceeded to its *inevitable* conclusion.

# The Adverbial Suffix *-LY*

### Rule 2

**In forming adverbs from adjectives ending in *-al*, simply add *-ly* to the original word.**

**adjective + *ly* = adverb**

**EXAMPLE**

verbal + *ly* = verbally

## Exercise 3

*Form the adverbs of the following adjectives:*

1. accidental
2. critical
3. elemental
4. equal
5. exceptional
6. final
7. general (adj.)
8. incidental
9. intentional
10. ironical
11. logical
12. mathematical
13. practical
14. professional
15. real
16. typical
17. usual
18. verbal
19. global

# Words Ending in -*OUS*

## -*OUS* before a Consonant

| Rule 3 |
| --- |
| When adding -*ous* to a noun ending in a consonant, do *not* change the spelling of the noun. |

**-*OUS* Before a Consonant**

| Noun | Suffix | | Adjective | Noun | Suffix | | Adjective |
| --- | --- | --- | --- | --- | --- | --- | --- |
| danger | + *ous* | = | dangerous | mountain | + *ous* | = | mountainous |
| hazard | + *ous* | = | hazardous | murder | + *ous* | = | murderous |
| humor | + *ous* | = | humorous | peril | + *ous* | = | perilous |
| libel | + *ous* | = | libelous | poison | + *ous* | = | poisonous |
| marvel | + *ous* | = | marvelous | riot | + *ous* | = | riotous |
| moment | + *ous* | = | momentous | slander | + *ous* | = | slanderous |

| Caution! |
| --- |
| Nouns ending in -*f* change the *f* to *v* when -*ous* is added. |

**EXAMPLES**

grief + *ous*   = grievous (*not* grievious)
mischief + *ous* = mischievous (*not* mischievious)

| Remember! |
| --- |
| Nouns ending in -*y* drop the *y* and add *e* before -*ous*. |

**EXAMPLES**

beauty + *ous* = beauteous
bounty + *ous* = bounteous
duty + *ous*   = duteous
pity + *ous*    = piteous
plenty + *ous* = plenteous

## -*OUS* before a Vowel

| Rule 4 |
| --- |

**When adding -*ous* to a noun ending in -*e*, drop the *e*.**

### EXAMPLES
adventure + *ous* = adventurous
analogue + *ous* = analogous
desire + *ous* = desirous
trouble + *ous* = troublous

| Note! |
| --- |

**Occasionally the final -*e* is retained before -*ous* for phonetic reasons, as explained on page 181.**

### EXAMPLES
courage + *ous* = courageous
advantage + *ous* = advantageous
outrage + *ous* = outrageous

## Exercise 4

*Write the correct adjectives of the following nouns by adding the suffix -ous.*

| | |
| --- | --- |
| 1. advantage _____ | 11. plenty _____ |
| 2. courage _____ | 12. adventure _____ |
| 3. dolor _____ | 13. bounty _____ |
| 4. peril _____ | 14. danger _____ |
| 5. mountain _____ | 15. grief _____ |
| 6. beauty _____ | 16. humor _____ |
| 7. desire _____ | 17. outrage _____ |
| 8. pity _____ | 18. duty _____ |
| 9. trouble _____ | 19. libel _____ |
| 10. mischief _____ | 20. poison _____ |

# Troublesome Affixes *-AL*, *-EL*, *-LE*

The endings, *-al*, *-el*, and *-le* are called affixes. They are added to the end of words and are a source of many spelling difficulties because they are pronounced in approximately the same way.

Although there are no hard-and-fast rules governing their use, here are some guide lines which will help you spell correctly most of the words in which they occur.

## The Affix *-AL*

| Rule 5 |
| --- |
| The affix *-al* is added to nouns and adjectives only. <br> The affix *-al* means *of*, *belonging to*, *pertaining to*, or *appropriate to*. |

If you remember these meanings, you will scarcely make a mistake.

**EXAMPLES**
personal  — *of* the person
autumnal — *belonging* to autumn
royal      — *pertaining* to a king
nautical  — *appropriate* to ships

---

**Common Words Ending in *-AL***

| Adjectives | | Adjectives | |
| --- | --- | --- | --- |
| additional | fatal | magical | penal |
| adverbial | fiscal | mechanical | personal |
| annual | general | medical | regal |
| brutal | jovial | neutral | several |
| classical | legal | normal | trivial |
| clerical | logical | original | |
| comical | | oval | |

| Nouns | |
| --- | --- |
| acquittal | proposal |
| arrival | recital |
| betrayal | refusal |
| capital | rival |
| denial | signal |

---

| Caution! |
| --- |

**Do not confuse *capital*, a city, with *capitol*, a building.**

---

# The Affix *-EL*

The affix *-el* originally diminished the meaning of a word to which it was attached. For example, tunnel once meant a small barrel or tun, and chapel meant a small church. Nowadays the original significance of *-el* is forgotten.

If you remember that *-el* is used less frequently than *-al* and if you memorize the spelling of the common words below, you will greatly reduce the possibility of misspelling words in which it appears.

### Common Words Ending in *-EL*

| | | | |
| --- | --- | --- | --- |
| bushel | jewel | novel | satchel |
| cancel | kennel | nickel | shovel |
| channel | kernel | panel | swivel |
| flannel | model | parcel | travel |
| funnel | morsel | quarrel | trowel |

# The Affix *-LE*

The affix *-le* is used far more frequently than *-al* or *-el*. This method will help you to remember the words that end in *-le*.

1. Examine the following list carefully.
2. Form a mental image of each word.
3. Pronounce each word aloud. Then write it in the air with your finger. Underline the *le* after you complete writing the word in the air.
4. Pronounce the word again.

When you perform these steps, you are visualizing, feeling, and hearing. In other words you are employing three senses to help you remember the correct spelling.

## Common Words Ending in *-LE*

| | | | |
|---|---|---|---|
| able | double | muffle | scuttle |
| ample | dribble | muscle | settle |
| angle | drizzle | muzzle | shuffle |
| apostle | fable | myrtle | shackle |
| article | fickle | needle | shuttle |
| ankle | fiddle | nestle | sickle |
| baffle | frizzle | nettle | sizzle |
| battle | gable | nibble | sparkle |
| beetle | gentle | nuzzle | sprinkle |
| bottle | giggle | paddle | squabble |
| brittle | girdle | peaceable | strangle |
| buckle | gristle | people | subtle |
| bundle | grizzle | pestle | tackle |
| bungle | handle | pickle | thimble |
| cattle | huddle | possible | thistle |
| chuckle | humble | prattle | treble |
| circle | hurdle | principle | tremble |
| couple | jangle | puzzle | trestle |
| cripple | jingle | raffle | trickle |
| castle | juggle | rankle | trifle |
| corpuscle | jungle | riddle | triple |
| dangle | knuckle | ruffle | trouble |
| dazzle | ladle | scribble | turtle |
| disciple | mantle | scruple | twinkle |
| | miracle | scuffle | |

## Exercise 5

*Select the word in each pair which is correctly spelled.*

1. a. brutel      b. brutal      _____
2. a. proposal      b. proposale      _____
3. a. flannel      b. flannal      _____
4. a. dangle      b. dangel      _____
5. a. drizzel      b. drizzle      _____
6. a. corpuscle      b. corpuscel      _____
7. a. fatal      b. fatel      _____
8. a. swivle      b. swivel      _____
9. a. tripel      b. triple      _____
10. a. signel      b. signal      _____
11. a. battle      b. battel      _____
12. a. quarrle      b. quarrel      _____
13. a. rankel      b. rankle      _____

14. a. mechanicle    b. mechanical     _____
15. a. angal    b. angle     _____
16. a. rival    b. rivle     _____
17. a. jewel    b. jewal     _____
18. a. nickel    b. nickle     _____
19. a. girdel    b. girdle     _____
20. a. tragicle    b. tragical     _____
21. a. thimble    b. thimbel     _____
22. a. capital    b. capitle     _____
23. a. knuckel    b. knuckle     _____
24. a. parcle    b. parcel     _____
25. a. regel    b. regal     _____

# Words Ending in *-ER* or *-OR*

The suffixes *-er* and *-or* mean *one who* or *that which*. For example, a *visitor* is *one who visits* and an *indicator* is *that which indicates*.

When should you use *-er* and when should you use *-or*?

---

### Caution!

**Although there are many words with these suffixes, there is no rule governing their use.**

---

The lack of rule, however, need not disturb you. Simply remember that most words end in *-or*. Then study the list of *-er* words below and pay attention to those you use most often.

---

**Common Words Ending in *-OR, -ER***

| -OR | | | -ER | |
|---|---|---|---|---|
| actor | contractor | investigator | advertiser | manager |
| administrator | counselor | operator | beginner | manufacturer |
| author | editor | radiator | bookkeeper | passenger |
| aviator | educator | refrigerator | consumer | purchaser |
| bachelor | elevator | senator | employer | receiver |
| collector | escalator | spectator | farmer | stenographer |
| commentator | governor | sponsor | interpreter | treasurer |
| conductor | indicator | supervisor | laborer | writer |
| | inventor | | | |

# Words Ending in -*AR*

A relatively small number of words end in -*ar*. The most common are listed below. If you study the list, this ending should never cause you trouble.

---

**Common Words Ending in -*AR***

| | |
|---|---|
| beggar | dollar |
| calendar | regular |
| collar | singular |

---

> **Notice!**
>
> **Distinguish between *hangar*, a shelter for housing airplanes, and *hanger*, one who hangs or that which hangs.**

## Exercise 6

*Add the suffix* -or, -er, *or* -ar *to each of the following words:*

1. begg __ __
2. receiv __ __
3. conduct __ __
4. passeng __ __
5. govern __ __
6. labor __ __
7. operat __ __
8. doll __ __
9. supervis __ __
10. stenograph __ __

# Words Ending in -*ANCE*, -*ENCE*

There are no simple ways of learning when to add -*ance* or -*ence*. It is best to study each of the following lists, using the words as often as possible until you habitually spell them correctly.

## Common *-ANCE, -ANCY, -ANT* Words

| | | | |
|---|---|---|---|
| abundant | descendant | inheritance | remembrance |
| abundance | elegance | irrelevancy | remonstrance |
| acquaintance | elegant | irrelevant | repentance |
| appearance | endurance | lieutenant | repentant |
| assistance | entrance | maintenance | restaurant |
| assistant | entrant | nuisance | sergeant |
| balance | grievance | observance | significance |
| brilliance | guidance | observant | significant |
| brilliancy | hindrance | pendant | stimulant |
| brilliant | ignorance | perseverance | tenancy |
| clearance | ignorant | pleasant | tenant |
| countenance | importance | preponderant | tolerance |
| defendant | important | | |

## Common *-ENCE, -ENCY, -ENT* Words

| | | | |
|---|---|---|---|
| absence | correspondent | impertinence | permanence |
| absent | deference | impertinent | permanent |
| abstinence | (deferential) | imprudence | persistence |
| abstinent | dependence | imprudent | persistent |
| adherence | dependent | independence | pestilence |
| adherent | difference | independent | precedence |
| antecedent | different | indulgence | preference |
| apparent | diffidence | indulgent | presence |
| audience | diffident | inference | present |
| coherence | diligence | influence | prominence |
| coherent | diligent | (influential) | prominent |
| coincidence | divergence | insistence | providence |
| concurrence | divergent | insolence | provident |
| concurrent | efficiency | insolent | reference |
| conference | efficient | intelligence | repellent |
| confidence | eminence | intelligent | reverence |
| confident | eminent | intermittent | reverent |
| conscience | essence | magnificence | residence |
| consequence | (essential) | magnificent | resident |
| consequent | equivalent | occurrence | sentence |
| competence | excellence | opponent | sufficient |
| competent | excellent | patent | superintendent |
| compliment (praise) | existence | patience | tendency |
| convenience | existent | patient | violence |
| convenient | experience | penitence | violent |
| correspondence | government | penitent | |

# Words Ending in *-ENSE*

There are only a few words ending in *-ense*.

---
**Words Ending in *-ENSE***
---

defense or defence (British)
expense
immense
offense or offence
pretense or pretence
suspense

---

## ___ Exercise 7 ___

*Insert* a *or* e *in the space indicated for the following words:*

1. complim __ nt
2. remembr __ nce
3. consist __ nt
4. superintend __ nt
5. depend __ nt
6. exist __ nce
7. descend __ nt
8. acquaint __ nce
9. griev __ nce
10. perman __ nt
11. magnific __ nt
12. brilli __ nce
13. compl __ mentary
14. conveni __ nce
15. abund __ nce
16. guid __ nce
17. consci __ nce
18. coincid __ nce
19. appar __ nt
20. consequ __ ntial

# Words Ending in *-ARY*, *-ERY*

There are more than 300 words ending in *-ary*. There are only two commonly used words ending in *-ery*.

---

**Common Words Ending in *-ERY***

---

cemetery            stationery

---

Perhaps it may help you to remember that in cemetery only *e*'s are used. Recall that station*ery* is used to write a lett*er*.

---

**Common Words Ending in *-ARY***

---

| | | |
|---|---|---|
| auxiliary | honorary | secretary |
| boundary | imaginary | secondary |
| centenary | infirmary | tertiary |
| dictionary | library | tributary |
| elementary | revolutionary | vocabulary |
| evolutionary | | involuntary |

---

## Exercise 8

*Select the word in each pair which is correctly spelled, and write it in the blank.*

1. a. boundery        b. boundary        _____
2. a. revolutionary   b. revolutionery   _____
3. a. cemetary        b. cemetery        _____
4. a. imaginery       b. imaginary       _____
5. a. tributery       b. tributary       _____
6. a. corollary       b. corollery       _____
7. a. coronery        b. coronary        _____
8. a. solitary        b. solitery        _____
9. a. militery        b. military        _____
10. a. infirmary      b. infirmery       _____

# Words Ending in *-ISE*, *-IZE*

There are no hard and fast rules to differentiate between the words ending in *-ise* and *-ize*. Perhaps the best procedure would be to master the list of *-ise* words and then remember that all others are spelled *-ize*.

---

### Common Words Ending in *-ISE*, *-IZE*

---

#### *-ISE*

| | |
|---|---|
| advertise | franchise |
|   (advertisement) | merchandise |
| advise | revise |
| adviser |   (revision) |
| arise | supervise |
| chastise |   (supervision) |
|   (chastisement) | surmise |
| compromise | surprise |
| demise | reprise |
| despise |   (reprisal) |
| disguise | |
| enterprise | |
| exercise | |

#### *-IZE*

| | |
|---|---|
| agonize | hypnotize |
| antagonize | idolization |
| authorize | itemize |
|   (authorization) | legitimatize |
| baptize (but baptism) | localize |
| burglarize | modernize |
| capsize | neutralize |
| centralize | ostracize |
| characterize | patronize |
|   (characterization) | pulverize |
| demoralize | realize |
| dramatize | recognize |
| emphasize (but emphasis) | solemnize |
| familiarize | specialize |
| fertilize | symbolize |
| generalize | tantalize |
| generalization | terrorize |
| humanize | visualize |

---

**Note!**

**There are only two words ending in -YZE:**
### analyze          paralyze

---

## Exercise 9

*Add the suffix -ise or -ize to each of the following stems.*

1. agon _____
2. chast _____
3. exerc _____
4. surpr _____
5. visual _____

6. superv _____
7. modern _____
8. enterpr _____
9. fertil _____
10. general _____

# Plurals Of Nouns

*S* or *ES*? That is the question. Word endings are a basic clue in forming plurals.

# Plurals Of Nouns

## Regular Plurals

| Rule 1 |
| --- |
| Most English nouns add -*S* to form the plural. |

EXAMPLES
cat + *s*     = cats
hat + *s*     = hats
house + *s* = houses

## Nouns Endings in a Sibilant Sound

| Rule 2 |
| --- |
| Nouns ending in a sibilant sound (-*s*, -*ss*, -*sh*, soft -*ch*, -*x*, or -*z*) add -ES to form the plural. |

**Nouns Ending in a Sibilant Sound Add -ES for Plural**

| Sibilant Sound | Plural Nouns | Sibilant Sound | Plural Nouns |
|---|---|---|---|
| -S | bus + *es* = bus*es* | -*SH* | *fish* + *es* = fish*es* |
| | gas + *es* = gas*es* | | parish + *es* = parish*es* |
| -SS | kiss + *es* = kiss*es* | -CH | church + *es* = church*es* |
| | loss + *es* = loss*es* | | lunch + *es* = lunch*es* |
| | pass + *es* = pass*es* | | bunch + *es* = bunch*es* |
| | class + *es* = class*es* | | wench + *es* = wench*es* |
| | mass + *es* = mass*es* | | punch + *es* = punch*es* |
| | business + *es* = business*es* | -X | box + *es* = box*es* |
| | | | tax + *es* = tax*es* |
| | | -Z | buzz + *es* = buzz*es* |
| | | | quartz + *es* = quartz*es* |

# Nouns Ending in Long $\bar{O}$

A number of nouns ending in long $\bar{o}$ add -ES for the plural. Learn this entire list.

**Nouns Ending in Long $\bar{O}$ with -ES Plural**

| | | | |
|---|---|---|---|
| buffalo*es* | domino*es* | mosquito*es* | tomato*es* |
| calico*es* | echo*es* | motto*es* | torpedo*es* |
| cargo*es* | embargo*es* | negro*es* | veto*es* |
| desperado*es* | hero*es* | potato*es* | virago*es* |
| | | | volcano*es* |

A few nouns ending in $\bar{o}$, add only an -S. Remember them by groups.

**Nouns Ending in Long $\bar{O}$ with -S Plural**

*Music*

alto*s*
soprano*s*
contralto*s*  } all are borrowed from Italian
piano*s*
solo*s*

*Circular Appearance*

dynamo*s*      silo*s*
cameo*s*

# Nouns Ending in *-F* or *-FE*

## Rule 3

Certain nouns ending in *-f* or *-fe* form the plural by changing *f* to *v* and adding *-S* or *-ES*.

---

### Nouns Changing Final *F* or *-FE* to *-V* and Adding *-S* or *-ES* for Plural

#### Common Nouns

| | | |
|---|---|---|
| beef | → | beeves |
| calf | → | calves |
| elf | → | elves |
| knife | → | knives |
| leaf | → | leaves |
| life | → | lives |
| loaf | → | loaves |
| sheaf | → | sheaves |
| thief | → | thieves |
| wife | → | wives |
| wolf | → | wolves |

#### Nouns with e̅e̅ Sound

| | | |
|---|---|---|
| beef | → | beeves |
| leaf | → | leaves |
| sheaf | → | sheaves |
| thief | → | thieves |

#### Nouns with ī Sound

| | | |
|---|---|---|
| knife | → | knives |
| life | → | lives |
| wife | → | wives |

#### Nouns with ei Sound

| | | |
|---|---|---|
| elf | → | elves |
| self | → | selves |
| shelf | → | shelves |

---

### Nouns Ending in *-F* and Adding Only *-S* for Plural

*-IEF*

| | | |
|---|---|---|
| belief | → | beliefs |
| brief | → | briefs |
| chief | → | chiefs |
| grief | → | griefs |
| handkerchief | → | handkerchiefs |

| | -OOF | |
|---|---|---|
| hoof | → | hoofs (rarely hooves) |
| proof | → | proofs |
| roof | → | roofs |
| | -RF | |
| dwarf | → | dwarfs |
| scarf | → | scarfs (*or* scarves) |
| turf | → | turfs |
| wharf | → | wharfs (*or* wharves) |

## Exercise 1

*Write plurals for the following words:*

| | | | |
|---|---|---|---|
| 1. reproof | _____ | 11. slough | _____ |
| 2. reprieve | _____ | 12. basso | _____ |
| 3. sieve | _____ | 13. mambo | _____ |
| 4. halo | _____ | 14. surf | _____ |
| 5. gulf | _____ | 15. trough | _____ |
| 6. coif | _____ | 16. stiletto | _____ |
| 7. albino | _____ | 17. sheaf | _____ |
| 8. shelf | _____ | 18. radio | _____ |
| 9. puff | _____ | 19. calf | _____ |
| 10. muff | _____ | 20. sylph | _____ |

# Nouns Ending in -*Y*

### Rule 4

**Words ending in *y* preceded by a *vowel* form their plural by adding -*S*.**

**Ending in -*Y*, Preceded by a Vowel, Adding -*S* for Plural**

| | | |
|---|---|---|
| day | → | days |
| boy | → | boys |
| monkey | → | monkeys |
| valley | → | valleys |
| volley | → | volleys |

## Exercise 2

*Write the plurals of these words:*

1. abbey
2. alley
3. attorney
4. buoy
5. chimney
6. donkey
7. journey
8. key
9. pulley
10. turkey

_____
_____
_____
_____
_____
_____
_____
_____
_____
_____

### Rule 5

When the final *-y* is preceded by a *consonant* the *-y* changes to *i* and *-ES* is added to form the plural.

**Words Ending in *-Y*, Preceded by a Consonant, Changing *-Y* to *-I* and Adding *-ES* for Plural**

| | |
|---|---|
| academy | → | academ*ies* |
| actuary | → | actuar*ies* |
| ally | → | all*ies* |
| army | → | arm*ies* |
| caddy | → | cadd*ies* |
| cry | → | cr*ies* |

# Special Situations

## Compound Nouns

### Rule 6

Compound nouns add *-S* or *-ES* to only the principal word to form the plural.

**EXAMPLES**

In the *in-law* series, the principal word is son, brother, etc.

brother*s*-in-law

mother*s*-in-law

---

| Notice! |
| --- |

   **A few compound words are practically single words and add the -*S* at the end. This explains such cases as**

| spoonful*s* | bowlful*s* |
| --- | --- |
| cupful*s* | handful*s* |

---

# Old English Plurals

A long time ago the English language had quite a list of words whose plurals ended not in -*S* but in -*EN*. Only a few are left today, but they never give any trouble because they are learned in the very early grades of school. Other variations follow:

**Old English Plurals**

### General Words

| child | → | child*ren* |
| --- | --- | --- |
| brother | → | breth*ren* (of a congregation) |
| ox | → | ox*en* |
| | | |
| foot | → | *fee*t |
| tooth | → | t*ee*th |
| goose | → | g*ee*se |
| | | |
| cannon | → | cannon (*or* cannon*s*) |
| deer | → | deer |
| sheep | → | sheep |
| swine | → | swine |

### Animals

| louse | → | l*ice* |
| --- | --- | --- |
| mouse | → | m*ice* |

### The Sexes

| man | → | m*e*n |
| --- | --- | --- |
| woman | → | wom*e*n |

### French Words

| madam | → | m*e*sdam*es* |
| --- | --- | --- |
| monsieur | → | m*e*ssieur*s* |

# Names of People

| Rule 7 |
| --- |
| As a general rule add S to form the plural of names of people. |

**EXAMPLES**
All the Johns in the school.
All the Jennys in this class.

# Letters, Signs, Figures

| Rule 8 |
| --- |
| Letters, signs and figures form their plural by adding 'S. |

**EXAMPLES**
Cross your t's
Mind your P's and Q's
Underline the 3's in the line.

# Foreign Words

Foreign words act differently when their plurals are formed. Since many of these foreign plurals are from the Latin, the Latin plurals are used. Other foreign plurals are also given.

1. Many **Latin** words ending in *-us* form their plural by changing the *us* to *i*. The most familiar of such words are

**Latin Words changing Final *-US* to *I* for Plural**

| | | |
| --- | --- | --- |
| alumnus | → | alumn*i* |
| fungus | → | fung*i* |
| focus | → | foc*i* |
| radius | → | radi*i* |
| bacillus | → | bacill*i* |
| terminus | → | termin*i* |

2. Some Latin words ending in *-um* change it to *a* to form the plural. A familiar word to us is *datum, data* (the facts in the case).

---

**Latin Words Changing Final *-UM* to *-A* for Plural**

| | |
|---|---|
| medium | → media (means of doing things) |
| addendum | → addenda (things added to a book or program) |
| bacterium | → bacteria |
| candelabrum | → candelabra |
| curriculum | → curricula |
| desideratum | → desiderata |
| erratum | → errata |
| maximum | → maxima |
| memorandum | → memoranda |
| minimum | → minima |
| stadium | → stadia |
| stratum | → strata |

---

3. **Greek** has a group of nouns ending in *-is* singular, *-es* plural. A familiar case is *crisis, crises*.

---

**Greek Words Changing *-IS* to *-ES* for Plural**

| | |
|---|---|
| analysis | → analyses |
| antithesis | → antitheses (opposite) |
| axis | → axes (center) |
| ellipsis | → ellipses |
| hypothesis | → hypotheses (assumption) |
| oasis | → oases |
| parenthesis | → parentheses |
| synopsis | → synopses |

---

4. The Greek language has given us a few words ending in *-on* singular, *-a* plural. These are from the ancient Greeks.

---

**Greek Plurals**

| | |
|---|---|
| automaton | → automata (mechanical figures working by themselves) |
| criterion | → criteria (standard of judgment) |

5. From the **French** have come these plurals:

---
**French Plurals**
---

| | |
|---|---|
| beau | → beaux (or beaus) |
| tableau | → tableaux (or tableaus) |
| chateau | → chateaux |
| portmanteau | → portmanteaux (or portmanteaus) |

---

6. These familiar words are all **Italian** plural forms:

---
**Italian Plurals**
---

spaghetti
confetti
banditti
ravioli

---

# Exercise 3

*Plurals of nouns.*
*Form the plurals of the following nouns:*

1. t
2. Mary
3. anniversary
4. dromedary
5. kerchief
6. 4
7. court-martial
8. lieutenant colonel
9. bay
10. tray
11. flurry
12. sulky
13. surrey
14. inequity
15. satellite
16. functionary
17. avocado
18. dynamo

## Exercise 4

*Have someone dictate the following passage containing many singular nouns for which you will write the plurals.*

Mother sent Mary to the Grand Union to purchase some *grocery* _____ for the long week end. Among the *thing* _____ she wanted to obtain were: *tomato* _____ , *potato* _____ , and *avocado* _____ . She also asked for several *quart* _____ of milk, two *pound* _____ of butter, several *piece* _____ of cake, and a pound of caramel-filled *chocolate* _____ .

After making these and several other *purchase* _____ , Mary started to return home. Several interesting *adventure* _____ occurred to her on the way. She met her friend Nancy who was one of the best *soprano* _____ in the church choir. Mary herself was usually placed among the *alto* _____ . After wandering up and down several narrow *alley* _____ , she ended one of the most interesting *journey* _____ by finding a bundle of *key* _____ , which she had lost several *day* _____ before. Such *event* _____ happen too seldom, and Mary will not forget this for a long time.

# The Final -Y

**Why should the Final -Y cause so much trouble?**

**Two simple rules will take care of all such words.**

# The Final -Y

Notice these words:

| Singular | | Plural |
|----------|---|--------|
| abb(ey) | → | abbeys |
| journ(ey) | → | journeys |
| monk(ey) | → | monkeys |

## The -Y Preceded by a Vowel

**Rule 1**

**The final -*Y* following a *vowel* remains *Y* when suffixes are added.**

These suffixes may be:

1. The letter -*S* to form the plural.

   ### EXAMPLES
   attorney + *s* = attorneys
   chimney + *s* = chimneys
   donkey + *s* = donkeys
   medley + *s* = medleys
   pulley + *s* = pulleys
   trolley + *s* = trolleys
   valley + *s* = valleys
   volley + *s* = volleys

167

2. The suffix *-ING* or *-ED*.

**EXAMPLES**
allay + *ed*   = allay*ed*
annoy + *ed* = annoy*ed*
buy           *not applicable*
allay + *ing*  = allay*ing*
annoy + *ing* = annoy*ing*
buy + *ing*   = buy*ing*

3. The suffix *-ER* meaning *one who*.

**EXAMPLES**
buy + *er*    = buy*er*
employ + *er* = employ*er*

4. The suffix *-ANCE*.

**EXAMPLE**
convey + *ance* = convey*ance*

5. The suffix *-AL*.

**EXAMPLE**
portray + *al* = portray*al*

## Exercise 1

*Spell the following words correctly.*

1. *tourney* in plural
2. The past tense of *allay*
3. The past tense of *volley*
4. *alley* in plural
5. Past tense of *survey*
6. Present participle of *portray*
7. Past tense of *journey*
8. Past tense of *relay*
9. Plural of *delay*
10. Past tense of *parlay*

# The -*Y* Preceded by a Consonant

## Rule 2

**When a *consonant* precedes the -*Y*, the *Y* changes to *I* when suffixes are added.**

Kinds of suffixes:

1. The plural of the noun formed with -*ES*.

   **EXAMPLES**
   ally + *es*      = all*ies*
   enemy + *es*   = enem*ies*
   salary + *es*   = salar*ies*
   tragedy + *es* = traged*ies*

2. The verb form with *he, she,* or *it*, formed by adding -*ES*, or -*ED*.

   **EXAMPLES**
   carry + *es*    = carr*ies*
   dignify + *es*  = dignif*ies*
   marry + *es*    = marr*ies*
   carry + *ed*    = carr*ied*
   dignify + *ed* = dignif*ied*
   merry + *ed*   = merr*ied*

3. Making an adjective by adding -*FUL*.

   **EXAMPLES**
   beauty + *ful* = beaut*iful*
   mercy + *ful* = merc*iful*
   pity + *ful*    = pit*iful*

4. Making a noun by adding -*NESS*.

   **EXAMPLES**
   busy + *ness* = bus*iness*
   cozy + *ness* = coz*iness*
   icy + *ness*    = ic*iness*

5. Making an adverb by adding -*LY*.

   **EXAMPLES**
   airy + *ly*      = air*ily*
   angry + *ly*    = angr*ily*
   busy + *ly*      = bus*ily*
   clumsy + *ly* = clums*ily*

| Caution! |
| --- |

**There is only one case in which the *Y* is retained. This is before *-ING*.**

**EXAMPLES**
carry + *ing* = carry*ing*
copy + *ing* = copy*ing*

## Exercise 2

*In the space to the right put the letter C if the spelling is correct. If it is incorrect, write the proper spelling.*

1. merciful  _____
2. beautiful  _____
3. cozily  _____
4. attornies  _____
5. valleys  _____
6. surveyor  _____
7. portraying  _____
8. pitying  _____
9. busied  _____
10. icyly  _____

## Exercise 3

*Write the correct spelling of the following words all of which end in final Y before adding a suffix.*

1. pretty + ness  _____
2. petty + ness  _____
3. steady + ing  _____
4. ready + ed  _____
5. bully + s  _____
6. airy + ness  _____
7. pity + ed  _____
8. tally + ing  _____
9. buy + er  _____
10. duty + ful  _____
11. ready + ness  _____
12. carry + ed  _____
13. hurry + ing  _____
14. copy + er  _____
15. sloppy + ness  _____
16. lively + hood  _____

| Remember! |
| --- |

**When adding the present participle (-*ing*) to verbs ending in -*Y*, do not change the *Y*.**

EXAMPLES

| Word | + ING | = | Present Participle |
| --- | --- | --- | --- |
| accompany | + ing | = | accompanying |
| bury | + ing | = | burying |
| hurry | + ing | = | hurrying |
| study | + ing | = | studying |
| worry | + ing | = | worrying |

# The Final *-E*

## *DyEing* or *Dying*?

## One *E* can make a world of difference.

# The Final -E

As you know, English has five *vowels:* A, E, I, O, U. The other letters are called *consonants*. Very often a consonant or group of consonants is added to a word and we get a second word. For example, let us consider the letters *-ry*. Add these to the following nouns (names of persons, places, acts, or things).

chemist   — one who analyzes things
chemist*ry* — the science of matter

forest     — the collection of trees
forest*ry*   — the study of care of forests

peasant   — worker of the soil
peasant*ry* — the group of peasants

mimic     — one who imitates another
mimic*ry*   — the art of imitation

You see that no change occurs in spelling. You simply add the final element to a familiar word and you get a second word of a different meaning.

There are many endings of this character. If you remember that they do not change the spelling of the original word, you will find that they are really old friends with new attachments.

## Exercise 1

*Write the following words correctly by adding the suffix indicated:*

1. pleasant + ry
2. artist + ry
3. portrait + ure
4. clock + wise
5. rocket + ry
6. sophist + ry
7. nation + ality
8. person + ality
9. dialectic + al
10. practical + ity

   Few writers have any trouble in spelling words with added parts such as those described. But when a silent -*E* occurs at the end of a word, problems arise. When should you retain the silent -*E* and when should you drop it?

# Dropping the Final -*E*

### Rule 1

   **Drop the final -*E* before a suffix beginning with a *vowel* (*a*, *e*, *i*, *o*, *u*).**

**Suffixes Beginning with a Vowel**

| | |
|---|---|
| -able | -ence |
| -ed | -ance |
| -er | -ing |
| -est | -ous |
| -ity | |

How to handle these suffixes.

1. Dropping the final *e* before **-*ER***.

   **EXAMPLES**
large + *er* = larg*er*
love + *er* = lov*er*
live + *er* = liv*er*

2. Dropping the final *e* before **-EST**.

**EXAMPLES**

large + *est* = larg*est*
die + *est* = (thou) di*est*

3. Dropping the final *e* before **-ABLE**.

**EXAMPLES**

love + *able* = lov*able*
imagine + *able* = imagin*able*
advise + *able* = advis*able*
desire + *able* = desir*able*

4. Dropping the final *e* before **-ING**.

**EXAMPLES**

come + *ing* = com*ing*
receive + *ing* = receiv*ing*
ache + *ing* = ach*ing*

Since many mistakes are made with the -*ing* words, the following list is provided. It contains some of your most useful words.

---

**Handling -ING**

| | | |
|---|---|---|
| whine | argue | advise |
| whin*ing* | argu*ing* | advis*ing* |
| write | surprise | dine |
| writ*ing* | surpris*ing* | din*ing* |
| shine | owe | lose |
| shin*ing* | ow*ing* | los*ing* |
| oblige | purchase | fascinate |
| oblig*ing* | purchas*ing* | fascinat*ing* |
| judge | pursue | become |
| judg*ing* | pursu*ing* | becom*ing* |
| choose | | use |
| choos*ing* | | us*ing* |

5. Dropping final *e* before **-OUS**.

### EXAMPLE

The suffix *-ous* is frequently added to a verb to make an adjective which always has the meaning, *full of*.

$$\text{desire} + ous = \text{desir}ous$$

### EXAMPLE

Sometimes the suffix *-ous* is added to a noun. Again an adjective results also meaning, *full of*.

$$\text{pore} + ous = \text{por}ous \text{ full of pores}$$

6. Dropping final *e* before **-ITY**.

### EXAMPLE

The suffix *-ity* may be added to an adjective to form a noun. The final *E* before the suffix disappears.

$$\text{divine} + ity = \text{divin}ity$$

The same thing happens with these words:

---

**Handling -ITY**

| | | |
|---|---|---|
| austere | extreme | immense |
| auster*ity* | extrem*ity* | immens*ity* |
| dense | facile | intense |
| dens*ity* | facil*ity* | intens*ity* |
| docile | grave | oblique |
| docil*ity* | grav*ity* | obliqu*ity* |
| opportune | passive | rare |
| opportun*ity* | passiv*ity* | rar*ity* |
| scarce | sincere | suave |
| scarc*ity* | sincer*ity* | suav*ity* |

---

## Exercise 2

*Form new words by spelling the following:*

1. revere + ing        _____
2. love + ly           _____
3. purchase + able     _____
4. extreme + ly        _____
5. pleasure + able     _____
6. large + ly          _____
7. nudge + ed          _____
8. state + ed          _____
9. fete + ed           _____
10. fine + ed          _____
11. dive + ing         _____
12. shove + ed         _____
13. devise + ing       _____
14. deceive + ed       _____
15. relieve + ing      _____
16. procrastinate + ing _____
17. imagine + ed       _____
18. besiege + ed       _____
19. receive + ing      _____

---

### Caution!

**Verbs ending in *oe* (canoe) retain the -*E* to preserve the pronunciation.**

canoeing   hoeing   shoeing   toeing.

*Dye* and *singe* retain the -*E* to differentiate the word from *die* and *sing*

**dyeing (one's hair)**
**dying (absence of life)**
**singeing (one's hair)**
**singing (a song)**

## Exercise 3

*Form the present participle (+ -ing) and the past participle (+ -ed) of the following verbs.*

| Word | Present Participle | Past Participle |
|------|--------------------|-----------------|
| 1. benefit | | |
| 2. commit | | |
| 3. lure | | |
| 4. refer | | |
| 5. pine | | |
| 6. elevate | | |
| 7. propel | | |
| 8. fit | | |
| 9. recur | | |
| 10. remit | | |
| 11. open | | |
| 12. club | | |
| 13. plunge | | |
| 14. singe | | |
| 15. pursue | | |
| 16. scare | | |
| 17. throb | | |
| 18. trot | | |
| 19. use | | |
| 20. whip | | |

# Retaining the Final -*E*

### Rule 2

**The final -*E* is retained when the suffix begins with a *consonant*.**

**Suffixes Beginning with a Consonant**

| | |
|------|------|
| -ness | -ful |
| -ment | -less |

How to handle these suffixes.

1. Adding the suffix **-*NESS***.
   Examine the following words which all belong in this class:

---

**Handling -*NESS***

---

| | | |
|---|---|---|
| complete | genuine | acute |
| complete*ness* | genuine*ness* | acute*ness* |
| expensive | large | appropriate |
| expensive*ness* | large*ness* | appropriate*ness* |
| coarse | fierce | vague |
| coarse*ness* | fierce*ness* | vague*ness* |
| like | polite | remote |
| like*ness* | polite*ness* | remote*ness* |
| rude | wide | white |
| rude*ness* | wide*ness* | white*ness* |

---

2. Adding the suffix **-*MENT***.
   Examine the following words which are all formed the same way:

---

**Handling -*MENT***

---

| | | |
|---|---|---|
| amuse | discourage | achieve |
| amuse*ment* | discourage*ment* | achieve*ment* |
| arrange | enforce | advance |
| arrange*ment* | enforce*ment* | advance*ment* |
| atone | engage | advertise |
| atone*ment* | engage*ment* | advertise*ment* |
| commence | excite | amaze |
| commence*ment* | excite*ment* | amaze*ment* |
| move | require | manage |
| move*ment* | require*ment* | manage*ment* |

---

3. Adding the suffix **-FUL**.
   The following words belong to this division:

---

**Handling -FUL**

---

| | |
|---|---|
| care | tune |
| care*ful* | tune*ful* |
| revenge | resource |
| revenge*ful* | resource*ful* |
| taste | remorse |
| taste*ful* | remorse*ful* |
| grace | hate |
| grace*ful* | hate*ful* |
| disgrace | shame |
| disgrace*ful* | shame*ful* |

---

4. Adding the suffix **-LESS**.
   Again the silent *E* is preserved because the suffix begins with the consonant *l*.

---

**Handling -LESS**

---

| | | | |
|---|---|---|---|
| age | grace | sense | taste |
| age*less* | grace*less* | sense*less* | taste*less* |
| care | guide | shape | voice |
| care*less* | guide*less* | shape*less* | voice*less* |
| shame | tongue | cease | name |
| shame*less* | tongue*less* | cease*less* | name*less* |
| change | noise | smoke | use |
| change*less* | noise*less* | smoke*less* | use*less* |

---

> ### Caution!
>
> **Some exceptions.**
> - *Due, true, whole*, drop the *-E* before *-LY—duly, truly, wholly.*
> - **Some words ending in *-E*, drop the *-E* before *-MENT* or *-FUL*.** *Argument* is an instance, as is *awful* (from awe).

# Unusual Situations

## Rule 3

**Some words retain the final -*E* regardless of the suffix in order to retain pronunciation.**

1. When the word ends in double -*EE*, the final -*E* is not dropped. This happens in order to retain the same pronunciation.

   **EXAMPLES**

   | | |
   |---|---|
   | agree | see |
   | agree*able* | see*able* |
   | agree*ing* | see*ing* |
   | agree*ment* | |

2. Words ending in -*OE* retain the final -*E*.

   **EXAMPLES**

   | | |
   |---|---|
   | canoe | shoe |
   | canoe*ing* | shoe*maker* |
   | woe | shoe*string* |
   | woe*ful* | shoe*ing* |
   | woe*begone* | hoe |
   | | hoe*ing* |

3. Words ending in -*CE* or -*GE* will retain the final -*E* before a suffix beginning with a vowel. This is necessary to keep the soft pronunciation.

   **EXAMPLES**

   | | | |
   |---|---|---|
   | notice | change | outrage |
   | notice*able* | change*able* | outrage*ous* |
   | service | courage | advantage |
   | service*able* | courage*ous* | advantage*ous* |

## Rule 4

**Certain words would lose their hard pronunciation of certain consonants unless a -*K* is added before a suffix beginning with *E*, *I*, or *Y* (used as vowel).**

## EXAMPLES

*mimic + ing* = mimicing would not be pronounced with the hard *c* (= to *k*). Hence the *k* is inserted between the final *c* and the beginning vowel of the suffix. Note the following.

colic → coli*cky*
frolic → froli*cking* → froli*cked*
mimic → mimi*cking* → mimi*cked*
panic → pani*cking* → pani*cked*
picnic → picni*cking* → picni*cked*
traffic → traffi*cking* → traffi*cked*

Explain why this is not done for *frolicsome* or *panic-stricken* or *traffic-cop*.

## Exercise 4

*Try your hand at spelling these words containing the final -E and a suffix.*

|     |          |         |     |     |
| --- | -------- | ------- | --- | --- |
| 1.  | agree    | +MENT   | =   | ____ |
| 2.  | amuse    | +MENT   | =   | ____ |
| 3.  | care     | +FUL    | =   | ____ |
| 4.  | canoe    | +ING    | =   | ____ |
| 5.  | come     | +ING    | =   | ____ |
| 6.  | disagree | +ABLE   | =   | ____ |
| 7.  | engage   | +MENT   | =   | ____ |
| 8.  | excite   | +MENT   | =   | ____ |
| 9.  | immense  | +ITY    | =   | ____ |
| 10. | like     | +LY     | =   | ____ |
| 11. | safe     | +TY     | =   | ____ |
| 12. | sense    | +LESS   | =   | ____ |
| 13. | shine    | +ING    | =   | ____ |
| 14. | enlarge  | +MENT   | =   | ____ |
| 15. | entice   | +ING    | =   | ____ |
| 16. | perceive | +ED     | =   | ____ |
| 17. | escape   | +ING    | =   | ____ |
| 18. | discharge| +ED     | =   | ____ |
| 19. | relieve  | +ING    | =   | ____ |
| 20. | contrive | +ANCE   | =   | ____ |

## Exercise 5

*Have someone read the following sentences from dictation as you spell the words correctly. There will be many examples of dropping or retaining the final -E.*

1. While they were *staring* at the stars, they saw something *stirring* in the bushes.
2. It takes much *planning* to build a house *preferred* by others.
3. The *cannery* used plenty of *cane* sugar with such fruits as *pineapples* and peaches.
4. Dressed *sloppily*, the tramps *plodded* along wearily on the *pitted* country road.
5. By using *scraps* of food, the cook managed to scrape together a fair meal after the *scrapping* of the parents was over.
6. The little *moppet* sat *moping* in her little chair while the mother *mopped* up the food which was lying *sloppily* on the floor.
7. After we *refused* to have anything to do with her, the discharged maid *fumed* and *fussed effusively* and finally stamped out of the room.
8. By *dotting* your *i*'s and *crossing* your *t*'s you can take a small step toward *better spelling*.
9. While a troop of cavalry was *ridding* the woods of the stragglers, a second troop was *riding* into the village.
10. As the giant airliner *hopped* off, my parents were praying and hoping that all would go well.

## Exercise 6

*Each of the following words has an error in the dropping or retention of final -E. Make the correction in the space to the right.*

| | | | |
|---|---|---|---|
| 1. scarcly | _____ | 10. wisedom | _____ |
| 2. vengance | _____ | 11. assureance | _____ |
| 3. truely | _____ | 12. insureance | _____ |
| 4. tastey | _____ | 13. outragous | _____ |
| 5. noticable | _____ | 14. servicable | _____ |
| 6. changable | _____ | 15. couragous | _____ |
| 7. perspireing | _____ | 16. gorgous | _____ |
| 8. retireing | _____ | 17. pronouncable | _____ |
| 9. aweful | _____ | | |

# Doubling Final Consonants

**Benefi*tt*ing?** **Benefi*t*ing?**
**Ri*d*ing?** **Ri*dd*ing?**

**Two rules can get the situation under control.**

# Doubling Final Consonants

Do you know the difference between *riding* a horse and *ridding* the house of undesirable visitors? Do you know when people are *hoping* and when they are *hopping*? These are some examples of words with doubled consonants. There is no reason why anyone should suffer while trying to remember whether to spell a word with one or with two final consonants, for there are rules which will take care of all cases.

How many times have you been puzzled about doubling a consonant?

Does *beginning* have two *n*'s in the middle?

Does *omitted* have two *t*'s?

Why has *benefiting* one *t*, while *admitting* has two?

These and all other questions are easily answered if you will remember these two rules. There are very few rules in English as sure to help you as these.

## One-Syllable Words

First you must recall the meaning of the word *syllable*. A syllable is a unit of spoken language forming either a whole word (as *men*) or a division of a word (as *priv* in *priv·i·lege*). Look at these words.

*run*        *swim*        *hop*

Each of these has a vowel in the middle and a consonant at the end. These make up one syllable and such a word is called a one-syllable word. But look at these:

*con·fer*        *pre·fer*        *trans·fer*

You notice that we have at least *two* syllables in each word. Now we can proceed to the rules. Notice what happens to our three friends when we add *-ing*.

ru*nn*ing        swi*mm*ing        ho*pp*ing

**185**

The final consonant (*n, m, p*) has been doubled before a suffix beginning with a vowel. We could have added the suffix *-er*.

ru*nn*er      swi*mm*er      ho*pp*er

Again the final consonant was doubled before a suffix beginning with a vowel.
    Now the rule is easy.

---

### Rule 1

**When a one-syllable word ends in one vowel and one consonant, that consonant is *doubled* before a suffix beginning with a vowel.**

---

    Now discover for yourself what would happen to the final consonants of these words.

**One-Syllable Words Doubling Consonant Before Suffix Beginning with Vowel**

| Word | + ER | + ING |
|------|------|-------|
| hit | → hi*tt*er | → hi*tt*ing |
| spin | → spi*nn*er | → spi*nn*ing |
| wrap | → wra*pp*er | → wra*pp*ing |
| trim | → tri*mm*er | → tri*mm*ing |

    These words are easy.
    The following words have more than one syllable but they follow the same rule as the words just described. They *double* their final consonant before a suffix beginning with a vowel.

| Word | + ER | + ING | + Other Suffix |
|------|------|-------|----------------|
| admit | ⟶ | admi*tt*ing | → admi*tt*edly |
| begin | → begi*nn*er → | begi*nn*ing | |
| compel | ⟶ | compe*ll*ing | |
| confer | ⟶ | confe*rr*ing | |
| control | ⟶ | contro*ll*ing | → contro*ll*able |
| commit | ⟶ | commi*tt*ing | |
| equip | ⟶ | equi*pp*ing | |
| omit | ⟶ | omi*tt*ing | |

# Words of More Than One Syllable

> ### Rule 2
>
> A word of more than one syllable ending in a single vowel and a single consonant, which has the accent on the final syllable, *doubles* that consonant before a suffix beginning with a vowel. *Remember, the accent must be on the last syllable*.
>
> occ·ur′        ad·mit′        per·mit′

If the final syllable has no accent, there will be no doubling of the consonant. Thus, *benefit* will not double the *t*, because the accent is on the first syllable.

be′·ne·fit·ing        tra′·vel·ed

> ### Note!
>
> Study the suffixes to the following words. Each word satisfies three conditions.
> 1. It is more than one syllable.
> 2. The last syllable has the accent.
> 3. The last syllable ends in *one* vowel and a *single* consonant.

### Two-Syllable Words Doubling Consonant Before Suffix Beginning with Vowel

| Word | + ING | + ED | + Other Suffix |
|------|-------|------|----------------|
| abet | → abetting | → abetted | → abettor |
| abhor | → abhorring | → abhorred | → abhorrence |
| admit | → admitting | → admitted | → admittance |
| allot | → allotting | → allotted | → allottance |
| annul | → annulling | → annulled | → annulment |
| | | | (one *l* because the suffix begins with a consonant) |
| confer | → conferring | → conferred | → conference |
| | | | (one *r* because the accent is not on *fer* but *con*) |
| concur | → concurring | → concurred | → concurrence |

| Word | + ING | + ED | + Other Suffix |
|---|---|---|---|
| defer | → deferring | → deferred | → deference (only one *r* because accent is *not* on last syllable) |
| dispel | → dispelling | → dispelled | |
| excel | → excelling | → excelled | |
| infer | → inferring | → inferred | → inference (one *r*. Why?) |
| occur | → occurring | → occurred | → occurrence |
| omit | → omitting | → omitted | |
| permit | → permitting | → permitted | |
| rebel | → rebelling | → rebelled | → rebellion |
| recur | → recurring | → recurred | → recurrence |
| refer | → referring | → referred | → reference (one *r*. Why?) |
| regret | → regretting | → regretted | |
| transfer | → transferring | → transferred | |

# Special Situations

## Rule 3

**When adding -*NESS* to a word, use *nn* if the original word ends in *n*.**

### EXAMPLES
mean + *ness* = mean*ness*
plain + *ness* = plain*ness*
thin + *ness* = thin*ness*

## Rule 4

**Words ending in -*FUL* have a single *l* unless -*ly* is added.**

### EXAMPLES
careful + *ly* = careful*ly*       hopeful + *ly* = hopeful*ly*
beautiful + *ly* = beautiful*ly*    useful + *ly* = useful*ly*
dutiful + *ly* = dutiful*ly*       youthful + *ly* = youthful*ly*
wonderful + *ly* = wonderful*ly*

## Exercise 1

*Below is a list of verbs of one syllable. Add* -ing *to each of them. Some will double their final consonant. Some will not. Why? Remember Rule 1. There must be only* one *vowel and* one *consonant.*

1. cramp           _____
2. drum           _____
3. grin           _____
4. hit           _____
5. look           _____
6. nod           _____
7. pain           _____
8. rest           _____
9. rig           _____
10. scrub           _____

*Six out of the ten doubled their consonants. The remaining four did not because they had a vowel and two consonants* (cr-a-mp) *or two vowels and consonant* (l-oo-k).

# How Consonants Determine Meaning

Now for a few pairs of words with different meanings, depending upon the doubling of the consonants.

| | | |
|---|---|---|
| bar | → | He *barred* the door. |
| bare | → | He *bared* his arm. |
| | | |
| din | → | The teacher *dinned* it into John's ear. |
| dine | → | We *dined* at four. |
| | | |
| pin | → | Mary *pinned* her dress. |
| pine | → | Mary *pined* away. |
| | | |
| plan | → | They *planned* a happy life. |
| plane | → | The carpenter *planed* the wood. |
| | | |
| scrap | → | The two dogs *scrapped*. |
| scrape | → | Walter *scraped* his new knife on the cement floor. |
| | | |
| wag | → | He *wagged* his head solemnly. |
| wage | → | He *waged* a bitter war. |

Notice how the meaning is determined by the single or double consonant and why correct spelling is so important to convey your meaning.

Notice these few exceptions to the rule: *chagrined, gaseous, transferable, transference, transferee, facility*.

## Exercise 2

*Write correctly the words formed as the exercise indicates:*

| | |
|---|---|
| 1. defer + ed _____ | 11. desire + ing _____ |
| 2. refer + ence _____ | 12. tire + less _____ |
| 3. shop + ing _____ | 13. true + ly _____ |
| 4. disapprove + al _____ | 14. swim + er _____ |
| 5. nine + teen _____ | 15. trim + er _____ |
| 6. hit + ing _____ | 16. occur + ence _____ |
| 7. singe + ing _____ | 17. move + able _____ |
| 8. fame + ous _____ | 18. commit + ed _____ |
| 9. control + ing _____ | 19. equip + age _____ |
| 10. repel + ent _____ | 20. excel + ing _____ |

## Exercise 3

*Write the* present participle *(+ing) and* past participle *(+ed) of the following verbs. Some will double the final consonant; others will not. When in doubt, refer to the rules on doubling final consonants.*

| Word | Present Participle | Past Participle |
|---|---|---|
| 1. adapt | | |
| 2. cramp | | |
| 3. design | | |
| 4. conceal | | |
| 5. congeal | | |
| 6. blot | | |
| 7. stop | | |
| 8. crush | | |
| 9. excel | | |
| 10. defer | | |
| 11. envelop | | |
| 12. extol | | |
| 13. flutter | | |
| 14. happen | | |
| 15. hum | | |
| 16. level | | |
| 17. quarrel | | |
| 18. rub | | |
| 19. signal | | |
| 20. retreat | | |

## Exercise 4

*By adding the various endings, make new words. In some instances, the final consonant of the original word will be doubled. When in doubt, refer to the rules about doubling final consonants.*

**EXAMPLE**
Form an adjective of the word *woman* by adding *-ish*.

| *Word* | *Suffix* | *New Word* |
|--------|----------|------------|
| woman  | -ish     | womanish   |

1. Form an adjective of *wit* by adding *-y*. _____
2. Form a noun from the verb *spin* by adding *-er*. _____
3. Form a noun from the noun *blot* by adding *-er*. _____
4. Form a noun by adding *-er* to *design*. _____
5. Form an adjective by adding *-ical* to *quiz*. _____
6. Form a noun by adding *-er* to *shut*. _____
7. Form a noun by adding *-er* to *slip*. _____
8. Form a noun by adding *-eer* to *profit*. _____
9. Form a noun by adding *-ing* to *meet*. _____
10. Form a noun by adding *-er* to *dry*. _____
11. Add *-able* to *inhabit* to form an adjective. _____
12. Add *-er* to *toil* to form a noun. _____
13. Add *-er* to *put* to form a noun. _____
14. Add *-ment* to *develop* to form a noun. _____
15. Add *-ment* to *defer* to form a noun. _____
16. Add *-er* to *rub* to form a noun. _____
17. Add *-er* to *develop* to form a noun. _____
18. Make the feminine of *god*. _____
19. Name the man who sells you drugs. _____
20. Add *-er* to *trap* to form a noun. _____

## Exercise 5

*Add the indicated ending to each of the following words.*

1. tearful + ly _____
2. careful + ly _____
3. open + ness _____
4. dutiful + ly _____
5. bountiful + ly _____
6. common + ness _____
7. mimic + ed _____
8. picnic + ing _____
9. mimic + ing _____
10. panic + y _____

# British and American Spelling

**Remember to follow American usage unless there is a compelling reason for adopting a British variant.**

# British and American Spelling

American spelling does not differ extensively from British spelling, but there are differences. Some of the more important differences are listed below.

## British and American Spelling Equivalents

| American | | British | American | | British |
|---|---|---|---|---|---|
| *-er* | *versus* | *-re* | *-or* | *versus* | *-our* |
| center | | centre | color | | colour |
| kilometer | | kilometre | labor | | labour |
| theater | | theatre | humor | | humour |
| *l* | *versus* | *ll* | *-se* | *versus* | *-ce* |
| counselor | | counsellor | defense | | defence |
| labeled | | labelled | offense | | offence |
| traveled | | travelled | pretense | | pretence |
| *ll* | *versus* | *l* | *-ze/z* | *versus* | *-se/s* |
| enrollment | | enrolment | analyze | | analyse |
| skillful | | skilful | criticize | | criticise |
| installment | | instalment | organization | | organisation |

## Exercise

*The following words are spelled as they are in Great Britain. On the line opposite each word write the American form.*

1. candour _____
2. theatre _____
3. labour _____
4. labelled _____
5. traveller _____
6. realisation _____
7. criticise _____
8. skilful _____
9. defence _____
10. analyse _____

# English
# as a
# Second
# Language

# Help for Spanish-Speaking Students

**Spanish spelling is more logical than English spelling. The following hints can help you overcome your problems with English.**

# Help for Spanish-Speaking Students

Spanish words are easy to spell because almost every letter represents only one sound and every letter is pronounced.

Spanish speakers find some English words difficult to spell because some letters represent more than one sound and some letters are not pronounced. Spanish spelling is logical and predictable. English spelling is inconsistent and not always controlled by rules.

If your native language is Spanish, the following hints will help you spell English words correctly.

## Different Spellings for the Same Sound

### F and PH

Spanish words with an *f* sound are sometimes spelled with a *ph* in English. The sound is the same but the spelling is different.

**F and PH Sound Alike**

| Spanish | English | Spanish | English |
|---------|---------|---------|---------|
| catástrofe | catastrophe | geografía | geography |
| farmacéutico | pharmacist | hemisferio | hemisphere |
| farmacia | pharmacy | párrafo | paragraph |
| frase | phrase | teléfono | telephone |
| filósofo | philosopher | triunfante | triumphant |
| fotografía | photograph | | |

| Notice! |
|---|
| All the words in the above list are derived from Greek. In such words the sound of *f* is spelled *ph* in English. In most other English words *f* is used; for example, *f*riend, pre*f*er, scar*f*. |

# *CU* and *QU*

The sound represented by *cu* in Spanish is spelled *qu* in English, as you may see from the following words:

### *CU* and *QU* Sound Alike

| Spanish | English |
|---|---|
| cuestión | *qu*estion |
| frecuente | fre*qu*ent |
| frecuentemente | fre*qu*ently |

# Spanish *i* and Its Equivalents

The vowel in s*i*, qu*i*, am*i*go is also an English sound. In Spanish this sound is represented by *i*. In English there are ten different ways of representing this sound as shown below.

### Spanish *i* and Its Equivalents

| Spanish | English |
|---|---|
| | ae — as in *Ae*sop, C*ae*sar |
| | ay — as in qu*ay* |
| | e — as in *e*ternal, sc*e*nic, conv*e*ne |
| | ea — as in *ea*ch, b*ea*n, t*ea* |
| *i* as in qu*i*, s*i* | ee — as in *ee*ry, sl*ee*k |
| | ei — as in *ei*ther, rec*ei*ve |
| | eo —as in p*eo*ple |
| | ey — as in k*ey* |
| | i — as in mach*i*ne, rav*i*ne, fat*i*gue, cl*i*que |
| | ie — as in pr*ie*st, ser*ie*s |

## Exercise 1

*Indicate at the right whether the following English words are correctly spelled. Place a C if correct and an X if wrong. If a word is misspelled, spell it correctly.*

1. farmacy _____
2. photograf _____
3. philosopher _____
4. geography _____
5. frecuently _____
6. eather _____
7. machene _____
8. triumfant _____
9. peeple _____
10. priest _____
11. recieve _____
12. paragraf _____
13. sereis _____
14. convean _____
15. fatiegue _____

## Spanish *u* and Its Equivalents

In Spanish the letter *u* (p*u*ro, C*u*ba) represents a sound which is also used in English but spelled differently. Note that there are several ways of spelling this sound:

**Spanish *u* and Its Equivalents**

| Spanish | English |
|---------|---------|
| *u* as in p*u*ro, C*u*ba | oo — as in g*oo*se, al*oo*f, sp*oo*n, r*oo*ster, t*oo* |
| | ou — as in gr*ou*p, tr*ou*pe, ac*ou*stic, b*ou*quet |
| | ough — as in thr*ough* |
| | u — as in r*u*ler, br*u*tal |
| | ui — as in fr*ui*t, s*ui*table |
| | o — as in d*o*, t*o*, tw*o* |

# *To*, *Too*, and *Two*

| Notice! |
|---|
| **The confusion of *to*, *too*, and *two* is a common error. Be sure you know the difference.** |

|  | **To** | **Too** | **Two** |
|---|---|---|---|
| *Meaning* | a preposition meaning the *opposite of from*; the sign of the infinitive. | an adverb meaning *also* or more than enough. | an adverb meaning *twice* one. |
| *Examples* | to the theatre, to go | too late | two friends |

Here is a sentence in which the three words are used correctly: The *two* friends wanted *to* go *to* the theatre but they were *too* late.

## Exercise 2

*Every word below is misspelled. Cross it out and spell it correctly.*

1. truip     _____
2. brootal     _____
3. sootable     _____
4. ruster     _____
5. throo     _____
6. acoostic     _____
7. aluf     _____
8. ruiler     _____
9. booquet     _____
10. guis     _____

## Exercise 3

*Compose a sentence in which* to, too, *and* two *are used correctly.*

# Double Consonants

There are only two double consonants in Spanish, *ll* and *rr*. There are many in English.

## Double Consonants

| Spanish | English | |
|---------|---------|---------|
| ll | cc | mm |
| rr | ff | pp |
|  | gg | tt |
|  | ll | |

Observe that the English words listed below have double consonants while their Spanish counterparts have only one.

## English Double Consonants (with Spanish Equivalent)

| Consonant | English | Spanish |
|-----------|---------|---------|
| cc | accent | (el acento) |
|  | accord | (el acuerdo) |
|  | occult | (el oculto) |
|  | occupied | (ocupado) |
|  | occur | (ocurrir) |
|  | accept | (aceptar) |
| ff | different | (diferente) |
|  | suffer | (sufrir) |
|  | sufficient | (suficiente) |
| gg | exaggerated | (exagerado) |
| ll | alliance | (la alianza) |
|  | dollar | (el dólar) |
|  | intelligent | (inteligente) |
| mm | common | (común) |
|  | grammar | (gramática) |
| pp | appear | (aparecer) |
|  | appetite | (apetito) |
|  | applaud | (aplaudir) |
|  | apprehend | (aprender) |
|  | approximately | (aproximadamente) |
| tt | attack | (ataque) |
|  | attention | (atención) |
|  | battle | (batalla) |
|  | bottle | (botella) |
|  | button | (botón) |

## Exercise 4

*Some of the following words are spelled correctly and some are misspelled. Put a C on the blank if a word is spelled correctly. Re-write it correctly if it is misspelled.*

1. acord     _____
2. dollar     _____
3. ocurr     _____
4. appetite     _____
5. aprehend     _____
6. aproximately     _____
7. applaud     _____
8. sufer     _____
9. buton     _____
10. aliance     _____
11. accept     _____
12. ocupied     _____
13. diferent     _____
14. gramar     _____
15. exaggerated     _____
16. apear     _____
17. suficient     _____
18. atention     _____
19. battle     _____
20. occult     _____

---

### Notice!

**Double consonants are more common in English than in Spanish. Consult the rules on pages 186 – 188 for doubling consonants. You will find them helpful.**

# The English *J* Sound

In Spanish, *j* is pronounced like English *h* in *hello!*, *have*, and *here*. The English *j* sound does not exist in Spanish. It resembles Spanish *ch* in *muchacho* except that it is voiced.

To understand the meaning of a voiced consonant, put your fingers on each side of your voice box (larynx). Say the sounds of *m, n, r.* Can you feel your vocal cords vibrate? These are called voiced consonants because they are made with the aid of the vocal cords.

Now say the sound of *ch*. Notice that your vocal cords do not vibrate. A consonant made without vibration of the vocal cords is called a voiceless consonant.

## J Sound Spelling Variations

"J" Sound

- di — as in cor*di*al, sol*di*er
- dg — as in bri*dg*e, fu*dg*e, slu*dg*e
- g — as in *g*em, *g*ist, alle*g*e, ma*g*ic, lon*g*itude, lon*g*evity, an*g*el, dan*g*er
- gg — as in su*gg*est
- j — as in *j*ade, *j*ar, *J*apan, *j*ail, *j*eer, *j*ealousy, *j*elly, *j*ingle, *j*ockey, *j*ostle, *j*udge, *j*ury

## Exercise 5

*Each of the following words contains the sound of* j. *Insert the missing letter or letters.*

1. alle __ e
2. lon __ evity
3. an __ el
4. __ ostle
5. __ ealousy
6. su __ __ est
7. cor __ __ al
8. sol __ __ er
9. __ ist
10. __ eer

# Silent Letters

In many English words there are silent letters. They are written but not pronounced.

## Letters Which *May* Be Silent

d — as in We*d*nesday

g — as in *g*narled, *g*nash, *g*nat, forei*g*n, rei*g*n, soverei*g*n

h — as in *h*eir, *h*erb, *h*onor, *h*our, shep*h*erd, fore*h*ead

k — as in *k*nee, *k*night, *k*nock, *k*now, *k*nowledge

l — as in a*l*mond, a*l*ms, ca*l*f, ca*l*m, cha*l*k, fo*l*k, ha*l*f, Linco*l*n, psa*l*m, so*l*dier, ta*l*k, wa*l*k, yo*l*k n — as in condem*n*, dam*n*, hym*n*, solem*n*

p — as in cor*p*s, cu*p*board, *p*neumonia, *p*sychology, *p*tomaine, ras*p*berry

t — as in chas*t*en, fas*t*en, glis*t*en, has*t*en, lis*t*en, mois*t*en, of*t*en, sof*t*en, epis*t*le, hus*t*le, jos*t*le, nes*t*le, this*t*le

## Exercise 6

*Replace the silent letter in each of these words:*

1. __ night
2. __ salm
3. epis __ le
4. cor __ s
5. sof __ en
6. We __ nesday
7. __ naw
8. fas __ en

9. rei __ n
10. lis __ en
11. hym __
12. ras __ berry
13. __ onor
14. cu __ board
15. mois __ en

# The -*OUGH* Combination

The -*ough* combination causes everyone difficulty. There are no rules governing the spelling of words containing it. You must memorize each word individually.

Carefully examine the following words and memorize their spelling:

**The -*OUGH* Sound**

| Word | Pronounced Like: |
|---|---|
| although, thorough, thoroughfare | oh |
| through, throughout, slough (a swamp) | you |
| bought, ought, sought | saw |
| tough, slough (to shed or cast off) | cuff |
| cough | awful |
| hiccough | up |
| drought | cow |

## Exercise 7

*Fill in each blank with a word selected from the list above.*

1. He continued to work _____ he wasn't feeling well.
2. The _____ ran _____ the center of the city.
3. The purchaser _____ some _____ medicine in the drugstore.
4. People who are very ill _____ to see a doctor.
5. Hemp is a _____ fiber.
6. A long severe _____ ruined the crops _____ the countryside.
7. Some snakes _____ off their skins annually.
8. A _____ may be embarrassing.

# The *-IGH* and *-EIGH* Combinations

The *-igh* and *-eigh* combinations look frightening but they are really very simple and you can master the spelling of words in which they appear within a few minutes.

The combination *-igh* is always pronounced like the diphthong in Spanish h*ay* and fr*ai*le.

Native Spanish speakers tend to spell *might, sight,* and similar words as *mait* and *sait* in accordance with the Spanish pattern. If you carefully study the following list, which contains the most common *-igh* words, you will not make this mistake.

### Common *IGH* Words

| | |
|---|---|
| blight | night |
| bright | playwright |
| fight | sight |
| flight | slight |
| fright | tight |
| frighten | tighten |
| might | |

The combination *eigh* is pronounced like the diphthong in r*ei*na and l*ey*. There are only two exceptions to this rule, *height* and *sleight,* which are pronounced as if they were spelled *jait* and *slait* in Spanish.

| Notice! |
| --- |

Usually *i* precedes *e* in English (e.g. *grieve, piece*). However, in *eigh*, *e* precedes *i*.

---

## Common *EIGH* Words

| | |
| --- | --- |
| eight | sleigh |
| freight | weigh |
| neigh | weight |
| neighbor | |

---

## ___ Exercise 8 _____

*Fill the blanks with -igh or -eigh*:

1. fr _____ t
2. w _____ t
3. m _____ t
4. n _____ bor
5. sl _____ t

6. t _____ t
7. n _____ t
8. fr _____ t
9. playwr _____ t
10. s _____ t

---

# The *-TION* Ending

Words which end with *-ción* in Spanish (for example, *habitación*) are spelled with *-tion* in English.

The ending *-ción* does not occur in English. Examine the list below:

---

## *-TION* and its Spanish Equivalent

| Spanish | English | Spanish | English |
| --- | --- | --- | --- |
| admiración | admir*ation* | irritación | irrita*tion* |
| atención | atten*tion* | preposición | preposi*tion* |
| atracción | attrac*tion* | producción | produc*tion* |
| construcción | construc*tion* | pronunciación | pronuncia*tion* |
| distinción | distinc*tion* | tentación | tempta*tion* |
| excepción | excep*tion* | tradición | tradi*tion* |

# Words Beginning with *SP-* and *ST-*

Have you noticed that Spanish words beginning with *esp* and *est* drop the initial *e* when they become English? If you are aware of this, you will avoid a common spelling error.

## SP-, ST-, and Its Spanish Equivalents

| Spanish | English |
|---------|---------|
| especial | *sp*ecial |
| espacio | *sp*ace |
| espectáculo | *sp*ectacle |
| espíritu | *sp*irit |
| establo | *st*able |
| estación | *st*ation |
| estado | *st*ate |
| estatua | *st*atue |
| estilo | *st*yle |
| estómago | *st*omach |
| estudio | *st*udy |
| estudiante | *st*udent |

## Exercise 9

*Write the English equivalent of each of the following:*

1. espectaculo       _____
2. atención       _____
3. estatua       _____
4. construcción       _____
5. estudio       _____
6. pronunciación       _____
7. espacio       _____
8. tradición       _____
9. estómago       _____
10. producción       _____

# Special Devices

# The Hyphen

To save time in consulting your dictionary, learn the basics of compound words and word division.

# The Hyphen

English is a language rich in compound words. Sometimes two nouns are combined as in *secretary-treasurer* because the new term combines the functions of both. The hyphen here shows that you are talking about one man or woman. Many compound words are adjectives formed from various parts of speech. For example, to say that a *car is of low price* seems a little archaic. (We might say: *A pearl of great price*.) Hence, we write *low-priced* car.

In describing a suit which you could wear at once after you had bought it, you could write: *a garment that was already made*, or the much shorter, *ready-made* garment.

Many hyphenated words eventually become so familiar, that they are written as one word. Certain magazines like *Time* and *Newsweek*, frequently write as single words those which texts and dictionaries still hyphenate.

# Compound Adjectives

## When to Hyphenate

There are eight types of such hyphenated adjectives.
1. Noun or adjective + participle.

   **EXAMPLES**
   *fire-fighting* apparatus (noun + participle)
   *bad-looking* apples (adjective + participle)

2. Noun + adjective.

   **EXAMPLES**
   *city-wide* campaign
   *lily-white* hands

3. Compound numbers between 21 and 99.

**EXAMPLES**
*twenty-fifth* person
the three hundred and *seventy-fifth* bill

4. Number + nouns.

**EXAMPLES**
the *five-year* plan
*thirty-cent* seats
twelve *two-year* olds

5. Short adverbs (*best, far, ill, long, much, well*) + participle.

**EXAMPLES**
*best-known* author
*far-fetched* theory
*ill-gotten* gains
*long-needed* vacation
*well-looking* person

6. Adjectives of nationality.

**EXAMPLES**
*Franco-Prussian* War
*Anglo-Saxon*
*Anglo-Norman*

7. Two nouns forming an adjective.

**EXAMPLES**
a *father-son* banquet
a *brother-sister* act
a *mother-daughter* outfit

8. Verb plus other elements forming an adjective.

**EXAMPLES**
The *would-be* actor
The *wait-and-see* plan for peace
A *hit-and-run* driver

# When *Not* to Hyphenate

1. When the adjective follows the noun.

   **EXAMPLES**
   *She was an executive well known for her honesty.*
   *He was a man ill fitted for the job.*

2. When two independent adjectives precede the noun and are not combined.

   **EXAMPLES**
   *Napoleon wore his old blue uniform.*
   But: *Napoleon wore his sky-blue uniform* (only one adjective).
   *She carried the tired old dog.*

3. When an adverb modifies an adjective.

   **EXAMPLES**
   *He was a highly paid executive.*
   *This was a nicely kept room.*
   *It was a newly born calf.*

4. When a comparative or superlative form is one of the two modifiers.

   **EXAMPLES**
   *There was no kinder hearted person in the room.*
   *The lowest priced car was the compact.*
   But: *A low-priced car was desired.*

5. When the compound modifier is a proper noun of two words.

   **EXAMPLES**
   *Thomas Mann was a Nobel Prize winner.*
   *He was the South American representative in the Security Council.*

6. When one word in the compound modifier has an apostrophe.

   **EXAMPLES**
   *The first year's harvest was small.*
   *The third century's literature was most religious.*
   *The seventh day's fast was broken.*

## Exercise 1

*Indicate at the right whether the following words are properly hyphenated. Place a C if correct and an X if wrong.*

1. well-fed cattle _____
2. redcheeked youngster _____
3. tenday reducing diet _____
4. a three-month delay _____
5. the twenty-second victim _____
6. badly-lit interior of the hut _____
7. state-wide elections _____
8. redeyed Susan _____
9. a seven-day wonder _____
10. the kind-hearted minister _____
11. hornrimmed spectacles _____
12. the legend of the saber toothed tiger _____
13. This was indeed a well kept garden _____
14. His ill-fated story was common knowledge _____
15. My sister was a red-head _____
16. a first class performance _____
17. the silver plated fork _____
18. the sky-blue water _____
19. England's far-flung empire _____
20. the far-off hills of Dune _____

# Compound Nouns

By using the hyphen with two or more familiar words, new words have been added to our vocabulary.

1. Use the hyphen when two normally distinct functions are united in one person or thing.

   **EXAMPLES**
   *secretary-treasurer* ⎱ *united*
   *fighter-bomber* ⎰ *functions*

However, *do not* hyphenate double terms that represent a single office:

**EXAMPLES**
Major General
Secretary of Defense
General of the Army ⎱ *single*
Lieutenant Commander ⎰ office
General Manager
Executive Secretary

2. Use the hyphen when two nouns form a new noun. Usually the first acts with the force of an adjective.

**EXAMPLES**

*trade-mark*
*light-year*
*foot-pound*

3. Sometimes a noun will be combined with another part of speech to form an entirely new noun.

**EXAMPLES**

*passer-by* (a noun plus a word meaning direction or motion)
*son-in-law*
*jack-in-the-box* (a noun plus a phrase)

4. A verb may be combined with some other part of speech to make a noun.

**EXAMPLES**

A *know-all*
A *do-nothing* ⎱ verb plus object helps
A *cure-all* ⎰ make new nouns
A *know-nothing*

A *count-down* ⎫ verb plus
A *flare-up,*   *play-off* | preposition helps
A *lean-to,*   *drive-in* ⎬ make new
A *go-between,*   *shake-up* | nouns
A *stick-up* ⎭

# Compound Numbers and Fractions

1. Use the hyphen in numbers from twenty-one to ninety-nine.
2. In fractions use the hyphen when the fraction is used as an adjective.

   **EXAMPLES**
   *The three and one-half pounds of butter.*
   *Two and one-eighth quarts of milk.*

---

| Caution! |
| --- |
| **Do not use the hyphen when the fraction is not a single adjective.** |

**EXAMPLES**
The chairman asked *one third* of the group to stay.
He drank *one half* of the cup quickly.

# Compounds with Certain Particles

1. Most compounds with **self-** use the hyphen.

   **EXAMPLES**
   *self-sacrifice*
   *self-interest*
   *self-made* man

---

| Caution! |
| --- |
| **Do *not* hyphenate the reflexives such as *yourself, himself, herself,* or *self* in such adjectives as *selfless, selfsame*.** |

2. The prefix **RE-** takes the hyphen when it means *again*, especially if necessary to prevent confusion.

   **EXAMPLES**
   *re-form* the squad
   *re-enact* the crime
   *re-emerge* from retirement

> ## Note!
>
> • **Note the difference between *reform* the drunkard and *re-form* the broken line of infantry.**
> • **To eliminate the hyphen in *re-enact* and *re-emerge* might lead to mispronunciation or misunderstanding.**

3. Use a hyphen with prefixes ending in the same vowel that begins the next word.

   ### EXAMPLES
   *co-owner*
   *pre-election*

4. Use a hyphen when a prefix is added to a word beginning with a capital letter.

   ### EXAMPLES
   *mid-Atlantic*
   *anti-Russian*
   *pro-British*

5. Use a hyphen with titles which are preceded by *VICE-* or *EX-*, or are followed by *-ELECT*.

   ### EXAMPLES
   *Vice-Admiral*
   *Vice-President*
   *Senator-elect*
   *President-elect*
   *ex-Governor*

# Used for Clarity

Use a hyphen to avoid confusion of meaning. In the following sentence something is wrong.

> Did you ever see a nail polish like this?

Without the hyphen the *nail* appears to be an active agent. With the hyphen the *nail-polish* becomes what it should be.

Here are more boners that result when the hyphen is not used:
1. The master like pose of John. (Sounds like an Oriental valet speaking.)
2. The well kept house. (This must be a very versatile well, what with its job as water-producer, and now as house-cleaner.)

## Words Which Are NEVER Hyphenated

| | |
|---|---|
| airman | nevertheless |
| background | outline |
| downstairs | pastime |
| farewell | railroad |
| headline | semicolon |
| inasmuch | together |
| keyboard | warehouse |
| midday | yourself |

## Words Which Are ALWAYS Hyphenated

| | |
|---|---|
| brother-in-law | son-in-law |
| daughter-in-law | aide-de-camp |
| father-in-law | man-of-war |
| mother-in-law | runner-up |
| sister-in-law | jack-o'-lantern |

# Used to Divide Words

The hyphen has another use at the end of a line in a page of writing. It is inadvisable as a general principle to divide a word at the end of the line; but if it must be done, then a hyphen is placed at the end of the line, in accordance with the rules of syllabication. See our handy "10,000 Word Ready Reference Spelling List" beginning on page 5.

## Words ALWAYS Written Separately

| | | | |
|---|---|---|---|
| all ready | any day | each other | in fact |
| all right | any place | *en route* | in order |
| some way | by and by | every way | in spite |
| some day | by the bye | every time | *pro tempore* |
| some place | by the way | *ex officio* | no one |

---

**Caution!**

    Do not confuse *already*, an adverb expressing time, with *all ready*, an adjective meaning fully prepared.

---

### EXAMPLES
The members of the team were *all ready* to go.
He had *already* left.

## Exercise 2

*Spell the following words correctly by inserting the hyphen where it belongs. If the word is correctly spelled, write C in the space to the right.*

1. sisterinlaw      _____
2. man of war      _____
3. aidedecamp      _____
4. runon sentence      _____
5. down-stairs      _____
6. anti American activities      _____
7. ex-husband      _____
8. re-emerge      _____
9. self-centered child      _____
10. one quarter of the population      _____
11. runnerup      _____
12. drivein theatre      _____
13. secretary-treasurer      _____
14. Lieutenant General      _____
15. tradein      _____
16. fire-fighting engine      _____
17. pro-European policy      _____
18. builtin arch      _____
19. The final play-off      _____
20. broken-down houses      _____

# 16

# The Apostrophe

**This little mark of punctuation can show possession and the omission of a letter.**

**An understanding of it is essential.**

# The Apostrophe

## To Show Contraction

1. Use the apostrophe to indicate a lost vowel.

   **EXAMPLES**
   do n*ot* = don't
   can n*ot* = can't
   could n*ot* = couldn't
   you *a*re = you're
   they *a*re = they're

## To Show Possession

### To Show Possession: Common Nouns

1. Most frequently the apostrophe is used to show possession. A *singular noun* not ending in -*s* adds *'s*.

   **EXAMPLES**
   The hat of the girl = the girl's hat
   The rights of the man = the man's rights

2. Add *'s* to a *singular noun* which ends in -*s* or an s-sound if a new syllable is formed by pronouncing the possessive.

   **EXAMPLES**
   The hair of the actress = the actress's hair
   The daughter of the boss = the boss's daughter

**219**

3. To show possession with a *plural noun*, add *'s* if the noun does not end in *s*.

EXAMPLES
men's hosiery
women's hats
children's shoes

4. If the *plural noun* ends in -*s* (as most nouns do), add only the apostrophe.

EXAMPLES
the doctors' fees
the dentists' conference
the teachers' demands

## To Show Possession: Proper Nouns

1. To show possession of a *singular proper noun* not ending in -*s*, add *'s*.

EXAMPLES
Mr. Mann's library
Miss Smith's dog
Dr. Levitt's office

2. When the *proper noun* ends in -*s* and has only one syllable, add *'s*.

EXAMPLES
Alger Hiss's case
Rudolf Hess's escape

3. When the *proper noun* ending in -*s* has two or more syllables, add only the apostrophe.

EXAMPLES
Mr. Dickens' readings
Roger Williams' expulsion

## To Show Possession: Compound Nouns

1. The apostrophe is used only after the last noun in the compound.

EXAMPLES
my mother-in-law's house
the man-of-war's deck

## To Show Possession: Indefinite Pronouns

1. Use the same rules for indefinite pronouns as those above for common nouns.

   **EXAMPLES**
   One's honor is at stake. (*singular*)
   The others' hats were soiled while ours were clean. (*plural*)

## To Show Possession: Personal Pronouns

1. Personal pronouns *never* use the apostrophe for their possessive case.

   **EXAMPLE**
   his, hers, its, ours, theirs

2. Be especially careful with *whose*. What is the difference between:

   > Whose house is this?
   > *and*
   > Who's there?

# To Avoid Repetition of *S* Sound

1. To avoid the repetition of the *s*-sound, just add the apostrophe.

   **EXAMPLE**
   for mildness' sake

# To Indicate Double Ownership

1. When you wish to indicate *ownership by two or more* persons, use the apostrophe *only* for the last.

   **EXAMPLES**
   Lewis and Clark's Expedition
   Jim and Joe's locker
   Smith, Kline and French's drugs

2. If you are talking about *separate ownership*, use the apostrophe after each noun.

**EXAMPLE**

The President's and Secretary of State's reports
This means there were two reports, one by each officer.

---

| Remember! |
|---|
| **The apostrophe means "belonging to whatever immediately precedes it,"** *except* **when it is used to indicate a lost vowel.** |

**EXAMPLES**

children's—belonging to children
    men's—belonging to men
        boss's—belonging to a single boss
        bosses'—belonging to more than one boss

## Exercise

*Rewrite the following phrases in such a way as to use the apostrophe in showing possession:*

1. The hat of the young girl

    _____

2. The votes of the men

    _____

3. The styles of the ladies

    _____

4. The paws of the cats

    _____

5. The decorations of the sailors

    _____

6. The hat of the professor

    _____

7. A shoe of a woman

    _____

8. The voice of the soprano

    _____

9. The tail of the dog

    _____

*Add the apostrophe in the following sentences to show omission of a letter.*

10. They do not vote often.  _____
11. We have not any money.  _____
12. The allies could not agree on the campaign.  _____
13. You are always late.  _____
14. They can not always win.  _____
15. It is too late to go now.  _____
16. Let us wait a little longer.  _____
17. We would not have acted so if we were not hungry.  _____

# Capital Letters

**These grammatical signposts can be crucial to the meaning of your sentences.**

# Capital Letters

## Basic Principles

### What to Begin with a Capital Letter

1. The first word of a sentence.
2. The first word of a quoted sentence.
3. The first word of a line of poetry.
4. The first word, and important words, in titles of books or themes.
5. Proper nouns.
6. The pronoun *I*.

## Proper Nouns

**When to Capitalize**

| |
|---|
| *Proper Names* |
| Sioux City |
| Eastern District High School |
| State Legislature |
| United Nations |
| *Definite place names* |
| the North vs. the South |
| *Family relationships* |
| Aunt |
| Mother |
| *Substitute for person's name* (*especially in direct address*) |
| "Hurry up, Aunt!" |
| "Yes, Mother, I'm hurrying!" |
| *Definite events* |
| May Day |
| War of 1870 |

### Races, Languages

| | |
|---|---|
| German | Caucasian |
| Hindu | Mongolian |
| French | |

### Titles

Uncle Don

Dr. Jones

### Organization Names

The Odd Fellows (club)

Bethlehem Steel Corporation

Methodist Episcopal Church

The Farmer-Labor Party

### Deity (and words associated with Deity)

God

Christ

St. John

Scriptures

### Trade names

Arrow shirt

Revlon's lotion

---

| Note! |
|---|
| **Capitalize only the part of the *trade name* that differentiates it from all other brands.** |

---

## When NOT to Capitalize

### Words that are not a specific name

our high school

the cold stream

### Point of the compass

four degrees north

### The names of the seasons

| | |
|---|---|
| spring | autumn |
| summer | winter |

### Studies other than languages

chemistry

biology

### A title after a modifier

my uncle

a doctor

I have two brothers

my cousins arrived

# Books, Plays, Music

| |
|---|
| **Remember This Rule in Capitalizing a Title!** |

**Don't cap the "CAPS." The last "CAP" stands for**
**C—conjunctions (and, but, or, for, nor)**
**A—articles (the, a, an)**
**P—prepositions (of, to, for, from)**

## EXAMPLES

*Book:*      *Rose of the Rancho*
*Play:*      "The Way of the World"
             "Right You Are if You Think You Are"
*Music:*     "To a Wild Rose"
             "Pie in the Sky"

## Exercise

*Try your hand at capitalizing the words that need capitals.*

1. We stopped at the hotel westover.
2. The buick cars are well advertised.
3. We celebrate decoration day.
4. the north side high school
5. We saw mutiny on the bounty.
6. They sang old french folk songs.
7. In english courts the bible is kissed.
8. Harriet Beecher Stowe's uncle Tom is known wherever the book is read.
9. They walked along fifth avenue.
10. Many people ask for washington coffee.
11. Our vacation to britain lasted six weeks.
12. Bard college is in new york.
13. the taming of the shrew is a play written by shakespeare.
14. My courses in college include mathematics, english, and three years of french.
15. Last spring we visited aunt emily who lives out west.

# Spelling Abbreviations

*F.O.B.*   *Esq.*   *R.F.D.*
*E.S.T.*   *Hon.*   *WY*

**Some basics to know when dealing with the business world.**

# Spelling Abbreviations

## The Calendar

### Day, Month, Time

**Days of the Week**

| Abbreviation | Weekday |
|---|---|
| Sun. | Sunday |
| Mon. | Monday |
| Tues. | Tuesday |
| Wed. | Wednesday |
| Thurs. | Thursday |
| Fri. | Friday |
| Sat. | Saturday |

**Months of the Year**

| Abbreviation | Month |
|---|---|
| Jan. | January |
| Feb. | February |
| Mar. | March |
| Apr. | April |
| Aug. | August |
| Sept. | September |
| Oct. | October |
| Nov. | November |
| Dec. | December |

## Time

| Abbreviation | Time |
| --- | --- |
| A.D. | anno Domini (Latin for ''In the year of the Lord'') |
| B.C. | before Christ |
| | |
| A.M. | ante meridiem (Latin for ''before noon'') |
| P.M. | post meridiem (Latin for ''after noon'') |
| | |
| E.S.T. | Eastern Standard Time |

# Business and Postal Terms

## Business Terms

**Business Terms**

| Abbreviation | Term |
| --- | --- |
| acct. | account |
| ad | advertisement |
| ans. | answer |
| assn. | association |
| Ave. | avenue |
| bldg. | building |
| Blvd. | boulevard |
| bros. | brothers |
| C.O.D. | collect on delivery |
| dept. | department |
| Esq. | esquire |
| etc. | and so forth |
| F.O.B. | freight on board |
| Inc. | incorporated |
| Jr. | junior |
| Ltd. | limited |
| mfg. | manufacturing |
| Mts. | mountains |
| no. | number |
| P.O. | post office |
| P.S. | postscript (written after the letter) |
| recd. | received |

| Abbreviation | Term |
|---|---|
| R.F.D. | rural free delivery |
| R.R. | railroad |
| R.S.V.P. | reply, if you please (French: répondez s'il vous plâit) |
| Sr. | senior |
| SS | steamship |
| St. | street |
| ult. | last month |

# Postal Terms

When the postal authorities introduced Zip codes some years ago, they drew up a new list of state abbreviations. Each abbreviation consists of two capital letters.

## State Abbreviations

| Abbreviation | State | Abbreviation | State |
|---|---|---|---|
| AL | Alabama | MT | Montana |
| AK | Alaska | NE | Nebraska |
| AZ | Arizona | NV | Nevada |
| AR | Arkansas | NH | New Hampshire |
| CA | California | NJ | New Jersey |
| CO | Colorado | NM | New Mexico |
| CT | Connecticut | NY | New York |
| DE | Delaware | NC | North Carolina |
| DC | District of Columbia | ND | North Dakota |
| FL | Florida | OH | Ohio |
| GA | Georgia | OK | Oklahoma |
| HI | Hawaii | OR | Oregon |
| ID | Idaho | PA | Pennsylvania |
| IL | Illinois | PR | Puerto Rico |
| IN | Indiana | RI | Rhode Island |
| IA | Iowa | SC | South Carolina |
| KS | Kansas | SD | South Dakota |
| KY | Kentucky | TN | Tennessee |
| LA | Louisiana | TX | Texas |
| ME | Maine | UT | Utah |
| MD | Maryland | VT | Vermont |
| MA | Massachusetts | VA | Virginia |
| MI | Michigan | WA | Washington |
| MN | Minnesota | WV | West Virginia |
| MS | Mississippi | WI | Wisconsin |
| MO | Missouri | WY | Wyoming |

# Personal Titles

## Titles

| Abbreviation | Title |
|---|---|
| Asst. | Assistant |
| Capt. | Captain |
| Com. | commander |
| | commissioner |
| | commission |
| | committee |
| D.D.S. | Doctor of Dental Surgery |
| Dr. | Doctor |
| Gov. | Governor |
| Hon. | Honorable |
| Lt. | Lieutenant |
| M.D. | Doctor of Medicine |
| Messrs. | Messieurs |
| Mr. | Mister |
| Mrs. | Mistress |
| Ms. | Miss, Mrs. |
| Ph.D. | Doctor of Philosophy |
| Pres. | President |
| Prof. | Professor |
| Rev. | Reverend |
| R.N. | Registered Nurse |
| Supt. | Superintendent |
| Sec. or Secy. | Secretary |
| Treas. | Treasurer |

# Measurement Terms

## Standard Measurement

| Abbreviation | Term | Abbreviation | Term |
|---|---|---|---|
| in. | inch | bu. | bushel |
| ft. | foot | doz. | dozen |
| yd. | yard | | |
| | | hr. | hour |
| oz. | ounce | yr. | year |
| lb. | pound | | |

## Metric Measurement

| Abbreviation | Term |
|---|---|
| l. | liter |
| mg. | milligram |
| kg. | kilogram |
| | |
| cm. | centimeter |
| mm. | millimeter |
| km. | kilometer |

## Exercise 1

*In the space to the right, put the correct spelling of the abbreviations of the following words:*

1. Secretary  _____
2. Treasurer  _____
3. Collect on Delivery  _____
4. Before noon  _____
5. Junior  _____
6. dozen  _____
7. August  _____
8. Doctor of Medicine  _____
9. Honorable  _____
10. year  _____
11. Saturday  _____
12. Rural Free Delivery  _____
13. Reply if you please  _____
14. Esquire  _____
15. Department  _____
16. pound  _____
17. Messieurs  _____
18. Dentist  _____
19. Reverend  _____
20. Boulevard  _____

## Exercise 2

*Write the words for which the following abbreviations are given:*

1. Ph.D. _____
2. Ave. _____
3. in. _____
4. etc. _____
5. no. _____
6. Bros. _____
7. P.S. _____
8. R.R. _____
9. Sept. _____
10. F.O.B. _____
11. Prof. _____
12. Asst. _____
13. E.S.T. _____
14. Gov. _____
15. B.C. _____
16. A.D. _____
17. SS _____
18. St. _____
19. recd. _____
20. dept. _____
21. M.D. _____
22. Treas. _____
23. Sat. _____
24. Hon. _____
25. Rev. _____
26. Sec. _____
27. D.D.S. _____
28. Capt. _____
29. Mar. _____
30. P.M. _____

# Troublesome Words

# Homonyms and Homophones

**A careful review of these troublemakers can easily clear up some basic usage problems.**

# Homonyms
# and
# Homophones

Earlier in this book we pointed out the necessity of listening carefully. Careless listening may give you a wrong mental picture of a word and thus you take the first step toward misspelling it.

There are many words that are pronounced and spelled alike but differ in meaning. They are called HOMONYMS. *Quail*, meaning a bird, and *quail*, meaning to recoil in dread, are homonyms.

There are hundreds of other words which are pronounced alike but differ in spelling, derivation, and meaning. They are called HOMOPHONES. *Altar/alter*, *chord/cord*, and *minor/miner* are homophones.

In the following list, most of the confusing pairs that cause spelling difficulties are defined and illustrated in sentences. Spelling exercises appear at intervals.

## Homonyms and Homophones

**aisle,** n.     a narrow passage.
         The bridal couple walked down the **aisle.**

**isle,** n.     an island.
         Poets sometimes write about the Golden **Isles.**

**already,** adv.     earlier.
         We had **already** eaten our lunch.

    *Key*
     n. = noun
     v. = verb
   adj. = adjective
   pp. = past participle
  adv. = adverb
  pro. = pronoun
prep. = preposition

**all ready,** adj.     all are ready.
>  Mother called the chauffeur when we were **all ready.**

**altar,** n.     a tablelike structure used for religious purposes in a church or out of doors.
>  The bridal couple came toward the **altar.**

**alter,** v.     to make a change.
>  Plastic surgeons can **alter** features.

**altogether,** adv.     entirely.
>  I **altogether** disapprove of such behavior in children.

**all together,** adj.     all in one place.
>  The prisoners were placed **all together** in one room.

**berth,** n.     a place to sleep.
>  We ordered a **berth** on the train.

**birth,** n.     act of being born.
>  The **birth** of the prince caused much joy.

**born,** pp.     that which has been given birth.
>  The baby was **born** at dawn.

**borne,** pp.     carried.
>  The countess was **borne** in her sedan chair.

**brake,** n.     an instrument to stop something.
>  Because the **brake** was broken, the car rushed downhill.

**break,** v.     to smash, cause to fall apart.
>  Be careful not to **break** these rare glasses.

**bridal,** adj.     pertaining to a wedding.
>  The **bridal** gown was of taffeta.

**bridle,** n.     part of a harness.
>  The horse pulled at his **bridle.**

**bridle,** v.     to restrain.
>  Some gossips need to **bridle** their tongues.

**canvas,** n.     a kind of rough cloth.
>  The sailor's duffel bag was of **canvas.**

**canvass,** v.     to solicit.
>  Election workers went out to **canvass** the neighborhood.

**capital,** n.     a major city of a state or nation; also, something of extreme importance; also, stock of wealth.
>  Albany is the **capital** of New York.
>  Kidnapping in some states is a **capital** offense.
>  Liberia welcomes foreign **capital.**

**capitol,** n.     a building.

> In Washington the **capitol** is popular with visitors.

**censer,** n.     a religious article.

> The acolyte slowly swung the **censer.**

**censor,** n.     one who examines for possible evil.

> The British **censor** examines the script of every new play.

**censor,** v.     to act as a censor.

> Authors do not wish anyone to **censor** their books.

**chord,** n.     a pleasant combination of tones.

> The pianist electrified his audience with his opening **chords.**

**cord,** n.     a rope.

> Can you get me some **cord** to tie these books?

**cord,** n.     a unit to measure fuel wood.

> He chopped three **cords** of wood today.

## Exercise 1

*Select the correct word in parentheses, and underline:*

1. This story cannot (alter, altar) the situation.
2. Some experts think that cargo will soon be (born, borne) in submarines.
3. If you put your foot on the (break, brake) you will stop the car.
4. Many sincere people oppose (capital, capitol) punishment.
5. The center (aisle, isle) of the church was very wide.
6. When the search party arrived, the fire had (all ready, already) died out.
7. John soon learned that his answers on the examination were (all right, alright).
8. The town drunk was (altogether, all together) beyond help from any social agency.
9. When the attack was sounded, the marines were (all ready, already).
10. Many families have not had to touch their (capitol, capital) for a long time.

**coarse,** adj.     vulgar.

> Such **coarse** language cannot be permitted.

**course,** n.     a way to be followed.

> In this emergency, only one **course** was indicated.
> John took the academic **course** in high school.

**complement,** n. or v.     something that completes another.
> The fresh **complement** of soldiers saved the day.

**compliment,** n., v.     something said in praise.
> This was the greatest **compliment** he could have paid.
> The President **complimented** the commander of the submarine for his good work.

**council,** n.     a deliberative body.
> The city **council** was called into special session.

**counsel,** n.     advice; also an attorney.
> My **counsel** in this case is to avoid temperature extremes.
> The defendant's **counsel** made a stirring plea.

**councilor,** n.     one who is a member of a council.
> The newly elected **councilor** was given an ovation.

**counselor,** n.     an advisor, usually legal.
> In America we use the expression **counselor** whereas in Britain it is solicitor or barrister.

**core,** n.     a center of fruit.
> The **core** of my apple was rotten.

**corps,** n.     a unit of people.
> General Smith commanded the Second Army **Corps.**

**descent,** n.     a going down.
> Poe's "**Descent** into a Maelstrom" is still exciting to read.

**dissent,** n.     a disagreement.
> Justice Holmes' **dissents** were famous.

**desert,** v.     to leave behind.
> It is a terrible crime to **desert** one's child.

**dessert,** n.     the fruit or ice-cream course at the end of a meal.
> We had sliced peaches for **dessert.**

**dual,** adj.     double.
> Dr. Jekyll and Mr. Hyde were the **dual** personalities of one man.

**duel,** n.     combat of two men.
> Hamilton was killed in the **duel** with Burr.

**instance,** n.     example.
> The lawyer gave **instance** after **instance** of good behavior.

**instants,** n.     plural, meaning moments.
> Pain was stopped for several **instants** before the operation was continued.

**its,** pro.     The possessive case of it.
> The baby played with **its** finger.

**it's,**     abbreviated form of **it is.**
> **It's** too late to go to any restaurant now.

**led,** v.    the past tense of **lead.**

    The colonel **led** his men to safety.

**lead,** n.    (lĕd) a metal.

    Plumbers make use of **lead** frequently.

---

## Exercise 2

*Select the correct word in parentheses, and underline.*

1. England called its Privy (Council, Counsel) into session.
2. It takes an angle of 40° to (compliment, complement) an angle of 50° to make a right angle.
3. To get out of the swamp, there was only one (course, coarse) to follow.
4. The (desert, dessert) at the end of the banquet was delicious.
5. (It's, Its) amazing how much you can get in a library.
6. The legislature passed the bill without any (dissent, descent).
7. After many skirmishes the captain (lead, led) his company to victory.
8. The witness refused to answer any question without advice from his (counsel, council).
9. Joseph ate his apple down to the (corps, core).
10. The judge said that he had a (dual, duel) responsibility.

---

**miner,** n.    one who extracts minerals from the earth.

    Mark Twain frequently wrote about **miners** in the Old West.

**minor,** adj., n.    unimportant; below legal age.

    This injury to the skin was a **minor** one.

    Alcoholic beverages may not be sold to **minors.**

**peace,** n.    a state of quiet; freedom from war.

    The U.N. tries hard to keep the **peace.**

**piece,** n.    a portion.

    A **piece** of pie costs fifty cents here.

**plain,** adj., n.    *as an adjective,* simple, unadorned.

    In this small town we live in **plain** houses.

    *As a noun,* a flat area of land.

    Many pioneers perished while crossing this **plain.**

**plane,** n.    an airplane; a tool; a flat surface.

    The **plane** made a forced landing.

    To smooth the surface, the carpenter used a new type of **plane.**

    In high school **plane** geometry usually precedes solid geometry.

**principal,** adj., n.     *as an adjective,* main, important.
These were the **principal** points in Nixon's speech.
*As a noun,* the head official in a school.
A **principal** in a modern high school must be a good administrator.

**principle,** n.     a statement of a rule in conduct or in science or mathematics.
Archimedes discovered the **principle** of buoyancy in liquids.
A candidate for high office must be a man of **principle.**

**stationary,** adj.     fixed, attached.
The old-fashioned schoolroom had **stationary** desks and chairs.

**stationery,** n.     paper used in correspondence.
Hammerhill is making a new kind of typewriter **stationery.**

**there,** adv.     an adverb of place.
He placed the package **there.**

**their,** pro.     a possessive pronoun.
The soldiers opened **their** kits.

**they're** pro. + v.     contraction of they are.
"**They're** here," the colonel shouted.

**to,** prep.     *preposition with a verb to make an infinitive.*
**To** err is human; **to** forgive, divine.
*Preposition with noun or pronoun.*
Please take this book **to** him.
Deliver this package **to** mother.

**too,** adv.     also, more than enough.
Father arrived late for the ceremony **too.**
Such bad behavior in class was **too** much for the teacher.

**two,**     numeral, the number 2.
He received **two** dollars an hour.

**waist,** n.     middle section of the body; a garment.
Every woman admires a narrow **waist.**
Her **waist** was made of lace.

**waste,** v., n.     to squander material which is squandered.
To **waste** food is almost a crime when so many starve.
Many manufacturers dispose of their industrial **wastes** through incineration.

**who's,** personal pro.     a contraction of who is.
"**Who's** there?" she asked.

**whose,**     possessive of who.
We should like to know **whose** coat this is.

**your,**     possessive of you.
This is **your** hat.

**you're,**     a contraction of you are.
"**You're** elected," the chairman shouted.

## Exercise 3

*Select the correct word in parentheses, and underline.*

1. An appendectomy can hardly be considered (minor, miner) surgery.
2. He was a great admirer of (peace, piece) by friendly negotiation.
3. Because of motor difficulties the (plane, plain) had to make a forced landing on the (plane, plain).
4. The (principle, principal) causes of World War II are not easy to state.
5. The young girl placed the belt around her (waste, waist).
6. The sailors threw (their, there) caps into the air.
7. This insolence was (to, too, two) much to bear.
8. It is not necessary to use expensive (stationery, stationary) on minor occasions.
9. We could never discover (whose, who's) book it was.
10. "(They're, their) here," exclaimed the teacher.

# Other Confusing Words

There are many other word pairs that are often confused because they sound almost alike, as *illusion* and *allusion*. Strictly speaking, such pairs are not homonyms or homophones. However, they cause spelling difficulties and for that reason are listed and defined below. So, too, are words that resemble one another so closely in spelling that they are a frequent source of trouble, as *moral* and *morale*, and *dairy* and *diary*.

**advice,** n. counsel.
> We asked the teacher for **advice.**

**advise,** v. to give counsel.
> Our parents are ready to **advise** us.

**ally,** v. to join with.
> England can usually be expected to **ally** herself with the United States.

**ally,** n. one who joins with another.
> France was our **ally** in World War II.

**alley,** n. a narrow thoroughfare.
> The cat disappeared down the **alley.**

**allusion,** n. a reference to.
> The judge made an **allusion** to an old ruling.

**illusion,** n. a deception.
> Some people suffer from **illusions.**

**angel,** n.    a supernatural being.
   Disputes about **angels** are found in medieval thought.

**angle,** n.    corner; point of view.
   Advertisers are always looking for a new **angle.**

**beside,** prep.    by the side of.
   The bride stood **beside** her husband.

**besides,** adv.    in addition to.
   **Besides** a bonus, he received a raise.

**breath,** n.    an exhalation.
   The **breath** froze in the cold air.

**breathe,** v.    to take in or let out breath.
   The doctor asked the patient to **breathe** in deeply.

**cloths,** n.    bits of cloth.
   Try using new wash **cloths.**

**clothes,** n.    covering for the human body.
   Beau Brummel's **clothes** were the talk of London.

**consul,** n.    an official in one country representing another.
   The Russian **consul** in the United States represents his country's interests.

**counsel,** n.    an attorney.
   The **counsel** for the defense entered a plea of guilty.

**credible,** adj.    believable.
   The witness made her story **credible.**

**creditable,** adj.    praiseworthy.
   The soldier's action was **creditable.**

**device,** n.    a contrivance.
   The inventor showed his new **device** for producing electricity.

**devise,** v.    to make a contrivance.
   The inventor **devised** a new means of producing electricity.

**emigrant,** n.    one who leaves a country for another.
   America welcomes **emigrants** of good character from many lands.

**immigrant,** n.    one who comes to another country after leaving his own.
   Forty million **immigrants** brought many resources to America.

**formally,** adv.    done in a formal or regular manner.
   The bridegroom was dressed **formally.**

**formerly,** adv.    earlier.
   **Formerly,** soldiers had to wait a long time for promotion.

**ingenious,** adj.    clever, tricky.
   The device for operating the ship was **ingenious.**

**ingenuous,** adj.     open, frank, innocent.
> The **ingenuous** countenance of the pretty witness won over the jury.

**later,** adv.     comparative degree of late.
> It's **later** than you think.

**latter,** adj.     of two things, the one mentioned second.
> Of the two desserts, ice-cream or sherbet, I chose the **latter.**

## Exercise 4

*Select the correct word in parentheses, and underline.*

1. He likes to wear brightly colored (clothes, cloths).
2. This development in art comes in a (later, latter) period in history.
3. Refugees in Hong Kong rushed to the American (consul, counsel) for safety.
4. Before signing this contract, you should get legal (advice, advise).
5. He placed the boxes (beside, besides) the wall.
6. During the early part of this century, many (immigrants, emigrants) from England went to Australia.
7. All those who attended the banquet were (formerly, formally) attired.
8. The young child had an (ingenious, ingenuous) countenance.
9. During the last war, the United States was an (ally, alley) of England.
10. The orator's speech was full of literary (illusions, allusions).

**loose,** adj.     free, unattached.
> The screw was **loose.**

**lose,** v.     to miss from one's possession.
> I would not like to **lose** any more money at the races.

**moral,** adj., n.     pertaining to the good and proper.
> Man lives by **moral** law as well as man-made law.

**morale,** n.     state of well-being of a person or group.
> The **morale** of our troops in the Middle East was high.

**personal,** adj.     pertaining to a person or individual.
> Our quarrel in the office was not due to a business but to a **personal** argument.

**personnel,** n.     the body of persons employed in some service.
> Because he had a deep understanding of people, he was appointed **personnel** manager.

**quiet,** adj.     free from noise.
> In hospital areas, **quiet** must be preserved.

**quite,** adj.    entirely, completely.
      The patient was **quite** conscious throughout the operation.

**than,**    a conjunction.
      Gold is heavier **than** silver.

**then,** adv.    an adverb of time.
      We shall await you **then.**

## Exercise 5

*Select the correct word in parentheses, and underline.*

1. Good food cannot always contribute to high (moral, morale) in the army.
2. Such demands are (quiet, quite) impossible to meet.
3. Problems of (personal, personnel) always arise where there are many employees.
4. The (loose, lose) stone caused the scout to slip.
5. Love is more powerful (then, than) hate.
6. I was (formally, formerly) dressed for the occasion.
7. Where did you (lose, loose) the money?
8. Every fable has a (moral, morale).
9. The tree-shaded street was (quite, quiet) deserted.
10. Rather (than, then) take a risk, he put his money in a bank.

# Exercises in Word Building

**Being familiar with common language families can save you a great deal of time.**

# Exercises in Word Building

Almost every one of us at least once in his life has wanted to strangle his neighbor's daughter for playing her scale exercises on the piano. The monotony of the same arrangement of notes hour after hour is almost beyond human endurance. Without these scales, however, no virtuoso would ever develop. Spelling, too, has its scales and exercises. They may seem just as boring as the musical exercises, but they are similarly valuable.

Study the following word families. Sometimes you will forget the spelling of one of these words. If you can remember its brother or sister, you will not have to consult the dictionary. A little time spent with these now will mean much time saved later.

## Word Families

### Words and Variations

| Word | | Related Words | |
|---|---|---|---|
| abolish | abolished | abolishing | abolition |
| accomplish | accomplished | accomplishing | accomplishment |
| account | accounted | accounting | accountant |
| acknowledge | acknowledged | acknowledging | acknowledgment |
| advise | advised | advising | adviser (or advisor) |
| allude | alluded | alluding | allusion |
| almost | always | already | altogether |
| appear | appeared | appearing | appearance |
| arrange | arranged | arranging | arrangement |
| arrive | arrived | arriving | arrival |
| assist | assisted | assisting | assistance |

| Word | Related Words | | |
|---|---|---|---|
| **begin** | beg*an* | begin*ning* | beginn*er* |
| **believe** | believ*ed* | believ*ing* | believ*er* |
| **busy** | bus*ied* | busy*ing* | bus*iness* |
| | | | |
| **change** | chang*ed* | chang*ing* | change*able* |
| **choose** | cho*se* | choos*ing* | cho*sen* |
| **complete** | complet*ed* | complet*ely* | comple*tion* |
| **confide** | confid*ent* | confid*ence* | confid*entially* |
| **conscience** | conscien*tious* | *sub*conscious | *un*conscious |
| **consider** | consider*ed* | consider*able* | consider*ation* |
| **continue** | continu*ed* | continu*ation* | continu*ally* |
| **control** | control*ling* | control*ler* | control*lable* |
| **critic** | critic*al* | critic*ize* | critic*ism* |
| | | | |
| **deceive** | deceit | dece*ption* | deceiv*er* |
| **decide** | decid*ed* | deci*sion* | decid*ing* |
| **define** | defin*ite* | defin*ition* | defin*itely* |
| **describe** | descri*ptive* | describ*ing* | descri*ption* |
| **desire** | desir*ous* | desir*ing* | desir*able* |
| | | | |
| **embarrass** | embarrass*ed* | embarrass*ing* | embarrass*ment* |
| **endure** | endur*ed* | endur*able* | endur*ance* |
| **equip** | equip*ped* | equip*ping* | equip*ment* |
| **every** | every*body* | every*where* | every*one* |
| **exceed** | exceed*ed* | exceed*ing* | exceed*ingly* |
| **excel** | excel*led* | excel*lent* | excel*lence* |
| **excite** | excit*ing* | excite*ment* | excit*able* |
| **exist** | exist*ed* | exist*ing* | exist*ence* |
| **experience** | experienc*ed* | experienc*ing* | experi*ment* |
| **extend** | extend*ed* | exten*sive* | exten*sion* |
| | | | |
| **impress** | impress*ed* | impress*ive* | impres*sion* |
| **intend** | intend*ed* | inten*sive* | inten*sion* |
| **interfere** | interfer*ed* | interfer*ing* | interfer*ence* |
| **interrupt** | interrupt*ed* | interrupt*ing* | interrup*tion* |
| | | | |
| **obey** | obe*dient* | obe*dience* | obe*isance* |
| **occasion** | occasion*ed* | occasion*al* | occasion*ally* |

| Word | | Related Words | |
|---|---|---|---|
| **peace** | peace*ful* | peace*able* | peace*ably* |
| **permit** | permit*ted* | permi*ssible* | permi*ssion* |
| **persist** | persist*ed* | persist*ent* | persist*ence* |
| **pity** | pit*ied* | pity*ing* | pit*iable* |
| **possess** | possess*ed* | possess*ive* | possess*ion* |
| **practice** | practic*al* | practic*ed* | practic*able* |
| **prefer** | prefer*red* | prefer*ring* | prefer*ence* |
| **recognize** | recogniz*ed* | recogni*tion* | recogniz*able* |
| **separate** | separat*ion* | *in*separ*able* | separat*ely* |
| **sincere** | sincer*ity* | *in*sincere | sincer*ely* |
| **surprise** | surpris*ed* | surpris*ingly* | surpris*ing* |

## Exercise

*Indicate by the letter* C *if the following words are correctly spelled. Correct all errors in the space to the right.*

1. arranger _____
2. choosers _____
3. difinative _____
4. preferential _____
5. inseparable _____
6. hypocritical _____
7. undefineable _____
8. undesireable _____
9. pityless _____
10. unaccountable _____
11. unchangeable _____
12. incompletely _____
13. disarrange _____
14. confiding _____
15. confidential _____
16. indecisive _____
17. non-existant _____
18. preferrable _____
19. experiential _____
20. unendureable _____

21. necessarly _____
22. transferred _____
23. cancel _____
24. changable _____
25. judgement _____
26. accomadate _____
27. gaurantee _____
28. reciepts _____
29. secretary _____
30. business _____
31. choosen _____
32. posessed _____
33. reconized _____
34. sincereity _____
35. existance _____
36. embarassed _____
37. excellent _____
38. exciteable _____
39. prefered _____
40. ocassion _____

# Words Most Frequently Misspelled

**Match your skills on commonly misspelled words.**

# Words Most Frequently Misspelled

## The One Hundred Pests

### The 100 Pests

| | | | | |
|---|---|---|---|---|
| ache | dear | instead | raise | too |
| again | doctor | | read | trouble |
| always | does | just | ready | truly |
| among | done | | | Tuesday |
| answer | don't | knew | said | two |
| any | | know | says | |
| | early | | seems | used |
| been | easy | | separate | |
| beginning | enough | laid | shoes | |
| believe | every | loose | since | very |
| blue | | lose | some | |
| break | February | | | wear |
| built | forty | making | straight | Wednesday |
| business | friend | many | sugar | week |
| busy | | meant | sure | where |
| buy | grammar | minute | | whether |
| | guess | much | | which |
| | | | tear | |
| can't | half | | their | whole |
| choose | having | none | there | women |
| color | hear | | they | won't |
| coming | heard | often | though | would |
| cough | here | once | through | write |
| could | hoarse | | tired | writing |
| country | hour | piece | tonight | wrote |

251

# Business Terms

The 500 words which follow are those which are most commonly misspelled in business correspondence. If you want to improve your business effectiveness, study these words closely until you can spell every one correctly.

The list was compiled by the National Office Management Association after a comprehensive study of 10,652 letters collected from business concerns and government agencies located throughout the country.

The words are not strange or unusual. They appear frequently in business letters. Many of them appear on other pages of this book. Mastery of this list will insure you against the spelling mistakes committed by many business men and women.

## Commonly Misspelled Business Terms

| A | aluminum | attractive |
|---|---|---|
| accept | analysis | auditor |
| accommodate | analyze | available |
| accountant | anniversary | aviation |
| accumulate | announcement | |
| acknowledgment | anthracite | |
| acquainted | anticipating | |
| acquire | anxiety | **B** |
| acquisition | apology | baggage |
| acquitted | apparatus | balance |
| actually | appearance | bankruptcy |
| additionally | applicant | banquet |
| address | appraisal | barrel |
| adjustable | appropriation | barter |
| administration | approval | becoming |
| advances | argument | beneficiary |
| advertisement | arrears | benefited |
| advisability | arrival | biased |
| advise | articles | bituminous |
| affects | assessable | bookkeeping |
| affidavit | assignment | borrower |
| affirmative | assistance | brief |
| agency | associate | broadcast |
| aggravate | assured | brokerage |
| allotment | attached | budget |
| allowance | attorney | bulletin |
| all right | attempt | bureau |
| alphabetic | attendance | business |

## C

calculator
calendar
campaign
canceled
candidate
capacity
capitalization
carbon
carrier
cartage
carton
certificate
chattel
circular
clearance
coincidence
collapsible
collateral
collision
column
combination
combustible
commerce
commission
committee
commodity
community
companies
comparative
compel
compensation
competent
complaint
complimentary
concession
condemn
conference
confirmation
congestion
conscientious
consequence
considerable
consignee

consolidated
construction
consumer
container
contemplating
contemporary
contingent
convenience
conveyance
cooperate
corporation
corroborate
corrugated
counterfeit
coupon
courteous
credentials
creditor
curiosity
currency
customer
cylinder

## D

decision
defendant
deferred
deficit
definite
defray
demonstration
depreciation
description
desperate
destination
deteriorate
determination
develop
dictionary
director
disappear
disappoint
disastrous
disbursements

discernible
discontinued
discrepancy
discuss
dispatch
dissatisfaction
dissolution
distinction
distinguish
distributor
dividend
document
doubt
duplicate
durable

## E

earliest
earnest
easier
economic
eighth
elevator
eligible
embarrass
emergency
enormous
enterprise
envelope
equally
equipped
especially
estimate
essentially
eventually
evidence
exaggerate
examination
exasperate
excellent
except
exchange
executive
exhibition

existence
expedite
explanation
extension

**F**

facilitate
February
financier
foreclosure
forehead
forfeit
formally
formerly
forty
franchise
fundamental
furniture
futile

**G**

generally
genuine
government
grammar

**H**

handkerchief
hastily
hazard
height
hoping
hosiery
humorous

**I**

illegible
immediately
impracticable
inasmuch
inconsistent
inconvenience
incorporated
incredible

increment
indelible
indemnity
indispensable
inducement
industrial
inevitable
inferred
inflation
infringement
initiate
inquiry
insolvency
inspection
instance
institution
instructor
insurance
integrity
intelligence
interpretation
inventory
investigate
invoice
involved
itemized
itinerary
its

**J**

jobber
journal

**K**

keenness
knowledge

**L**

laboratory
ladies
latter
leased
ledger
legitimate

leisure
liabilities
library
license
likable (*or* likeable)
liquidation
literature
lucrative
luscious
luxury

**M**

machinery
maintenance
management
manila
manufacturer
margin
material
maturity
mechanical
medicine
memorandum
mercantile
merchandise
merge
middleman
mimeograph
miniature
miscellaneous
misrepresent
misspelled
moistener
monopoly
mortgage
movie
mucilage
municipal

**N**

necessary
ninth
notary
noticeable

notwithstanding
nowadays

**O**

obliging
observation
obsolete
obstacle
occasionally
occurred
omission
oneself
opportunity
optimism
option
ordinance
organization
outrageous
overdraw
overhead
oxygen

**P**

pamphlet
parallel
parenthesis
parliament
particularly
pavilion
peaceable
peculiarities
pecuniary
percent
perforation
performance
permanent
permissible
perpendicular
perseverance
personal
personnel
persuade
perusal
petition

petroleum
photostat
physical
physician
plaintiff
plausible
policy
practically
precedence
precise
preface
preference
prescription
presence
presidency
prestige
primitive
principal
principle
privilege
procedure
process
professional
prominence
promissory
pronunciation
prospectus
psychology

**Q**

qualification
quantity
questionnaire
quotation

**R**

readjustment
really
reasonable
rebate
receipt
recognize
recommend
reconstruction

reference
regardless
register
reimburse
reinforcement
relations
remedied
remittance
representative
requisition
resign
respectfully
respectively
responsible
restaurant
ridiculous
rural

**S**

sacrifice
salary
salutation
sanitary
satisfactory
schedule
scissors
secretarial
security
seize
separate
several
significance
similar
simultaneous
sincerely
sociable
society
solemn
solvent
sometimes
source
southern
souvenir
specialize

specify
spectacular
speculate
statement
stationary
stationery
statistics
straightened
strenuous
strictly
sublet
subsidize
substantial
substitute
subtle
successful
suggestion
summary
superfluous
superintendent
surplus

surprise
susceptible
syllable
syndicate
systematize

**T**

tangible
tariff
tendency
testimonials
tickler
together
transferred
transparent
treasurer
triplicate
Tuesday
turnover
typewriter
typical
typographical

**U**

unanimous
university
unmistakable
utilities
utilize

**V**

verification
vicinity
visible
volume
voucher

**W**

waive
warrant
Wednesday
whatever
wholesale
wholly
women

# A National Examination

## Exercise

*The following words are among those office workers and students frequently misspell. You may notice that some of them have been discussed in previous pages of this book. You should profit from this repetition.*

*First, study the list carefully. Next, ask a friend to dictate the words to you and write them as dictated. Have your friend check off the words you misspelled. Study these words. Then have your friend dictate these words to you. You can repeat this process until you have mastered all the words.*

1. equation
2. bankruptcy
3. partially
4. effect (result)
5. likable

6. reward
7. advantageous
8. nominal
9. certificate
10. campaign

11. obsolete
12. earnest
13. excessive
14. triumph
15. youthfulness
16. atomic
17. manufacturer
18. jewelry
19. advertisement
20. believe
21. existence
22. deductible
23. benevolent
24. eighth
25. grammar
26. bargain
27. visible
28. offered
29. absence
30. deceive
31. decision
32. fluorescent
33. nominate
34. chair
35. length
36. advisable
37. beginning
38. totaling
39. dropping
40. scissors
41. research
42. exhaust
43. alliance
44. gesture
45. yield
46. ineligible
47. license
48. desk
49. already
50. recede
51. personnel
52. labeled
53. separate
54. turnover
55. impel

56. obscure
57. capacity
58. calendar (date)
59. erroneous
60. embarrassed
61. ceremony
62. manageable
63. wholesale
64. replace
65. magnify
66. humorous
67. noticeable
68. principle (rule)
69. tariff
70. disagreeable
71. durable
72. precision
73. malicious
74. punctuate
75. limited
76. require
77. illogical
78. fulfill
79. principal (head)
80. its (possessive)
81. leniency
82. remain
83. relay
84. where
85. agreeable
86. identical
87. likelihood
88. guarantee
89. opportunity
90. superintendent
91. loose
92. left
93. notifying
94. practicable
95. attorneys
96. meantime
97. nickel
98. committee
99. negotiate
100. concede

| | |
|---|---|
| 101. neutralize | 146. underwrite |
| 102. forfeit | 147. grasp |
| 103. omitted | 148. company |
| 104. installment | 149. sympathy |
| 105. seize | 150. lose |
| 106. irreparable | 151. unduly |
| 107. questionnaire | 152. imperative |
| 108. familiar | 153. diligent |
| 109. supersede | 154. messenger |
| 110. pessimistic | 155. usable |
| 111. valuable | 156. objectionable |
| 112. insistent | 157. analysis |
| 113. ninth | 158. recommend |
| 114. warehouse | 159. exercise |
| 115. remittance | 160. mediocre |
| 116. ambiguous | 161. genuine |
| 117. letterhead | 162. mailman |
| 118. salary | 163. equipped |
| 119. obstruct | 164. insignificant |
| 120. justified | 165. enforceable |
| 121. until | 166. knowledge |
| 122. franchise | 167. prepaid |
| 123. realize | 168. naive |
| 124. peculiar | 169. recurrence |
| 125. exceed | 170. issuing |
| 126. prescription | 171. surprise |
| 127. fragile | 172. incredible |
| 128. diplomatic | 173. testimonial |
| 129. essential | 174. opponent |
| 130. infinite | 175. wagered |
| 131. machinery | 176. illegible |
| 132. arguing | 177. advocate |
| 133. nineteenth | 178. impossible |
| 134. succeed | 179. voluntary |
| 135. concealed | 180. interpretation |
| 136. comparable | 181. summarize |
| 137. obtainable | 182. hindrance |
| 138. bookkeeper | 183. technical |
| 139. remind | 184. interfered |
| 140. impatient | 185. unnecessary |
| 141. occurrence | 186. generalize |
| 142. inferred | 187. whether (if) |
| 143. almanac | 188. indebtedness |
| 144. occasion | 189. beneath |
| 145. gauge | 190. indefensible |

| | |
|---|---|
| 191. triplicate | 236. effort |
| 192. contribute | 237. exhibitor |
| 193. obstinate | 238. preliminary |
| 194. confirm | 239. repair |
| 195. travel | 240. possession |
| 196. mileage | 241. employee |
| 197. assistance | 242. responsible |
| 198. minimum | 243. eligible |
| 199. apologies | 244. incidentally |
| 200. meanwhile | 245. balance |
| 201. sponsor | 246. claim |
| 202. moreover | 247. vocabulary |
| 203. appointment | 248. colleague |
| 204. merchandise | 249. vehicle |
| 205. athletics | 250. grateful |
| 206. aluminum | 251. verify |
| 207. electric | 252. grievance |
| 208. maintenance | 253. commodity |
| 209. continuous | 254. mailable |
| 210. mechanical | 255. sacrifice |
| 211. contain | 256. contrive |
| 212. mortgage | 257. transferring |
| 213. cooperate | 258. desolate |
| 214. literally | 259. excusable |
| 215. consistent | 260. conferred |
| 216. movable | 261. parallel |
| 217. authorize | 262. preference |
| 218. aspirant | 263. notable |
| 219. consensus | 264. earlier |
| 220. negative | 265. excellent |
| 221. annual | 266. amendment |
| 222. procedure | 267. expression |
| 223. dissatisfied | 268. counsel (advise) |
| 224. remove | 269. efficiency |
| 225. economical | 270. immediately |
| 226. receive | 271. disbursement |
| 227. expenditure | 272. difficulty |
| 228. prejudice | 273. literature |
| 229. disappoint | 274. benefited |
| 230. relieve | 275. miscellaneous |
| 231. equally | 276. concur |
| 232. pamphlet | 277. necessarily |
| 233. dilemma | 278. available |
| 234. communicate | 279. leisure |
| 235. package | 280. criticize |

281. oneself
282. deteriorate
283. accumulate
284. devastate
285. marriage
286. office
287. specialize
288. organize
289. controlled
290. dependent
291. statistical
292. envelope
293. formerly
294. liaison
295. secretary
296. dialect
297. schedule
298. diminish
299. encouragement
300. same
301. disappearance
302. scarcely
303. pastime
304. eccentric
305. favorable
306. referring
307. emphasis
308. privilege
309. fourth
310. similar
311. hesitate
312. universal
313. handsome
314. owing
315. development
316. compelled
317. uneasy
318. program
319. percentage
320. desirable
321. distributor
322. eliminate
323. equilibrium
324. lying
325. nevertheless

326. essence
327. allowance
328. adjustable
329. questionable
330. collect
331. enlightenment
332. futurity
333. municipal
334. modify
335. discipline
336. remorse
337. extremely
338. default
339. reimburse
340. revoke
341. multiply
342. financial
343. accustomed
344. executive
345. congenial
346. loneliness
347. dictionary
348. merge
349. record
350. especially
351. penalize
352. memorandum
353. commission
354. environment
355. mutually
356. gratis
357. logical
358. twentieth
359. tracer
360. unfortunately
361. deficient
362. imitation
363. coordinate
364. retainer
365. casualty
366. automatic
367. visualize
368. should
369. evidence
370. equity

| | | | |
|---|---|---|---|
| 371. counterfeit | | 416. bulletin |
| 372. accommodate | | 417. exceptional |
| 373. reparation | | 418. prestige |
| 374. inherent | | 419. remembrance |
| 375. nuisance | | 420. abundance |
| 376. tragedy | | 421. official |
| 377. corridor | | 422. arrears |
| 378. fortunate | | 423. unanimous |
| 379. innocence | | 424. difference |
| 380. auditor | | 425. censure |
| 381. forgetting | | 426. depository |
| 382. achievement | | 427. division |
| 383. exempt | | 428. victorious |
| 384. ownership | | 429. fiscal |
| 385. attention | | 430. destination |
| 386. indicative | | 431. considerably |
| 387. confidential | | 432. amount |
| 388. inspection | | 433. superior |
| 389. legacy | | 434. pedestrian |
| 390. repetition | | 435. experience |
| 391. luxury | | 436. traditional |
| 392. emergency | | 437. honorable |
| 393. vacation | | 438. periodical |
| 394. remarkable | | 439. illiterate |
| 395. reasonable | | 440. government |
| 396. spacious | | 441. legislate |
| 397. connect | | 442. penetrate |
| 398. conduct | | 443. readily |
| 399. nonchalant | | 444. proposal |
| 400. reinstate | | 445. insertion |
| 401. siege | | 446. perpetrate |
| 402. despair | | 447. regulation |
| 403. forcibly | | 448. specimen |
| 404. optimism | | 449. performance |
| 405. accountant | | 450. hazard |
| 406. manual | | 451. quotation |
| 407. announcement | | 452. suggestion |
| 408. profitable | | 453. distinction |
| 409. approach | | 454. studying |
| 410. actually | | 455. plan |
| 411. serviceable | | 456. congratulate |
| 412. defendant | | 457. influence |
| 413. pursuing | | 458. portrait |
| 414. sufficiency | | 459. substitute |
| 415. provision | | 460. frequency |

| | |
|---|---|
| 461. misspell | 506. scandal |
| 462. integrity | 507. significance |
| 463. unite | 508. circumstances |
| 464. appropriate | 509. reliable |
| 465. currency | 510. agencies |
| 466. presentation | 511. eventually |
| 467. misfortune | 512. initial |
| 468. strengthen | 513. addition |
| 469. apparently | 514. interrupt |
| 470. honorary | 515. ordinarily |
| 471. insurable | 516. dominant |
| 472. promissory | 517. conviction |
| 473. compensate | 518. reservation |
| 474. article | 519. pronunciation |
| 475. vacuum | 520. appraisal |
| 476. warrant | 521. correct |
| 477. diagram | 522. disposition |
| 478. recitation | 523. injustice |
| 479. beneficiary | 524. submission |
| 480. compromise | 525. amusement |
| 481. recuperate | 526. improbable |
| 482. acceptance | 527. reputation |
| 483. utilize | 528. opposite |
| 484. acknowledge | 529. serenity |
| 485. constitute | 530. skeptical |
| 486. number | 531. perseverance |
| 487. catastrophe | 532. equivalent |
| 488. liability | 533. applicable |
| 489. determination | 534. typewriter |
| 490. intentionally | 535. lien |
| 491. statute | 536. assume |
| 492. absolutely | 537. temporary |
| 493. late | 538. budgeting |
| 494. competent | 539. inevitably |
| 495. admittance | 540. maximum |
| 496. recreation | 541. auditorium |
| 497. restitution | 542. tax |
| 498. violence | 543. return |
| 499. scarcity | 544. persuade |
| 500. petition | 545. immovable |
| 501. filing | 546. reduction |
| 502. tangible | 547. spontaneous |
| 503. prepare | 548. scholastic |
| 504. diseases | 549. unconditional |
| 505. ignorant | 550. handling |

| | |
|---|---|
| 551. subtraction | 576. minority |
| 552. wrong | 577. patience |
| 553. structural | 578. security |
| 554. receipt | 579. observance |
| 555. engagement | 580. personality |
| 556. discuss | 581. amateur |
| 557. disability | 582. estimate |
| 558. unprofitable | 583. changeable |
| 559. ridiculous | 584. tolerant |
| 560. ruler | 585. examination |
| 561. tentative | 586. incentive |
| 562. probability | 587. simplicity |
| 563. demonstration | 588. collision |
| 564. impediment | 589. trivial |
| 565. opinion | 590. incurred |
| 566. endowment | 591. headache |
| 567. controversy | 592. carton |
| 568. resume | 593. competition |
| 569. guidance | 594. reconciliation |
| 570. departure | 595. abbreviate |
| 571. inconvenience | 596. illustration |
| 572. variety | 597. commerce |
| 573. renewal | 598. inadequate |
| 574. acquaintance | 599. suspicious |
| 575. texture | 600. dismissal |

# Demons and Superdemons

**Now you're ready to deal with some of the most difficult spelling words.**

# Demons
## and
## Superdemons

If you have studied the previous chapters, you are now probably an above-average speller. You spell better than 75 out of 100 randomly chosen persons.

Do you want to spell even better—to rank among the top ten per cent? To reach that exalted level, you must master some well-known spelling demons, words with which even superior spellers like yourself have trouble.

The demons listed below will test your ability. They are difficult and confusing but can be mastered with a little study. Admittedly some are rare, but not unusually so. They turn up in the reading and conversation of cultured people.

To help you master them, two kinds of help are given. First, infrequently used words are defined so that you will not have to run to a dictionary to discover their meaning. Secondly, the spelling difficulty in each word is italicized.

The exercises at the end of the chapter will test your spelling prowess. Don't undertake the exercises, however, without preliminary study. If you score a hundred in any exercise, you are one in ten thousand!

# Demons! Demons! Demons!

**Demons and Superdemons**

| | |
|---|---|
| abb*eys* | baci*llus* |
| a*berr*ation | bassin*et* |
| al*le*luia | bes*tial* |
| ap*i*ary (a place where bees are kept) | bib*u*lous (inclined to drink) |
| ap*pell*ation | b*oui*llon |
| a*que*ous | |
| ar*c*tic | |
| a*ver* | |

caduceus (the insignia of the Medical Corps, U.S. Army)

caitiff (a mean and wicked person)

calorie

calyx

cameos

cancellation

canticle (a little song or hymn)

canvass (the act of soliciting votes)

carafe (a glass water bottle for the table)

catarrh

caul (a membrane which sometimes covers the head of a child at birth)

cellar

cellular

cetacean (a whale)

chaise

chancre (a venereal sore)

chattel

cherubic

chiffonier (a high and narrow chest of drawers)

chrysalis (the cocoon in which butterflies develop)

clayey

clientele

cole slaw

colicky

colossal

complaisance (disposition to please)

condign (fit, suitable; for example: condign punishment)

connoisseur

contractible

coolly

cornucopia

corollary

corroborate

councilor (an advisor)

counsellor (a lawyer)

covey

coxswain

crevasse (a deep crevice)

crewel (worsted yarn, slackly twisted)

curacy (the office of a curate)

cynosure (a center of attraction)

deign

dieresis (two dots placed over a vowel to show that it is pronounced as a separate syllable)

diphtheria

distensible

donkeys

dowry

dyne (a unit of force)

dyspeptic

ebullient

empyrean (the heavens)

ephemeral (lasting only a day)

Eskimos

excel

exegesis (a critical explanation of a text)

expansible

expiable (capable of being atoned)

fezzes (felt Turkish hats)

fieriest (most fiery)

flexion (a movement of a joint)

fulsome

garlicky

garrote (to strangle)

genealogy

gneiss (a kind of rock)

gringos (as used contemptuously by Spanish-speaking people, especially about Americans)

hara–kiri (suicide by disembowelment)

hemorrhage

hoeing

imperceptible

infusible

isthmus

*j*inrik*isha* (a small two-wheeled vehicle
   drawn by a man)

*kh*aki
kil*os*
kimon*o*

labe*l*ed
lary*n*x
ligh*tn*ing
ling*oe*s

majordom*o*s
me*ll*ifluous (sweetened with honey)
*mn*emonics (the art of improving the
   memory)

penicil*l*in
perfect*i*ble
phleg*m*
picnic*k*ing

*queu*e

refe*r*rer
*rh*eum (a watery discharge from the eyes
   or nose)

sacri*l*egious
sar*s*aparilla
*sc*imitar (a curved sword)
shellac*k*ed
sibilan*c*y
sin*gei*ng
str*ait* jacket

tread*le*
troll*eys*

vend*i*ble (salable)

wir*y*
wr*ie*st (most wry)

zw*ei*back

# Stump Your Friends!

At your next party challenge the spelling ability of your friends. Distribute slips of paper and pencils, and dictate the following ten words. Scarcely anyone knows the spelling of all ten, as you will see.

A score of 7 is commendable; 8 is exceptional; 9 is incredible; and 10 is out of this world.

|  |  |
|---|---|
| altos | liquefy |
| colicky | plague |
| ecstasy | rarefy |
| hypocrisy | supersede |
| inoculate | vilify |

# Exercise

*Some of the following words are spelled correctly and some are misspelled. Put a check on the blank if a word is spelled correctly. Rewrite it correctly if it is misspelled.*

1. appelation                      _____
2. basinette                      _____
3. bouillon                      _____
4. calorie                      _____
5. cattarrh                      _____
6. celler                      _____
7. cold slaw                      _____
8. connoisseur                      _____
9. counsellor                      _____
10. dispeptic                      _____
11. donkeys                      _____
12. Eskimoes                      _____
13. excel                      _____
14. fulsome                      _____
15. garlicky                      _____
16. geneology                      _____
17. isthmus                      _____
18. kimona                      _____
19. labelled                      _____
20. penicillin                      _____
21. queue                      _____
22. sacriligious                      _____
23. sibbilancy                      _____
24. trolleys                      _____
25. wiry                      _____

# Space
# Age
# Words

**These twentieth century words and definitions can make your reading and writing more precise.**

# Space Age Words

Several hundred new words have entered our language to describe space age technology. Some are so recent that they have not yet been included in dictionaries although they frequently appear in newspapers and are part of our daily conversation.

You should know the spelling and meaning of the most common space age words. They are listed below and their spelling difficulties indicated when necessary.

## Space Abbreviations

**Space Age Abbreviations**

| Abbreviation | Term |
| --- | --- |
| AC | Alternating current |
| BMEWS | Ballistics Missiles Early Warning System |
| DOVAP | Doppler Velocity and Positions |
| G *or* g | Earth's gravity |
| ICBM | Intercontinental Ballistics Missile |
| LOX | Liquid oxygen |
| NASA | National Aeronautics and Space Administration |
| UHF | Ultra high frequency |
| VHF | Very high frequency |
| X | Experimental |
| Y | Prototype (a model used for operational tests) |

# Space Terms

## Common Space Age Words

| Term | Definition |
|------|------------|
| | **A** |
| abort | To terminate; to cut short |
| ac*c*eleration | Rate of change of speed |
| *aero*dynamics | Science dealing with force of air in motion (Note: a singular noun) |
| air-to-air miss*ile* | A missile launched in the air against an air-borne target (Use hyphens because the two nouns form an adjective) |
| air-to-surface miss*ile* | A missile launched in the air against a target on land or sea |
| antimiss*ile* miss*ile* | A missile designed to destroy other missiles in flight |
| antisatellite miss*ile* | A missile designed to destroy a satellite in flight |
| apog*ee* | The point of an orbit which is at the greatest distance from the earth |
| aster*oids* | The numerous small planets whose orbits lie between Mars and Jupiter |
| astron*aut* | A space flier |
| av*ionic*s system | Navigation instruments |
| | **B** |
| ballistic miss*ile* | A missile which follows a ballistic trajectory after the force of its initial thrust is ended |
| booster | An auxiliary rocket |
| | **C** |
| Cape Can*aver*al | Florida launching site |
| capsule | A sealed cabin in which humans can live during space flight; it contains mechanisms for the return of its occupants to earth |
| control rocket | A rocket used to guide a space vehicle |
| cos*mic* rays | Space radiations |
| cosmon*aut* | A space flier; an astronaut |
| countdown | The timed events preceding a launching expressed in minus quantities (T minus 5, etc.). After launching, plus time is used (T plus 5, etc.) |
| crater | A depression formed by the impact of a meteor |
| | **D** |
| digital computer | A computer which solves problems by mathematical processes |
| drone | An unmanned aircraft remotely controlled |

| Term | Definition |
|---|---|
| | **E** |
| elevons | Wing flaps |
| elliptical | Pertaining to an ellipse |
| | **F** |
| fuselage | Airplane body |
| | **G** |
| galaxy | A massive collection of stars |
| gamma ray | A form of electromagnetic radiation |
| gantry | A structure resembling a crane used to assemble and service large rockets |
| guided missile | A missile whose flight path can be changed by a mechanism within it |
| | **H** |
| hypersonic | Relating to speed faster than sound |
| | **I** |
| inclination | The angle formed by two lines or planes |
| interstellar | Relating to space between stars |
| ion | An atom minus an outer electron |
| | **J** |
| jet propulsion | A form of propulsion in which the propulsion unit obtains oxygen from the air (In rocket propulsion the unit carries its own oxygen-producing material) |
| | **L** |
| landing rocket | A rocket used to convey passengers from a spacecraft to the moon or earth |
| liftoff | The rising of a space vehicle from its launcher (Note that liftoff is not hyphenated) |
| light-year | The distance traveled by light in a year (Note the hyphen) |
| Loran | A long-range electrical navigation system (Note capitalization) |
| lunar | Relating to the moon |
| | **M** |
| Mach number | A number expressing the relationship between the speed of a body and the speed of sound (Notice that Mach is capitalized) |
| maneuvers | Military movements |
| mare | A lunar sea |
| microwave | A very short radio wavelength (Note that microwave is not hyphenated) |

| Term | Definition |
|---|---|
| **N** | |
| nu*clear* rocket | A rocket propelled by nuclear fission |
| **O** | |
| orbit | Path of space vehicle |
| orbital | Pertaining to an orbit |
| **P** | |
| pad | A launch pad; a base for a launcher |
| payload | The equipment or cargo carried on a space mission (Not hyphenated) |
| peri*gee* | The point of an orbit which is closest to the earth |
| pi*ck*aback | Carried as one might carry a person on his shoulders or back |
| planetary | Pertaining to planets |
| probe | An unmanned space vehicle used for purposes of exploration |
| prope*ll*ant | Liquid or solid fuel burned in rocket engines to provide thrust |
| **Q** | |
| quasars | Recently discovered radioactive objects billions of light years from the earth |
| **R** | |
| rad*ar* | A device which emits radio energy and receives reflections of that energy from objects |
| re-entry | The return of a space vehicle to the earth's atmosphere (Note hyphenation) |
| roger | A word signifying okay |
| **S** | |
| sate*ll*ite | An unpowered space vehicle in orbit around the moon or a planet |
| scrub | To cancel a launch |
| shuttle | Re-usable spacecraft |
| soft landing | A landing on the moon or on a planet without a crash |
| so*n*ic boom | The roar caused by an aircraft flying at speed faster than sound |
| spacelab | Experimental station developed by European Space Agency with NASA |
| **T** | |
| tel*em*etry | The radio connection between a missile and a ground station |
| ter*r*estrial | Relating to the earth |
| tra*j*ectory | A space vehicle's path through space |
| tro*po*sphere | The lower layer of the earth's atmosphere |

# Space Vehicles

Since 1957, when the Soviet Union opened the space age by launching Sputnik I, there have been many space projects and vehicles. They are listed below in alphabetical order for easy reference.

| Notice! |
| --- |

**All the space vehicle names are capitalized. The italicized letters indicate spelling difficulties.**

## Space Vehicle Names

| | | |
| --- | --- | --- |
| Able | Greb | Saturn |
| A*g*ena | Hitch-hiker | Score |
| A*l*ouette | (Observe the hyphen) | Scout |
| Anna | In*j*un | Soyuz |
| A*pollo* | Liberty Bell | Sputn*ik* |
| Ariel | Lofti | Star*ad* |
| Atlas | Luna | S*u*rcal |
| Beacon | Lunik | Sy*n*com |
| Cent*aur* | Ma*r*iner | Telstar |
| Columbia | Mars | Thor |
| Composite | Midas | T*i*ros |
| Cosmos | Oscar | Titan |
| Courier | Pion*ee*r | Tr*aa*c |
| Delta | Poly*ot* | Transit |
| Discoverer | Radose | Vanguard |
| Echo | Ranger | Venera |
| Ele*k*tron | Redstone | Venus Probe |
| Explorer | Relay | Viking |
| Freedom | Salyut | Voskhod |
| Friendship | Samos | Vosto*k* |
| Gemini | | |

# Exercise 1

*From each group select the correctly spelled word and place the letter before it in the space at the left.*

1. _____ a. Apollo  b. Appollo  c. Apolo  d. Appolo

2. _____ a. nuculear  b. nuclaer  c. nuclear  d. nucclear

3. _____ a. trajectory  b. tragectory  c. tradgectory  d. trajerectory

4. _____ a. Sputnick  b. Sputtnick  c. Sputtnik  d. Sputnik

5. _____ a. asteroyds  b. astaroids  c. astiroids  d. asteroids

6. _____ a. hypersonnic  b. hypersonic  c. hyppersonic  d. hyperssonic

7. _____ a. tropposphere  b. troposphere  c. tropospheer  d. troposphear

8. _____ a. astronnaut  b. astronaut  c. asternaut  d. astornaut

9. _____ a. lasser  b. lacer  c. laser  d. laiser

10. _____ a. acceleration  b. aceleration  c. accelleration  d. acelleration

11. _____ a. Marriner  b. Mariner  c. Marinar  d. Marinner

12. _____ a. apogge  b. apoggee  c. appoge  d. apogee

13. _____ a. rador  b. rader  c. radar  d. raydor

14. _____ a. interrstellar  b. intersteller  c. intersteler  d. interstellar

15. _____ a. missile  b. missil  c. misile  d. misle

# Measuring
# Your
# Progress

# Achievement Tests

## An overall chapter-by-chapter review so that you can test yourself.

SCORE _____

# Achievement Test 1

## Chapters 1–4

*Indicate by writing T or F to the right whether the following statements about English spelling are true or false.*

1. English spelling is difficult because it is not phonetic. ____
2. At one time in the history of English the endings in *through, thorough, plough* were pronounced. ____
3. The element *pt* in *ptomaine, pterodactyl*, and *ptarmigan* is pronounced in Modern English. ____
4. *Spaghetti, toreador, echelon*, and *sputnik* are derived from Italian, Spanish, French, and Russian respectively. ____
5. Such words as *birth—berth, air—heir* are called antonyms. ____
6. Many poor spellers do not hear words correctly. ____
7. Nervous tension never interferes with ability to spell. ____
8. There are no rules in spelling that are worth learning. ____
9. The most reliable source of information for spelling is in the dictionary. ____
10. Occasionally there are differences between British and American spelling. ____
11. The sounds of English vowels have not changed through the centuries. ____
12. The *k* in *knowledge*, and the *k* in *knee* were at one time pronounced in English. ____
13. Good examples of homonyms are *fright—freight; sleigh—sleight; tray—trait*. ____
14. Spelling *antidote* as *anecdote* may indicate poor or careless listening. ____
15. Dictionaries vary their spelling in accordance with the areas of the country. ____
16. To become a better speller you must read everything very slowly. ____
17. Many good spellers can tell that a word is misspelled by its appearance (or configuration). ____
18. All good spellers inherit this ability. ____
19. Sometimes you can discover your own spelling devices to help you. ____
20. A good way to recall the spelling of *stationary* is to think of *station*. ____

21. The British prefer to add an extra *u* in such words as *labour, favour,* and *armour.* ____
22. The section on correct spelling in a good dictionary is entitled *Orthography.* ____
23. The words *center* and *centre* are examples of *homonyms.* ____
24. The words *theater* and *theatre* are examples of *antonyms.* ____
25. There is little value in compiling your own list of misspelled words. ____
26. In learning how to spell the word *superintendent* it is advisable to pronounce each syllable distinctly. ____
27. The letter *b* in *debt* and *doubt* is not pronounced in Modern English. ____
28. In learning how to spell a new word it is helpful to write it several times correctly. ____
29. The trouble with English spelling is that there are no rules. ____
30. The ancient Sumerians used a language that was called hieroglyphics. ____
31. There is no difference in pronunciation between *trough* and *through.* ____
32. *Tough* and *rough* are homonyms. ____
33. *Through* and *true* have the same final sound. ____
34. The final sound in *knight* and *tight* is pronounced *īt.* ____
35. Many English words derived from ancient Greek have silent letters as in *psyllium* and *pseudonym.* ____
36. *Moat* and *mote* are examples of homophones. ____
37. Words like *privilege* and *government* are frequently misspelled by omitting a letter. ____
38. Skimming will make one a better speller. ____
39. Careful observation helps one to become a better speller. ____
40. It is possible to train your eyes so they can recognize misspelled words by their appearance. ____
41. You can fix the correct spelling of the word *principle* by associating it with ru*le.* ____
42. To fix the correct spelling of *separate*, think of *sepa* plus *rate.* ____
43. By recalling the spelling of *where*, you may spell *there* correctly. ____
44. The words *hair* and *heir* are pronounced the same. ____
45. Though "practice makes perfect" many professional writers are sometimes plagued by misspellings. ____
46. The ultimate aim of learning to spell is to avoid consulting the dictionary. ____
47. If you read a printed article containing the words *savour* and *connexion* you might conclude that the article was printed in England. ____
48. Some people might learn to spell *their* correctly by associating it with *heir.* ____

49. The words *rough* and *ruff* are true homophones.  ____
50. The words *sough* and *rough* are identical in sound.  ____
51. Words in English derived from ancient Greek are pronounced exactly as they were in Greece.  ____
52. English words are spelled exactly as they sound.  ____
53. The best way to study spelling is memorize all the words you need.  ____
54. *Beet* and *beat* are true antonyms.  ____
55. Because there are *gh* in *night* and *sight*, they should be pronounced.  ____
56. A person writing *litature* instead of *literature* has probably not heard the word correctly.  ____
57. Because the *b* in *debt* is silent, therefore the *b* in *debit* should also be silent.  ____
58. An error in spelling *magazine* and *temperament* is that the middle *a* is frequently omitted.  ____
59. To pronounce *scrambled* as *skwambled* may be due to infantile speech.  ____

# Achievement Test 2

## Chapter 6

*Underscore the word spelled correctly in the parentheses.*

1. The agent signed the (receipt, reciept) for the rent.
2. It was a great (relief, releif) to go home at last.
3. Mary gave a loud (shriek, shreik) and ran.
4. The marines refused to (yeild, yield) their positions.
5. He was a perfect (fiend, feind) in his behavior.
6. His (acheivement, achievement) was remarkable.
7. Once we have lost our reputation, it is difficult to (retreive, retrieve) it.
8. It takes a good (freind, friend) to make one.
9. The slain leader was carried to the (beir, bier).
10. He was (chief, cheif) of the whole island.
11. We were (receiveing, receiving) visitors all day.
12. It is difficult to (deceive, decieve) people all the time.
13. Strenuous efforts are required to (achieve, acheive) a scholarship.
14. Astronomers can now (percieve, perceive) stars that are quite small.
15. Our (neighbors, nieghbors) to the south were angry at our behavior.
16. Careless training may lead to such (mischievious, mischievous) behavior in childhood.
17. The last (frontier, fronteir) is now in space.
18. Although the (ceiling, cieling) was low, he bought the house.

SCORE _____

# Achievement Test 3

## Chapters 7–8

*In the following sentences the italic words are sometimes correctly spelled; sometimes misspelled. In the spaces to the right, place C if the spelling is correct. Write the correct spelling for all misspelled words.*

1. Our lighter team was at a *dissadvantage*. _____
2. Park all *disabled* cars here. _____
3. Any *mistatement* of fact will be punished. _____
4. The old man could not *reccollect* anything that had happened. _____
5. The doctor *recommended* an aspirin. _____
6. This procedure was an *inovation*. _____
7. Let us *rennovate* your apartment. _____
8. Actions such as these are *unatural*. _____
9. This apartment had been *unoccupied* for a month. _____
10. Congress tried to *overide* the veto. _____
11. For misbehaving the sergeant was *dimoted*. _____
12. Sugar will easily *disolve* in water. _____
13. As a lawyer Clarence Darrow was *preminent*. _____
14. One should always have some *anteseptic* handy for unexpected cuts. _____
15. His behavior under fire was *degrading*. _____

*Select the correct choice of the two in parentheses:*

16. By crossing the state border they ran into difficulty with the (intra-state, interstate) commission. _____
17. Do not (interrupt, interupt) an older person. _____
18. At the end of his letter he added a (poscript, postscript). _____
19. Many (suburban, subburban) communities are growing. _____
20. When the lights blew out we called the (superrintendent, superintendent). _____
21. Quite a few hotels here welcome (transient, transent) guests. _____
22. The judge ruled that this evidence was not (admissible, admissable). _____

23. Such arguments are (laughible, laughable). _____
24. It was (unthinkable, unthinkible) that he could lose the game. _____
25. For many years he was the most (eligible, eligable) bachelor in town. _____
26. England has always been (invincible, invincable) in a crisis. _____
27. (Legible, legable) handwriting is a delight for the reader. _____
28. Make yourself (comfortable, comfortible). _____
29. Many foods are (perishible, perishable) unless properly refrigerated. _____
30. Evidence of the disease was not yet (demonstrable, demonstrible). _____

*In the following sentences the italic words are sometimes correctly spelled; sometimes misspelled. In the spaces to the right, place C if the spelling is correct. Write the correct spelling for all misspelled words.*

31. The debater made a *mistake*. _____
32. I don't *reccolect* what happened. _____
33. *Professional* ball-players receive high salaries. _____
34. His sleight of hand was *unoticeable*. _____
35. That player is vastly *overated*. _____
36. Sometimes it is better if one doesn't know his *anticedents*. _____
37. Iodine is still a popular *antiseptic*. _____
38. "Don't *interrupt* me," she exclaimed. _____
39. Lincoln was not very happy when several states *seseded* from the Union. _____
40. The doctor diagnosed the disease as a *preforated* ulcer. _____
41. We must look at things in their proper *prespective*. _____
42. Let us *proceed* with the business. _____
43. Many a *percocious* child can learn how to play chess well. _____
44. This water is hardly *drinkible*. _____
45. Some mountains are *inaccessable*. _____
46. The *combustible* materials were placed in fire-proof bins. _____
47. Many an *eligable* bachelor has been attracted by a pretty young girl. _____
48. There are some schools for *incorrigible* youngsters. _____
49. "Such language is *detestable*," said the teacher. _____
50. He was an old *acquaintence*. _____

51. The face of the *defendent* became pale as the verdict was read. _____
52. Sometimes little things turn out to have great *significence*. _____
53. The mechanics overhauled the airplane motor in a *hanger*. _____
54. The *collar* of his shirt was frayed. _____
55. The businessman advertised in a local newspaper for an experienced *stenographer*. _____
56. Most department store customers prefer to use an *escalator* when they wish to ascend to another floor. _____
57. The *radiater* of the car started to boil over in the hot weather. _____
58. Readers who disagree with a newspaper's editorial position should write a letter to the *editor*. _____
59. One of the duties of a *superviser* is to train employees. _____
60. The *purchaser* is protected by a money-back guarantee. _____

_____ SCORE _____

# Achievement Test 4

## Chapters 9–11

*Underscore the word spelled correctly in the parentheses.*

1. All the (buffaloes, buffalos) were killed in this territory.
2. The President sent through his two (vetoes, vetos) to Congress.
3. All the (tomatoes, tomatos) had ripened.
4. We examined six (pianos, pianoes) before we selected one.
5. Cowboys learn how to do many stunts with their (lassoes, lassos).
6. Among the (calfs, calves) were some spotted ones.
7. All the (leafs, leaves) fell down.
8. Many old (beliefs, believes) must be disregarded.
9. Napoleon crushed many (armies, armys) in his time.
10. This farm still made use of (oxes, oxen).
11. Hailstones fell down several (chimneys, chimnies).
12. In this machine there were many levers and (pulleys, pullies).
13. The soldiers shot several (volleys, vollies) at their fleeing enemies.
14. The (salaries, salarys) of his employees were frequently raised.
15. The Greeks composed the greatest dramatic (tragedeys, tragedies).
16. The judge pronounced his sentence (angrily, angryly).
17. It is advisable occasionally to be (mercyful, merciful).
18. The band-leader played several (medleys, medlies).
19. A public (conveyance, conveyence) was supplied to the general.
20. Good carriage always (dignifies, dignifys) the person.
21. My father reminded us that we would be (dineing, dining) at six.
22. It was the loveliest sight (imagineable, imaginable).
23. (Judging, Judgeing) from the attendance, the play was a hit.
24. Her success in college was (surpriseing, surprising).
25. Thoreau was (writeing, writing) a great deal while staying at Walden Pond.
26. The wounded dog was (whining, whineing) all night long.
27. All those (desireous, desirous) of success must work hard.
28. The (density, denseity) of the atmosphere is being studied.
29. The lecturer spoke clearly and (sincerely, sincerly).
30. Certain traits sometimes run in (families, familys).
31. We both like (dining, dineing) out frequently.
32. This trail is not for the birds but for (donkeys, donkies).

33. Much (encouragment, encouragement) was required before the baby would walk.
34. Space travel is no longer (unimagineable, unimaginable).
35. This line had the fewest (casualties, casualtys).
36. We noticed that all the ants seemed (busily, busyly) engaged in building a new home.
37. Jascha Heifetz was (accompanied, accompanyed) by an accomplished pianist.
38. When her son did not return the mother was (worried, worryed).
39. Reynolds frequently (portrayed, portraied) the English nobility of the 18th Century.
40. His sermons frequently seemed touched with (sublimity, sublimeity).
41. Such actions at this time seemed (inadvisable, inadviseable).
42. By careless handling, she seemed to be (singing, singeing) her hair.
43. In expository writing (vagueness, vaguness) is not tolerated.
44. "Stop (argueing, arguing) and come away," the wife shouted to her husband.
45. Considering everything, it was a (lovely, lovly) wedding.
46. Such (couragous, courageous) action was rarely seen.
47. Dinner at this late hour was (tastless, tasteless).
48. Working long on the (contriveance, contrivance) made him a bit fanatic about it.
49. (Anniversaries, anniversarys) should be celebrated properly.
50. A pair of (oxes, oxen) is a rarity on a farm today.
51. The printer corrected the (proofs, prooves) of the new book.
52. My friend liked all his (brothers-in-law, brother-in-laws).
53. The castle was (beseiged, besieged) for ten days.
54. Mary's (likeness, likness) was obvious in the portrait.
55. After many lessons he learned to dance (gracfully, gracefully).
56. This celebration was (truly, truely) magnificent.
57. The comic made his living by (mimicing, mimicking) others.
58. Some ranches have as many as 10,000 (sheeps, sheep).
59. All the (alumni, alumnuses) of Fairweather College returned on Founder's Day.
60. Before the American public high schools, there were many (academies, academys).
61. It is very difficult to discover a single (curricula, curriculum) which can satisfy all people.
62. Ehrlich stained many (bacilli, bacilluses) in his career.

_____ SCORE _____

# Achievement Test 5

## Chapters 12–15

*Underscore the word spelled correctly in the parentheses.*

1. He wanted to buy a (low-priced, low priced) car.
2. This author was (best known, best-known) for his characterization.
3. She was the (thirty-first, thirty first) queen to be chosen.
4. This hypothesis was a little (far-fetched, far fetched).
5. The ewe was (newly-born, newly born).
6. It was the (highest priced, highest-priced) dress in the store.
7. It was a successful (pre-election, preelection) bet.
8. To get this loan, you must have a (coowner, co-owner).
9. They cheered the (exGovernor, ex-Governor).
10. (Vice-Admiral, Vice Admiral) Rooney was promoted.
11. The doctors (conferred, confered) for two hours.
12. We had no (preference, preferrence) in this matter.
13. After many trials, he was (transferred, transfered) to another prison.
14. The girl quickly tore the (wrapings, wrappings) from the package.
15. Many new bills are thrown into the legislative (hoper, hopper).
16. Mulvaney was the best (hitter, hiter) in the league.
17. Turkey, plus all the (trimings, trimmings) was served yesterday.
18. The Dupont Company had a (controlling, controling) interest in the firm.
19. Our graduates (excelled, exceled) all others at Yale.
20. The prisoner never (regretted, regreted) his misdeeds.
21. The house had a (low-ceiling, low ceiling).
22. (One half, one-half) of the audience left at the end of the first act.
23. All night the tune kept (dining, dinning) in her head.
24. The duchess wore a (low necked, low-necked) gown at the party.
25. The employer demanded several (references, referrences).
26. We are all (hoping, hopping) for permanent peace.
27. Such freak accidents (occured, occurred) seldom.
28. The guilty culprit wore a (hangdog, hang-dog) look.
29. America at that time had (unparalleled, unparaleled) prosperity.
30. It was the (twenty ninth, twenty-ninth) celebration of the ending of the war.
31. The (pre-dawn, predawn) flight was a success.

32. My cousin was the (high scorer, high-scorer) in the game.
33. My mother always (prefered, preferred) to save rather than spend everything.
34. The (ex policeman, ex-policeman) was found guilty of perjury.
35. The judge and the attorneys (conferred, confered) for three hours.
36. The athlete (chined, chinned) thirty times on the horizontal bar.
37. The (Pro-Temperance, Pro Temperance) Party won few votes.
38. The poor little bird (flaped, flapped) her wings feebly and then remained still.
39. The (red-cheeked, red cheeked) youngster seemed shy.
40. Some of the guests at the home were over (eighty eight, eighty-eight) years old.
41. Television has been accused of (sub-liminal, subliminal) advertising.
42. The soldier seemed (regretful, regrettful) of his actions.
43. This rouge seems to be the (lowest priced, lowest-priced) in the entire shop.
44. Adolescents are frequently (smitten, smiten) with puppy love.
45. His appearance at the trial was (well-timed, well timed).
46. He was (hiting, hitting) well in that game.
47. The boy kept (running, runing) despite the cries of his mother.
48. Many guards (patroled, patrolled) the prison on the day of the execution.
49. Passengers should be (already, all ready) at 10 P.M.
50. A (run-on, run on) sentence contains more than enough for one complete sentence.
51. We greeted the (Senator-elect, Senator elect).
52. Rescue boats went back and forth in the (mid Atlantic, mid-Atlantic) area.
53. Her praises were (extoled, extolled) for her amazing performance.
54. Eisenhower's (aide-de-camp, aidedecamp) was later decorated for his contributions.
55. After a little encouragement the guitarist (regaled, regalled) the picnickers with many songs.
56. Mary won first prize; but Susan was (runner up, runner-up).
57. Mills for (spining, spinning) cotton have long supported the town.
58. A few parts of the story were (omitted, omited) by the defendant.
59. Children frequently (scraped, scrapped) their elbows at the corner.
60. Periods of prosperity have (recurred, recured) with regularity in this state.
61. Their marriage was (annuled, annulled) by mutual consent.
62. The nurse (scrubed, scrubbed) the baby's face until it was gleaming.
63. The crowd (paniced, panicked) after the accident.
64. South America (rebeled, rebelled) against the mother country.
65. Judge Harmon (deferred, defered) sentence until Friday.

SCORE _____

# Achievement Test 6

## Chapters 16–17

*Underscore the word spelled correctly in the parentheses.*

1. Many college freshmen (don't, dont) know how to study.
2. This salesman specialized in (mens', men's) hosiery.
3. It was (his, his') greatest victory.
4. (Who'se, Who's) there?
5. Dot all the (i's, is) and cross the (ts, t's).
6. "(Youve, You've) won your battle," said the trainer.
7. The shopper specialized in (lady's, ladies') shoes.
8. This was my (brother-in-law's, brother's-in-law's) house.
9. It was the (children's, childrens') ward to which we hurried.
10. This (couldn't, could'nt) have happened to a nicer chap.
11. It was once more a conflict between (East, east) and (West, west).
12. The young artists admired the works of (grandma Moses, Grandma Moses).
13. At the Sorbonne, he specialized in the (hindu, Hindu) languages.
14. My uncle belonged to the (elks, Elks).
15. The hit of the week was ("For my Beloved," "For My Beloved").
16. A popular novel in high school is (*A Tale of two Cities*, *A Tale of Two Cities*).
17. They traveled (North, north) for twenty miles.
18. On (Columbus Day, Columbus day), many stores are closed.
19. One of the greatest musical hits is (*My fair Lady*, *My Fair Lady*).
20. He was recently elected to the (house of representatives, House of Representatives).
21. The (boy's, boys') hat was on crooked.
22. ("They're, theyr'e) here," the Captain shouted.
23. The conference passed a resolution against all high (doctor's, doctors') fees.
24. The numerous (teacher's, teachers') contributions were finally rewarded.
25. Count all the (7's, 7s) in this line!
26. We enjoyed (Harrigan and Hart's, Harrigan's and Hart's) humor.
27. The sale took place in the (women's, womens') hosiery department.
28. "I never want to touch a penny of (their's, theirs)," she shouted.
29. All the (ts, t's) in this word are left uncrossed.

30. He admired his (lawyer's, lawyers') integrity.
31. The "Ivy League" colleges are situated mostly in the (east, East).
32. After studying (french, French) literature he began to appreciate Moliere.
33. Higher (Mathematics, mathematics) fascinated Einstein at an early age.
34. (Governor, governor) Rockefeller attempted to balance the state budget.
35. Several (captains, Captains) won their promotions in this campaign.
36. The fiftieth state in the union is (hawaii, Hawaii).
37. Mrs. Morrow wrote *North to the* (*Orient, orient*).
38. There are one hundred members of the U.S. (Senate, senate).
39. On (arbor day, Arbor Day) an interesting ceremony took place.
40. Of all the novels read in high school (*Silas Marner, Silas marner*) seems to be most popular.
41. Great praise has come recently to (admiral, Admiral) Rickover.
42. A famous radio personality years ago was (uncle Don, Uncle Don).
43. This store had good bargains in (boys', boy's) shoes.
44. There are many fine students from the (south, South) in the colleges today.

SCORE _____

# Achievement Test 7

## Chapter 19

*Select the correctly spelled word from the two in parentheses:*

1. Teachers frequently give good (advice, advise) to their students. _____
2. England and the U.S. have long been (alleys, allies). _____
3. There is nothing as beautiful as a happy bride walking down the (isle, aisle). _____
4. My parents said that they were (already, all ready). _____
5. Frequently one can have an optical (illusion, allusion) after eyestrain. _____
6. The judge refused to (altar, alter) his decision. _____
7. (Altogether, All together) there were twelve cents in his pocket. _____
8. The casket was (borne, born) on the shoulders of the pallbearers. _____
9. There were several (angles, angels) in this picture by Raphael. _____
10. We ordered an upper (berth, birth) on the train to Chicago. _____
11. Father was almost (besides, beside) himself with grief. _____
12. (Break, Brake) the news gently. _____
13. The baby's (breath, breathe) came in short spasms. _____
14. The cowboy grasped the horse by the (bridal, bridle). _____
15. Ward leaders tried to (canvass, canvas) the district. _____
16. In Washington we visited the beautiful (Capital, Capitol). _____
17. The angry principal began to (censure, censor) the students for misbehavior. _____
18. He could chop several (cords, chords) of wood each day. _____
19. The salesmen showed me several suits of (clothes, cloths). _____
20. In college, my brother took the pre-medical (course, coarse). _____
21. Don't forget to (complement, compliment) him on his good grades. _____

22. The German (consul, council) telegraphed to his ambassador in Washington. _____

23. The cook removed the (corps, core) of the apple. _____

24. Scientists are often (incredulous, incredible) of new theories. _____

25. Many authors like to keep (diaries, dairies) when they are young. _____

26. Justice Oliver Wendell Holmes frequently would (dissent, descent) from his colleagues. _____

27. After the meat course, we had a delicious (dessert, dissert). _____

28. Da Vinci invented a (devise, device) to hurl cannonballs. _____

29. Hamilton and Burr fought a (duel, dual) in New Jersey. _____

30. This spot was (formally, formerly) a cemetery. _____

31. For several (instance, instants) he remained quiet. _____

32. Through an (ingenious, ingenuous) trick the prisoner escaped. _____

33. Actresses like to receive (complements, compliments) for their performances. _____

34. There were thirteen delicious (deserts, desserts) on the menu. _____

35. The Dutch (consul, counsel) in New York helped us to obtain a visa. _____

36. The new President was (formally, formerly) inaugurated. _____

37. Good food in the barracks will help produce good (moral, morale). _____

38. A graduate of Harvard was the (personal, personnel) manager of the store. _____

39. Avogadro's (principal, principle) led to many other important discoveries. _____

40. This company advertises a fine quality of (stationery, stationary). _____

41. Standing in line for a token is often a (waste, waist) of valuable time. _____

42. New inventions (supersede, supercede) old customs. _____

43. It was an (excedingly, exceedingly) hot day. _____

44. Nothing (succeeds, suceeds) like success. _____

45. The parade (proceded, proceeded) without further interruption. _____

46. The magician created an optical (allusion, illusion) for us. _____

47. The West will not (accede, acede) to these demands.  _____
48. After the waters (receeded, receded), we returned to  _____
   our home.
49. The (corps, corpse) was taken to the morgue.  _____
50. The baby liked (it's, its) finger.  _____
51. "It's (later, latter) than you think," the preacher said.  _____
52. Four black-robed monks (led, lead) the way yesterday.  _____
53. After the battle, the general called his (council, counsel)  _____
   together.
54. Several (lose, loose) shingles fell down.  _____
55. Liquor is not permitted to (minors, miners).  _____
56. A world at (peace, piece) is a world of security.  _____
57. It was as (plane, plain) as the nose on his face.  _____
58. After the hike, the boys were (quite, quiet) starved.  _____

# Answer
# Key

# Answer Key

## For Chapters 5–23

**CHAPTER 5**

Exercise 1/Page 119
1. bo·nan·za
2. re·pent
3. fa·tigue
4. pun·ish·ment
5. or·deal
6. rum·mage
7. miss·ing
8. gas·o·line
9. ex·ca·vate
10. ty·ran·ni·cal

Exercise 2/Page 122
1. grammar
2. separate
3. usually
4. C
5. calendar
6. C
7. C
8. until
9. C
10. C
11. C
12. accommodate
13. professor
14. government
15. C
16. across
17. illegible
18. equivalent
19. C
20. C

Exercise 3/Page 123
1. hundred
2. modern
3. perspiration
4. western
5. relevant
6. cavalry
7. children
8. jewelry
9. larynx
10. pattern

## CHAPTER 6

Exercise 1/Page 126
No answers are needed for this exercise since the correct spellings are given.

Exercise 2/Page 127
1. aggrieve
2. brief
3. friend
4. grieve
5. frontier
6. mischief
7. shield
8. shriek
9. wield
10. species
11. relieve
12. leisure
13. handkerchief
14. receipt
15. seize
16. perceive
17. grief
18. niece
19. conceive
20. veil

Exercise 3/Page 128
The answers to this exercise are incorporated in the sentences.

Exercise 4/Page 130
The answers to this exercise are found in the passage.

## CHAPTER 7

Exercise 1/Page 135
1. dissolve
2. dissimilar
3. misspell
4. disappear
5. mistake

Exercise 2/Page 135
circumscribe—draw limits
transcribe—write a copy
subscribe—sign one's name
describe—represent by words
proscribe—denounce and condemn
prescribe—dictate directions

Exercise 3/Page 136
1. misstep
2. misunderstood
3. dissimilar
4. re-echo
5. substandard
6. supersonic
7. pre-Columbian
8. anti-imperialist
9. circumnavigates
10. postoperative

Exercise 4/Page 137
1. persecuted
2. proceed
3. precocious
4. perspective
5. prescribe
6. perforated
7. produce
8. persist
9. perpetual
10. propose

## CHAPTER 8

Exercise 1/Page 141
The answers are contained in the exercise.

Exercise 2/Page 142
The answers are contained in the exercise.

Exercise 3/Page 142

1. accidentally
2. critically
3. elementally
4. equally
5. exceptionally
6. finally
7. generally
8. incidentally
9. intentionally
10. ironically
11. logically
12. mathematically
13. practically
14. professionally
15. really
16. typically
17. usually
18. verbally
19. globally

Exercise 4/Page 144

1. advantageous
2. courageous
3. dolorous
4. perilous
5. mountainous
6. beauteous
7. desirous
8. piteous
9. troublous
10. mischievous
11. plenteous
12. adventurous
13. bounteous
14. dangerous
15. grievous
16. humorous
17. outrageous
18. duteous
19. libelous
20. poisonous

Exercise 5/Page 147

1. b
2. a
3. a
4. a
5. b
6. a
7. a
8. b
9. b
10. b
11. a
12. b
13. b
14. b
15. b
16. a
17. a
18. a
19. b
20. b
21. a
22. a
23. b
24. b
25. b

Exercise 6/Page 149

1. beggar
2. receiver
3. conductor
4. passenger
5. governor
6. laborer
7. operator
8. dollar
9. supervisor
10. stenographer

Exercise 7/Page 151
1. compliment
2. remembrance
3. consistent
4. superintendent
5. dependent
6. existence
7. descendant
8. acquaintance
9. grievance
10. permanent
11. magnificent
12. brilliance
13. complimentary or complementary, depending upon meaning
14. convenience
15. abundance
16. guidance
17. conscience
18. coincidence
19. apparent
20. consequential

Exercise 8/Page 152
1. b
2. a
3. b
4. b
5. b
6. a
7. b
8. a
9. b
10. a

Exercise 9/Page 154
1. agonize
2. chastise
3. exercise
4. surprise
5. visualize
6. supervise
7. modernize
8. enterprise
9. fertilize
10. generalize

**CHAPTER 9**

Exercise 1/Page 159
1. reproofs
2. reprieves
3. sieves
4. halos or haloes
5. gulfs
6. coifs
7. albinos
8. shelves
9. puffs
10. muffs
11. sloughs
12. bassos or bassi, (Italian)
13. mambos
14. surfs
15. troughs
16. stilettos or stilettoes
17. sheaves
18. radios
19. calves
20. sylphs

Exercise 2/Page 160
1. abbeys
2. alleys
3. attorneys
4. buoys
5. chimneys
6. donkeys
7. journeys
8. keys
9. pulleys
10. turkeys

Exercise 3/Page 164
1. t's
2. Marys
3. anniversaries
4. dromedaries
5. kerchiefs
6. 4's
7. courts-martial
8. lieutenant colonels
9. bays
10. trays
11. flurries
12. sulkies
13. surreys
14. inequities
15. satellites
16. functionaries
17. avocados
18. dynamos

Exercise 4/Page 165
1. groceries
2. things
3. tomatoes
4. potatoes
5. avocados
6. quarts
7. pounds
8. pieces
9. chocolates
10. purchases
11. adventures
12. sopranos or soprani (Ital.)
13. altos or alti (Ital.)
14. alleys
15. journeys
16. keys
17. days
18. events

## CHAPTER 10

Exercise 1/Page 168
1. tourneys
2. allayed
3. volleyed
4. alleys
5. surveyed
6. portraying
7. journeyed
8. relayed
9. delays
10. parlayed

Exercise 2/Page 170
1. C
2. C
3. C
4. attorneys
5. C
6. C
7. C
8. C
9. C
10. icily

Exercise 3/Page 170
1. prettiness
2. pettiness
3. steadying
4. readied
5. bullies
6. airiness
7. pitied
8. tallying
9. buyer
10. dutiful
11. readiness
12. carried
13. hurrying
14. copier
15. sloppiness
16. livelihood

## CHAPTER 11

Exercise 1/Page 174
1. pleasantry
2. artistry
3. portraiture
4. clockwise
5. rocketry
6. sophistry
7. nationality
8. personality
9. dialectical
10. practicality

Exercise 2/Page 177

1. revering
2. lovely
3. purchasable
4. extremely
5. pleasurable
6. largely
7. nudged
8. stated
9. feted
10. fined
11. diving
12. shoved
13. devising
14. deceived
15. relieving
16. procrastinating
17. imagined
18. besieged
19. receiving

Exercise 3/Page 178

| | | |
|---|---|---|
| 1. benefit | benefiting | benefited |
| 2. commit | committing | committed |
| 3. lure | luring | lured |
| 4. refer | referring | referred |
| 5. pine | pining | pined |
| 6. elevate | elevating | elevated |
| 7. propel | propelling | propelled |
| 8. fit | fitting | fitted |
| 9. recur | recurring | recurred |
| 10. remit | remitting | remitted |
| 11. open | opening | opened |
| 12. club | clubbing | clubbed |
| 13. plunge | plunging | plunged |
| 14. singe | singeing | singed |
| 15. pursue | pursuing | pursued |
| 16. scare | scaring | scared |
| 17. throb | throbbing | throbbed |
| 18. trot | trotting | trotted |
| 19. use | using | used |
| 20. whip | whipping | whipped |

Exercise 4/Page 182

1. agreement
2. amusement
3. careful
4. canoeing
5. coming
6. disagreeable
7. engagement
8. excitement
9. immensity
10. likely
11. safety
12. senseless
13. shining
14. enlargement
15. enticing
16. perceived
17. escaping
18. discharged
19. relieving
20. contrivance

Exercise 5/Page 183

The answers to this exercise are contained in the sentences among the words italicized.

Exercise 6/Page 183

| | | |
|---|---|---|
| 1. scarcely | 7. perspiring | 13. outrageous |
| 2. vengeance | 8. retiring | 14. serviceable |
| 3. truly | 9. awful | 15. courageous |
| 4. tasty | 10. wisdom | 16. gorgeous |
| 5. noticeable | 11. assurance | 17. pronounceable |
| 6. changeable | 12. insurance | |

## CHAPTER 12

Exercise 1/Page 189

| | | |
|---|---|---|
| 1. cramping | 5. looking | 8. resting |
| 2. drumming | 6. nodding | 9. rigging |
| 3. grinning | 7. paining | 10. scrubbing |
| 4. hitting | | |

Exercise 2/Page 190

| | | |
|---|---|---|
| 1. deferred | 8. famous | 15. trimmer |
| 2. reference | 9. controlling | 16. occurrence |
| 3. shopping | 10. repellent | 17. movable |
| 4. disapproval | 11. desiring | 18. committed |
| 5. nineteen | 12. tireless | 19. equipage |
| 6. hitting | 13. truly | 20. excelling |
| 7. singeing | 14. swimmer | |

Exercise 3/Page 190

| | | |
|---|---|---|
| 1. adapt | adapting | adapted |
| 2. cramp | cramping | cramped |
| 3. design | designing | designed |
| 4. conceal | concealing | concealed |
| 5. congeal | congealing | congealed |
| 6. blot | blotting | blotted |
| 7. stop | stopping | stopped |
| 8. crush | crushing | crushed |
| 9. excel | excelling | excelled |
| 10. defer | deferring | deferred |
| 11. envelop | enveloping | enveloped |
| 12. extol | extolling | extolled |
| 13. flutter | fluttering | fluttered |
| 14. happen | happening | happened |
| 15. hum | humming | hummed |
| 16. level | leveling | leveled |
| 17. quarrel | quarreling | quarreled |
| 18. rub | rubbing | rubbed |
| 19. signal | signaling | signaled |
| 20. retreat | retreating | retreated |

Exercise 4/Page 191

1. witty
2. spinner
3. blotter
4. designer
5. quizzical
6. shutter
7. slipper
8. profiteer
9. meeting
10. dryer
11. inhabitable
12. toiler
13. putter
14. development
15. deferment
16. rubber
17. developer
18. goddess
19. druggist
20. trapper

Exercise 5/Page 191

1. tearfully
2. carefully
3. openness
4. dutifully
5. bountifully
6. commonness
7. mimicked
8. picnicking
9. mimicking
10. panicky

## CHAPTER 13

Exercise/Page 193

1. candor
2. theater
3. labor
4. labeled
5. traveler
6. realization
7. criticize
8. skillful
9. defense
10. analyze

## CHAPTER 14

Exercise 1/Page 198

1. pharmacy
2. photograph
3. C
4. C
5. frequently
6. either
7. machine
8. triumphant
9. people
10. C
11. receive
12. paragraph
13. series
14. convene
15. fatigue

Exercise 2/Page 199

1. troop
2. brutal
3. suitable
4. rooster
5. through
6. acoustic
7. aloof
8. ruler
9. bouquet
10. goose

Exercise 3/Page 199

Example: The *two* boys took *too* long *to* get dressed.

## Exercise 4/Page 201

| | | |
|---|---|---|
| 1. accord | 8. suffer | 15. C |
| 2. C | 9. button | 16. appear |
| 3. occur | 10. alliance | 17. sufficient |
| 4. C | 11. C | 18. attention |
| 5. apprehend | 12. occupied | 19. C |
| 6. approximately | 13. different | 20. C |
| 7. C | 14. grammar | |

## Exercise 5/Page 202

| | | |
|---|---|---|
| 1. allege | 5. jealousy | 8. soldier |
| 2. longevity | 6. suggest | 9. gist |
| 3. angel | 7. cordial | 10. jeer |
| 4. jostle | | |

## Exercise 6/Page 203

| | | |
|---|---|---|
| 1. k | 6. d | 11. n |
| 2. p | 7. g | 12. p |
| 3. t | 8. t | 13. h |
| 4. p | 9. g | 14. p |
| 5. t | 10. t | 15. t |

## Exercise 7/Page 204

| | |
|---|---|
| 1. although | 5. tough |
| 2. thoroughfare—through | 6. drought—throughout |
| 3. bought—cough | 7. slough |
| 4. ought | 8. cough |

## Exercise 8/Page 205

| | | |
|---|---|---|
| 1. fright or freight | 5. slight | 8. freight or fright |
| 2. weight | 6. tight | 9. playwright |
| 3. might | 7. night | 10. sight |
| 4. neighbor | | |

## Exercise 9/Page 206

| | | |
|---|---|---|
| 1. spectacle | 5. study | 8. tradition |
| 2. attention | 6. pronunciation | 9. stomach |
| 3. statue | 7. space | 10. production |
| 4. construction | | |

## CHAPTER 15

Exercise 1/Page 212

| | | | |
|---|---|---|---|
| 1. C | 6. C | 11. X | 16. X |
| 2. X | 7. C | 12. X | 17. X |
| 3. X | 8. X | 13. X | 18. C |
| 4. C | 9. C | 14. C | 19. C |
| 5. C | 10. C | 15. X | 20. C |

Exercise 2/Page 217

| | | |
|---|---|---|
| 1. sister-in-law | 8. C | 15. trade-in |
| 2. man-of-war | 9. C | 16. C |
| 3. aide-de-camp | 10. C | 17. C |
| 4. run-on | 11. runner-up | 18. built-in |
| 5. downstairs | 12. drive-in | 19. C |
| 6. anti-American | 13. C | 20. C |
| 7. C | 14. C | |

## CHAPTER 16

Exercise/Page 222

| | |
|---|---|
| 1. The young girl's hat | 10. don't |
| 2. The men's votes | 11. haven't |
| 3. The ladies' styles | 12. couldn't |
| 4. The cats' paws | 13. You're |
| 5. The sailors' decorations | 14. can't |
| 6. The professor's hat | 15. It's |
| 7. The woman's shoe | 16. Let's |
| 8. The soprano's voice | 17. wouldn't |
| 9. The dog's tail | |

## CHAPTER 17

Exercise/Page 226

| | |
|---|---|
| 1. Hotel Westover | 9. Fifth Avenue |
| 2. Buick | 10. Washington coffee |
| 3. Decoration Day | 11. Britain |
| 4. North Side High School | 12. Bard College, New York |
| 5. *Mutiny on the Bounty* | 13. *The Taming of the Shrew*, Shakespeare |
| 6. Old French | 14. English, French |
| 7. English, Bible | 15. Aunt Emily, West |
| 8. Uncle | |

## CHAPTER 18

Exercise 1/Page 232

| | | |
|---|---|---|
| 1. Sec. or Secy. | 8. M.D. | 15. Dept. |
| 2. Treas. | 9. Hon. | 16. lb. |
| 3. C.O.D. | 10. yr. | 17. Messrs. |
| 4. A.M. | 11. Sat. | 18. D.D.S. |
| 5. Jr. | 12. R.F.D. | 19. Rev. |
| 6. doz. | 13. R.S.V.P. | 20. Blvd. |
| 7. Aug. | 14. Esq. | |

Exercise 2/Page 233

| | |
|---|---|
| 1. Doctor of Philosophy | 16. anno Domini |
| 2. Avenue | 17. Steamship |
| 3. inch | 18. Street |
| 4. et cetera (and so forth) | 19. received |
| 5. number | 20. department |
| 6. Brothers | 21. Doctor of Medicine |
| 7. Postscript | 22. Treasurer |
| 8. Railroad | 23. Saturday |
| 9. September | 24. Honorable |
| 10. Freight on Board | 25. Reverend |
| 11. Professor | 26. Secretary |
| 12. Assistant | 27. Doctor of Dental Surgery |
| 13. Eastern Standard Time | 28. Captain |
| 14. Governor | 29. March |
| 15. before Christ | 30. post meridiem (after noon) |

## CHAPTER 19

Exercise 1/Page 238

| | | |
|---|---|---|
| 1. alter | 5. aisle | 8. altogether |
| 2. borne | 6. already | 9. all ready |
| 3. brake | 7. all right | 10. capital |
| 4. capital | | |

Exercise 2/Page 240

| | | |
|---|---|---|
| 1. Council | 5. It's | 8. counsel |
| 2. complement | 6. dissent | 9. core |
| 3. course | 7. led | 10. dual |
| 4. dessert | | |

Exercise 3/Page 242

| | | |
|---|---|---|
| 1. minor | 5. waist | 8. stationery |
| 2. peace | 6. their | 9. whose |
| 3. plane—plain | 7. too | 10. They're |
| 4. principal | | |

Exercise 4/Page 244

1. clothes
2. later
3. consul
4. advice
5. beside
6. emigrants
7. formally
8. ingenuous
9. ally
10. allusions

Exercise 5/Page 245

1. morale
2. quite
3. personnel
4. loose
5. than
6. formally
7. lose
8. moral
9. quite
10. than

**CHAPTER 20**

Exercise/Page 249

1. C
2. C
3. definitive
4. C
5. C
6. C
7. undefinable
8. undesirable
9. pitiless
10. C
11. C
12. C
13. C
14. C
15. C
16. C
17. non-existent
18. preferable
19. C
20. unendurable
21. necessarily
22. C
23. C
24. changeable
25. judgment or
    judgement
26. accommodate
27. guarantee
28. receipts
29. C
30. C
31. chosen
32. possessed
33. recognized
34. sincerity
35. existence
36. embarrassed
37. C
38. excitable
39. preferred
40. occasion

**CHAPTER 22**

Exercise/Page 268

1. appellation
2. bassinet
3. C
4. C
5. catarrh
6. cellar
7. cole slaw
8. C
9. C
10. dyspeptic
11. C
12. Eskimos
13. C
14. C
15. C
16. genealogy
17. C
18. kimono
19. labeled
20. C
21. C
22. sacrilegious
23. sibilancy
24. C
25. C

## CHAPTER 23

Exercise/Page 275

| | | |
|---|---|---|
| 1. a | 6. b | 11. b |
| 2. c | 7. b | 12. d |
| 3. a | 8. b | 13. c |
| 4. d | 9. c | 14. d |
| 5. d | 10. a | 15. a |

# For Achievement Tests 1–7

## ACHIEVEMENT TEST 1

Chapters 1–4/Page 278

| | | | |
|---|---|---|---|
| 1. T | 16. F | 31. F | 46. T |
| 2. T | 17. T | 32. F | 47. T |
| 3. F | 18. F | 33. T | 48. T |
| 4. T | 19. T | 34. T | 49. T |
| 5. F | 20. T | 35. T | 50. F |
| 6. T | 21. T | 36. T | 51. F |
| 7. F | 22. T | 37. T | 52. F |
| 8. F | 23. F | 38. F | 53. F |
| 9. T | 24. F | 39. T | 54. F |
| 10. T | 25. F | 40. T | 55. F |
| 11. F | 26. T | 41. T | 56. T |
| 12. T | 27. T | 42. F | 57. F |
| 13. F | 28. T | 43. T | 58. T |
| 14. T | 29. F | 44. F | 59. T |
| 15. F | 30. F | 45. T | |

## ACHIEVEMENT TEST 2

Chapter 6/Page 281

| | | |
|---|---|---|
| 1. receipt | 7. retrieve | 13. achieve |
| 2. relief | 8. friend | 14. perceive |
| 3. shriek | 9. bier | 15. neighbors |
| 4. yield | 10. chief | 16. mischievous |
| 5. fiend | 11. receiving | 17. frontier |
| 6. achievement | 12. deceive | 18. ceiling |

## ACHIEVEMENT TEST 3

Chapters 7–8/Page 282

| | | |
|---|---|---|
| 1. disadvantage | 3. misstatement | 5. C |
| 2. C | 4. recollect | 6. innovation |

7. renovate
8. unnatural
9. C
10. override
11. demoted
12. dissolve
13. pre-eminent
14. antiseptic
15. C
16. interstate
17. interrupt
18. postscript
19. suburban
20. superintendent
21. transient
22. admissible
23. laughable
24. unthinkable
25. eligible
26. invincible
27. legible
28. comfortable
29. perishable
30. demonstrable
31. C
32. recollect
33. C
34. unnoticeable
35. overrated
36. antecedents
37. C
38. C
39. seceded
40. perforated
41. perspective
42. C
43. precocious
44. drinkable
45. inaccessible
46. C
47. eligible
48. C
49. C
50. acquaintance
51. defendant
52. significance
53. hangar
54. C
55. C
56. C
57. radiator
58. C
59. supervisor
60. C

## ACHIEVEMENT TEST 4

Chapters 9–11/Page 285
1. buffaloes, buffalos, buffalo
2. vetoes
3. tomatoes
4. pianos
5. lassos, lassoes
6. calves
7. leaves
8. beliefs
9. armies
10. oxen
11. chimneys
12. pulleys
13. volleys
14. salaries
15. tragedies
16. angrily
17. merciful
18. medleys
19. conveyance
20. dignifies
21. dining
22. imaginable
23. judging
24. surprising
25. writing
26. whining
27. desirous
28. density
29. sincerely
30. families
31. dining
32. donkeys
33. encouragement
34. unimaginable
35. casualties
36. busily
37. accompanied
38. worried
39. portrayed
40. sublimity
41. inadvisable
42. singeing
43. vagueness
44. arguing
45. lovely
46. courageous
47. tasteless
48. contrivance
49. anniversaries
50. oxen
51. proofs
52. brothers-in-law
53. besieged
54. likeness
55. gracefully
56. truly
57. mimicking
58. sheep
59. alumni
60. academies
61. curriculum
62. bacilli

## ACHIEVEMENT TEST 5

Chapters 12–15/Page 287
1. low-priced
2. best-known
3. thirty-first
4. far-fetched
5. newly born
6. highest priced
7. pre-election
8. co-owner
9. ex-Governor
10. Vice-Admiral
11. conferred
12. preference
13. transferred
14. wrappings
15. hopper
16. hitter
17. trimmings
18. controlling
19. excelled
20. regretted
21. low ceiling
22. one half
23. dinning
24. low-necked
25. references
26. hoping
27. occurred
28. hangdog
29. unparalleled
30. twenty-ninth
31. predawn
32. high scorer
33. preferred
34. ex-policeman
35. conferred
36. chinned
37. Pro-Temperance
38. flapped
39. red-cheeked
40. eighty-eight
41. subliminal
42. regretful
43. lowest priced
44. smitten
45. well-timed
46. hitting
47. running
48. patrolled
49. all ready
50. run-on
51. Senator-elect
52. mid-Atlantic
53. extolled
54. aide-de-camp
55. regaled
56. runner-up
57. spinning
58. omitted
59. scraped
60. recurred
61. annulled
62. scrubbed
63. panicked
64. rebelled
65. deferred

## ACHIEVEMENT TEST 6

Chapters 16–17/Page 289
1. don't
2. men's
3. his
4. who's
5. i's, t's
6. you've
7. ladies'
8. brother-in-law's
9. children's
10. couldn't
11. East, West
12. Grandma Moses
13. Hindu
14. Elks
15. "For My Beloved"
16. *A Tale of Two Cities*
17. north
18. Columbus Day
19. My Fair Lady
20. House of Representatives
21. boy's
22. They're
23. doctors'
24. teachers'
25. 7's
26. Harrigan and Hart's
27. women's
28. theirs
29. t's
30. lawyer's
31. East
32. French
33. mathematics
34. Governor
35. captains
36. Hawaii
37. Orient
38. Senate
39. Arbor Day
40. *Silas Marner*
41. Admiral
42. Uncle Don
43. boys'
44. south

## ACHIEVEMENT TEST 7

Chapter 19/Page 291

1. advice
2. allies
3. aisle
4. all ready
5. illusion
6. alter
7. altogether
8. borne
9. angels
10. berth
11. beside
12. break
13. breath
14. bridle
15. canvass
16. Capitol
17. censure
18. cords
19. clothes
20. course

21. compliment
22. consul
23. core
24. incredulous
25. diaries
26. dissent
27. dessert
28. device
29. duel
30. formerly
31. instance
32. ingenious
33. compliments
34. desserts
35. consul
36. formally
37. morale
38. personnel
39. principle

40. stationery
41. waste
42. supersede
43. exceedingly
44. succeeds
45. proceeded
46. illusion
47. accede
48. receded
49. corpse
50. its
51. later
52. led
53. council
54. loose
55. minors
56. peace
57. plain
58. quite